FEB 1967

Six Cultures Series: Volume III

The Rājpūts
of Khalapur, India

Six Cultures ✻ Studies of Child Rearing Series

Editor:
Beatrice B. Whiting, *Harvard University*

Senior Investigators
Irwin L. Child, *Yale University*
William W. Lambert, *Cornell University*
John W. M. Whiting, *Harvard University*

Six Cultures Series ✻ Volume III

The Rājpūts
of Khalapur, India

Leigh Minturn
John T. Hitchcock

John Wiley and Sons, Inc.

New York · London · Sydney

Library of Congress Catalog Card Number: 66-17632
Printed in the United States of America

Introduction

The six monographs in this series report research undertaken in 1954 by a group of social scientists from Harvard, Yale, and Cornell universities. In its broadest conception, the research aimed at exploring cross-culturally the relation between different patterns of child rearing and subsequent differences in personality. The overall research was designed to study the degree to which the experiences of a child in the first years of life determine his behavior and in adult life influence his perception of the world, his philosophy, religion, and code of ethics.

Theories of the relationship between specific types of treatment in early childhood and subsequent personality differences have been advanced by psychologists and anthropologists. This project was established with the hope of being able to test some of these hypotheses using material collected in a standard manner in six parts of the world where families have divergent ways of life and theories and methods of training young children.

The intellectual history of this project begins with the work of Margaret Mead, Ruth Benedict, Edward Sapir, Ralph Linton, Abram Kardiner, John Dollard, and other pioneers in the field of culture and personality whose work formed the foundation of this study. To detail the contribution of these pioneers would demand an essay on the entire new discipline that grew out of the integration of anthropological and psychological theory, an undertaking not practical in this introduction. A brief historical summary by John Whiting appears in the preface to Volume I of this series.

Specifically, the impetus for the present study came from the cross-cultural work on socialization done by two of the senior investigators, John W. M. Whiting and Irvin L. Child, while they were colleagues at the Institute of Human Relations at Yale University. The results of this research were published in *Child Training and Personality* (1953). Using theories of disease as measures of adult personality, the authors attempted to test certain psychological theories relating the treatment of the basic behavior systems in infancy and childhood to adult personality characteristics.

The data on the 75 societies used in these studies were taken from published ethnographies which varied greatly in detail and areas of coverage. The dream of the investigators was to send field teams out to get comparable detailed material on 100 societies. As a first step in accomplishing this aim, the present study was planned.

In 1953 the Committee on Social Behavior of the Social Science Research Council sponsored a seminar* and a conference† to discuss cross-cultural work on socialization. As a result, the *Field Manual for the Cross-Cultural Study of Child Rearing* was prepared (Whiting et al., 1953), and Whiting and Child persuaded William W. Lambert of Cornell University to join them in seeking funds to conduct a comparative study of child rearing. A generous grant from the Behavioral Science Division of the Ford Foundation made it possible to carry out these plans. The fieldwork and part of the analysis and writing of five of the six reports in this volume were financed by this grant. Later analysis and editing were supported by a grant from the United States Public Health Service.

Intensive planning for the study was carried on at Cornell, Harvard, and Yale during the following year under the direction of the senior investigators, William W. Lambert, Irvin L. Child, and John W. M. Whiting. As part of the over-all research plan, further cross-cultural studies were undertaken at Cornell, Harvard, and Yale. Irvin Child, with the assistance of Margaret Bacon and Herbert Barry, investigated the consequences of various types of training on nurturance, responsibility, obedience, self-reliance, and achievement using ethnographic accounts for cross-cultural comparison (Bacon, Child, and Barry, 1963; Barry, Bacon, and Child, 1957; Barry, Child, and Bacon, 1959). William Lambert and Leigh Minturn did further cross-cultural work on aggres-

---

* The contributing members of the seminar were Barbara Chartier Ayers, Hildreth Geertz, George Goethals, Charles Holzinger, Edgar Lowell, Eleanor E. Maccoby, A. Kimball Romney, Richard Salisbury, William Steward, and John W. Thibaut.

† Attending the conference were Robert R. Sears (Chairman), A. L. Baldwin, R. A. Bauer, Irvin L. Child, L. S. Cottrell, Jr., Leon Festinger, J. G. Gewirtz, A. Inkeles, Harry Levin, Gardner Lindzey, Eleanor E. Maccoby, Carson McGuire, G. P. Murdock, B. Paul, John M. Roberts, R. R. Sarbin, Pauline S. Sears, M. Brewster Smith, R. L. Solomon, John W. Thibaut, and John W. M. Whiting.

sion (Lambert, Triandis, and Wolf, 1959; Triandis and Lambert, 1961), and John Whiting worked on measures of guilt and other mechanisms of internalized controls (Burton and Whiting, 1961).

During June and July of 1954, a Social Science Research Council Summer Conference was held at the Laboratory of Human Development at Harvard. All the research personnel, with the aid of David Aberle of Michigan, Alfred Baldwin and James J. Gibson of Cornell, and Robert Sears of Stanford, wrote the *Field Guide for a Study of Socialization in Five Societies.** This guide appears as Volume 1 of the six culture series. It presents in detail the research plan, the hypotheses to be tested, and the research instruments agreed on by the field teams and the senior investigators. The reader should study this volume in order to understand the content and organization of the monographs and the methods employed in data collection. The theoretical background and the intellectual history of the project are presented in the preface by John W. M. Whiting.†

The five original field teams started work in the fall of 1954 and spent from 6 to 14 months in the field. Although the original design of the study called for a sample of societies whose culture had already been studied by ethnologists, the temperament and motivation of young anthropologists were such that they tended to choose groups who are relatively unknown and who, often from some personal reason, appealed to their interests. The actual groups chosen represent a compromise between the advantages of previous coverage and these personal interests, and also provide the great range of differences desired by the project planners.

Thomas and Hatsumi Maretzki chose the village of Taira on the northeast coast of Okinawa, the largest of the Ryukyu Islands in the Pacific. At the time, Thomas Maretzki was an advanced graduate student in the Anthropology Department at Yale University. Hatsumi Maretzki, a graduate of the University of Hawaii, was on the staff of the Gesell Institute Nursery School. Thomas Maretzki is now an associate professor of anthropology at the University of Hawaii.

Leigh Minturn worked with a group of families of the Rājpūt caste in the town of Khalapur in Uttar Pradesh in northern India. Unmarried at the time of the study, she used the facilities of Morris Opler's Cornell field station in Khalapur which then was directed by John Hitchcock, who collaborated with her in the study. Leigh Min-

---

* Published in mimeographed form by the Laboratory of Human Development, Harvard University, 1954.

† See also, Lambert, W. W., 1960.

turn received her doctorate from the Social Relations Department of Radcliffe College and Harvard University, and was, at the time of the study, a research associate at Cornell University. She is now an associate professor of psychology at the University of Illinois. John Hitchcock received his doctorate in anthropology from Cornell University and is at present an associate professor of anthropology at University of California, Los Angeles.

William and Corinne Nydegger chose a group of Ilocano-speaking families living in hamlets in northern Luzon in the Philippines. At the time of the study, William Nydegger was an advanced graduate student at Cornell University. His wife had done graduate work in anthropology at the University of Wisconsin. William Nydegger is now an associate professor of anthropology at Pennsylvania State University.

A. Kimball and Romaine Romney chose a group of families in the Mixtecan barrio of Santo Domingo in the town of Juxtlahuaca in Oaxaca State, Mexico. At the time of the study, A. Kimball Romney was an advanced graduate student at Harvard University. His wife attended the University of Colorado. A. Kimball Romney is now an associate professor of anthropology at Stanford University.

John and Ann Fischer agreed to take on the task of establishing bench marks for comparison by studying a group of mothers in the United States. They moved into a neighborhood in Orchard Town in New England. John Fischer, who has a doctorate in social relations from Harvard University, was at the time of the study an assistant professor at Harvard and his wife Ann was an advanced graduate student in anthropology. John Fischer is at present a professor of anthropology at Tulane University and his wife is an associate professor of anthropology at the same university. When they undertook the study, the Fischers had just returned from three years in the Caroline Islands in the Pacific where John Fischer had served as district anthropologist and as native affairs officer on the islands of Truk and Ponape in Micronesia. During this time, Ann Fischer was gathering material on child rearing in Truk; on the basis of this work she received her doctorate from Harvard.

In 1955 a sixth team, Robert and Barbara LeVine, left for Kenya, Africa where they studied a group of homesteads in the Kisii Highlands of South Nyanza District. They were financed by a Ford Foundation fellowship and a National Science Foundation predoctoral fellowship. At the time of the study Robert LeVine was an advanced graduate student in the department of social relations at Harvard University. Barbara LeVine was a graduate student of psychology at

Boston University. She subsequently received a doctorate in social psychology from Northwestern University. Now Barbara Lloyd, she is a lecturer in social psychology at the University of Birmingham in England. Robert LeVine is at present an associate professor of anthropology in the Committee on Human Development, University of Chicago.

To help insure comparability of data, a central clearing house was set up at the Laboratory of Human Development under the supervision of Beatrice B. Whiting, a Yale-trained anthropologist who was a research associate at the Laboratory of Human Development at Harvard. Field notes were mailed in periodically and field problems were discussed by correspondence.

The research design, agreed on by all the field teams, was set up to measure as accurately as possible the child-training practices and the hypothesized individual and cultural differences in personality, especially in the areas of aggression, dependency, and the internalization of various mechanisms of behavior control—areas of special theoretical interest to the senior investigators at Cornell, Yale, and Harvard universities, respectively. Previous research had been done in these areas at the Institute of Human Relations at Yale, at the Iowa Child Welfare Station under the direction of Robert Sears, and subsequently at the Laboratory of Human Development at Harvard University. The research conducted at Iowa and Harvard focused on a study of individual differences among groups of mothers and children in Iowa, Massachusetts, and in three different cultural groups in the Southwest (Sears, Whiting, Nowlis, and Sears, 1953; Whiting, Chasdi, Antonovsky, and Ayres, in press).

In designing the field research reported in this volume, an attempt has been made to assess individual as well as cultural differences. This is one of the unique aspects of the design. The hope was to test hypotheses about the relations of child-rearing practices and consequent personality, both intraculturally and cross-culturally. In the first instance, 24 mothers in each society were studied as individuals in their relationship to one of their children, and each of the 24 children (ages 3 to 10) was observed and interviewed in a standard manner in the hope of detecting behavioral and personality differences. (The mother interviews, child interviews, child T.A.T.'s, and the description of the observations of the children used in the study can be found in Chapter 5 of the *Field Guide for the Study of Socialization*.) The cross-cultural measures included material on child-training practices and also religious beliefs, theories of disease, recreational activities, and so on, collected by standard ethnographic techniques. The outlines for studying these are to be found in Chapter 2 of the *Field Guide for the Study of Socialization*.

A word should be said here about the nature of the social unit each field team chose to study. It was decided to choose a group large enough to yield an adequate sample of individual families. For our design this meant that a group of at least 50 families would be needed to draw our sample of 24, since at least half the families would have grown-up children, children under 3, or no children at all. On the other hand, we wanted a group who knew each other and shared beliefs, values, and practices so that it would be possible to use ethnographic techniques in collecting data and in describing certain aspects of the daily life in cultural terms. The techniques used to locate the Primary Social Unit (P.S.U.) are described in detail in the *Field Guide for the Study of Socialization*, Chapter 6.

In Taira, Okinawa, the Maretzkis visited 63 households in the central part of town and recorded the relationships among the occupants and their kin. The census included about 330 individuals, 83 of which were children under the age of 11.

In Khalapur, India, Leigh Minturn gathered census material in 38 courtyards; all were owned by members of the Rājpūt caste who constitute 40% of the total population of 5000. The courtyards are in a neighborhood inhabited exclusively by members of the Rājpūt caste; the area is bounded on two sides by a river and fields and is separated from the rest of the town on the third side by a temple, school, and meeting house and by a street occupied by another caste group, and on the fourth by a patti division line. (Khalapur is divided into seven political units or pattis.)

In Juxtlahuaca, a town of 3600, the Romneys made a census of 31 courtyards in the Mixtecan barrio of Santo Domingo. This section is separated from the rest of the town, which is inhabited by Spanish-speaking ladinos, by a deep barranca. The census of 31 courtyards included 90 children under 11 years of age.

In Orchard Town, population 5000, a census was made of 42 households, most of them on three adjoining streets in North Village, which has a population of 1000 and is one of the three centers of the town. The families participated together in P.T.A., school functions, women's clubs, and church, as well as in local politics. There were 83 children under 11 in the sample.

In the barrio of Tarong, Luzon, it was necessary to make a census of six adjacent hamlets before a sample of 24 children of the right age could be drawn. The barrio encompasses an area of about two square miles of land crosscut by steep ridges and valleys. The hamlets consisted of from 3 to 17 families. The sample was drawn from 58 families who had 76 children under 11 years of age. The genealogical material collected by the Nydeggers indicates that all but six of the 61 families in the barrio were descended from seven families who settled the area around 1860 (Minturn and Lambert, 1964, p. 18).

In Nyansongo, 18 contiguous homesteads were visited. The families in these homesteads all belong to one clan, and neighboring homesteads often belong to the same patrilineage. The census from which the sample was drawn included 208 individuals of whom 92 were children under 11.

In each of the six societies all the families knew each other and associated at certain times during the year and presumably met our criterion of sharing basic cultural values. If I were to judge the societies on the degree of intimacy of the mothers of the total P.S.U., I would rank the families in Taira as most intimate and those in Juxtlahuaca second. In the other societies there is intimacy in subgroups but not in the entire P.S.U. Although the Khalapur families live close to one another, the women are confined to courtyards, and most of their everyday contacts are limited to women in the same block who can be visited by crossing roof tops.

Women in groups of homesteads in Nyansongo are members of cooperative work teams and hence are on intimate terms with one another. There were three such work groups in the sample. The members of each belonged to the same subclan. Hamlet groups in Tarong are very intimate, especially when families face on the same yard. Visiting, kin ties, and a central school all unite the members of the P.S.U.

The Orchard Town mothers seem to be the least intimate in the sample, although they knew one another by name and knew the names of one another's children.

The P.S.U. groups are defined and selected to maximize the homogeneity which is essential for the use of standard ethnographic techniques. In gathering the background material and much of the material on socialization, the field teams used informants and participant observation. In areas that were not covered by standardized instruments, the data presented in the ethnographies is often based on a combination of discussion with from four to eight informants checked by observation of the daily life of the group. All the field teams lived in the communities they studied for the better part of a year or longer. Three of the field teams had children who played with the sample children. All the ethnographers visited the houses daily, participated in community activities, and became socialized in the habits of the group.

For the individual measures, 24 children were selected from the census material sent in by the field teams according to the following criteria: the sample consisted of four sex-age groups, six boys and six girls from 3-to-5 years of age and an equal number from 7-to-10 years of age.* To maximize the independence of cases, no more than one child was selected from each family. The sample mothers were interviewed and the children interviewed and observed in a standard manner for 12 five-minute periods.

Implicit in the research design is a general concept of the relation of personality to culture, which may be presented as follows: the ecology of an area determines the maintenance systems, which include basic economy and the most elementary variables of social structure. In other words, the type of crops grown, the presence or absence of herding, fishing, and so on, depend on the nature of the terrain, the temperature and amount of rainfall, and the location of the area vis-à-vis centers of invention and diffusion. These basic conditions partly determine the arrangement of people in space, the type of houses, and household composition. These in turn set the limits for child-rearing practices. The basic innate needs of both children and parents must be met within this framework.

It is obvious that ecology does no more than determine gross limits for the social structure. Within these limits the nature of the composition of households, neighborhoods, and other social groups will lead to variance in child training. Whether or not a grandmother lives in the house, or whether other relatives are close at hand, will influence a mother's behavior toward her child.

We assume that different patterns of child rearing will lead to differences in the personality of children and thus to differences in adult personality. Since personality may only be inferred, the problem of measurement is difficult on both the individual and the cultural levels. Individual children may be given tests of various kinds, interviewed, or observed. On a cultural level, we may analyze the patterning of child or adult behavior, for example, the games and recreational activity, the rituals or ceremonial life, or we may assess beliefs about the supernatural, theories of disease, or popular folk tales in terms of personality dimensions.

---

* The LeVines' sample was aberrant. They studied six sex-age groups consisting of four children each. They included a group 10-to-14 years of age since they wanted to follow the children through initiation. The Romneys' sample of older children was limited to five girls and five boys 7-to-10 years old.

Chart I indicates this conceptual system in a simple manner. To summarize the conceptual background in another way, the researchers viewed ecology, economics, and social and political organization as largely determining the behavior of the agents of child rearing. They viewed child behavior as an index of child personality and saw adult behavior, beliefs, and values as indices of adult personality. The causal relationships implied in this scheme are open to discussion. Such discussions, with the knowledge available at present, ultimately end with a problem similar to that of the priority of the chicken or the egg.

A word should be said about the type of ecology and economy represented in the sample. Five of the six cultures are agricultural. There are no fishing or hunting and gathering economies, nor are there pastoral people. With the exception of Orchard Town, most of the men in the six societies are farmers. In Tarong, Philippines and in Taira, Okinawa, the most important staple crop is wet rice. In Juxtlahuaca, Mexico and in Nyansongo, Kenya, corn is the important staple. In the latter, eleusine, a grain, is also important. In Khalapur, wheat and other grains are the main food crops.

Chart I   The Relation of Personality to Culture

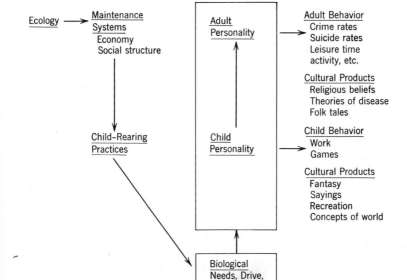

The ecology of the areas, however, makes the farming techniques different: in Taira and Tarong, men and women work together in the fields; in Khalapur and Juxtlahuaca only men work in the fields; in Nyansongo, with the exception of ploughing and building fences, all the agricultural work is done by women. An important variable in determining the amount of agricultural work women do is the distance of the gardens and fields from the dwellings. The gardens are closest in Nyansongo and Tarong, furthest away in Juxtlahuaca and Khalapur. Every Nyansongo woman has gardens close to her house, and she and a group of women who are members of her cooperative work group are responsible for all the gardening. In Tarong the fields and paddies lie directly below the houses which are built on the ridges. The town Juxtlahuaca is situated in a long, narrow river valley. Most of the cornfields near the town and in the valley belong to the ladinos in the Mexican part of town. The Mixtecans' main fields are usually a half-hour walk from home on the slopes of the mountains which follow the river valley. Women do not work in the fields in Juxtlahuaca. Clearing the mountain gardens is done by cutting the trees and undergrowth and burning it off, a technique called slash and burn agriculture. Khalapur is surrounded by fields that are a 15-to-20-minute walk from the courtyards. As in Juxtlahuaca, the Rājpūt women do not work in the fields; however, their enforced seclusion as married women would make such work impossible even if the fields were closer by. In Taira the rice paddies are also on the outskirts of the town. They are closer at hand, however, than are the fields in Khalapur and Juxtlahuaca, although not so close as are the paddies in Tarong. Both the Tarong and Taira women help in the fields, although it is my impression that the Taira women spend more time working in the gardens than the Tarong women do. It is interesting to note that, in the five agricultural societies, the women do more gardening work when the gardens are nearby. It also appears that in rice cultures women are especially good at transplanting the young shoots, a backbreaking and fussy job which requires manual dexterity and patience. Women do not work when slash and burn techniques are use. In all the five societies, men do whatever plowing is done. Buffaloes are used as draft animals in Khalapur, India, the carabao in Tarong, Philippines, and oxen in Juxtlahuaca, Mexico and in Nyansongo, Africa. In Taira, Okinawa there are few large animals. Because Nyansongo families cannot afford to hire ploughs, the women prepare the soil with hoes.

If the model of the influence of the maintenance systems on child rearing is correct, the amount of time and effort women exert in agricultural work is one of the several ecological and economic variables which influence their child-training techniques. The amount of time the fathers spend in the agricultural work and the distance of the fields from the house will influence the amount of time men spend around the house and the amount of time the children see them.

The majority of the families in Nyansongo in Kenya, in Tarong in the Philippines, and in Khalapur, India have large animals which must be watered and pastured. There are no adequate fences in any of these three societies, so humans must see that the cattle do not get into crops. This is done either by tethering the animals, the technique employed by the Tarongans, or by employing a herd boy when the cows are in pasture, the technique used by the Nyansongo and by the Rājpūts of Khalapur. The latter keep the cattle in pens adjoining the courtyards for much of the day and bring fodder into town. The Nyansongo shut the cattle up only at night. During the day, young boys or occasionally younger girls tend the herds. Where the herding technique is used, children are important in the economy and their negligence may ruin the crops essential for the food supply. As a consequence, training in responsibility is early and irresponsibility is severely punished.* Although there are sheep, goats, and burros in Juxtlahuaca, only a few of the families in the sample owned these animals. Here also herdboys are used.

Besides doing whatever agricultural work is expected, some of the women are involved in other economic pursuits. Most of the sample mothers in Taira helped their husbands in lumbering, carrying faggots down from the mountains and bundling them for sale. Some of the Juxtlahuacan mothers cooked for the markets. Some of the Tarongan and Nyansongo women occasionally sold surplus vegetables in the markets. In Orchard Town some women worked outside the home at wage-earning jobs. Only the Rājpūt women had no possible way of earning money.

In sum, the amount of work, excluding child care and housework, required of women varies with the economy and ecology. The Nyansongo women have the heaviest work load, the Orchard Town and Rājpūt mothers the lightest. The Taira and Tarong women seem to rank second and third in economic work load, the Juxtlahuaca fourth. The burden of housework and child care also varies. Here comparisons are difficult, and there are several factors that should be considered. Technological development in the processing of food and in the procurement of water and fuel is one of the determinants of the number

---

* See Barry, Child, and Bacon, 1959 for a discussion of responsibility training in economies having large animals. The authors interpret the relationship in terms of the amount of property accumulated and owned by members of a society.

of hours a woman spends in cooking and cleaning. For example, the women in Tarong, Philippines, must pound their own rice whereas the women in Taira take theirs to a mill to be processed. Both the Rājpūt women of Khalapur and the Juxtlahuacan women spend long hours preparing grain for cooking. The Orchard Town mother certainly has the easiest lot in this domain; furthermore, she alone has water and fuel readily available in her kitchen.

A second factor that must be considered is the availability of help. As will be described later, in the kin-based hamlet groups in Tarong, Philippines, in the extended family courtyards in Juxtlahuaca, Mexico, and in Khalapur, India, and in the stem family households in Taira, Okinawa, other adult women are available to help with the daily routine of living. In the Nyansongo homestead, there may be co-wives and mothers-in-law within shouting distance. It should be noted, however, that the degree to which women help each other when they live close by and are related varies. In our sample, the closest cooperation between women occurs in Tarong, Philippines; here the kin group is often bilateral and a woman has her own relatives as well as her husband's close at hand. Similarly, in Juxtlahuaca a woman may have her own relatives nearby to help. Affinal relatives seem to be less predictably helpful. In Khalapur the mothers report that they receive little or no help from their sisters- and mothers-in-law, although these relatives are at hand in emergencies.*

In Nyansongo homesteads the cooperation between co-wives varies with the personality, with the difference in age of the wives, and with the executive ability of the husband. It appears that when the second wife is considerably younger than the senior wife, there is more likely to be cooperation. Most Nyansongo mothers, however, use children, usually siblings or cousins, between the ages of 5 and 8 to take over the care of their infants, and these children are the constant companions of their little charges until they can walk and travel with the rest of the children. The Taira mother who is lucky enough to have a mother-in-law or her own mother living in the house receives help with the daily care of her infant. The Orchard Town mother, in contrast to the mothers in the other five societies, has the least help. She can hire baby-sitters, but in general she seldom does so. Even when her own mother or her husband's mother lives in the same town, or even next door, she is not in the habit of asking them to do more than occasional baby-sitting.

---

* It should be noted that the Rājpūt mothers have outside help from sweepers, washers, and water carriers who do some of the daily housework.

Even in child care, however, it should be noted that technological development is important. In our sample, for example, only the Orchard Town mother has a baby carriage. In all the other societies infants must be carried, and children are used in lieu of carriages. Similarly, there are no playpens or high chairs to confine the infant safely while the mother works.

Still a further dimension of comparison is the degree of loneliness of mothers. It is here that the Orchard Town mother is unique: she spends most of her day in the company of her children, isolated from other adults. This is especially true in winter, when it is an effort to bundle up the family and go on a visit.

Associated with loneliness is boredom, and here the Orchard Town mother is similar to the Rājpūt mother in Khalapur who is confined to the courtyard day after day. Both enjoy seeing and talking to someone new and look forward to any breaks in the monotony of the daily routine. Although the Rājpūt mothers usually have adult companionship, they cannot wander downtown or break the monotony either by watching people interact on television or by reading about them in books.

As suggested earlier, the climate influences daily living routine and arrangements in many ways. Children react to excessive heat and cold and grow restive if continuous rains confine them to the dwelling. In all the societies there are days when the temperature is uncomfortably cool (see Chart II). During November through March children may feel cold in the early morning in Juxtlahuaca, Mexico. In June, July, August, and September the nights may be uncomfortably cool in Nyansongo, Kenya. In both of these societies and in Khalapur, India, winter nights probably seem colder than they actually are because of the diurnal variation which averages over 25 degrees. Orchard Town, U.S.A., has by far the most prolonged period of cold and the most days with temperatures that drop below freezing. However, it has insulated buildings and central heating; the children have special winter clothes and hence probably suffer less from the cold than any of the other children in the sample. On the other hand, the Orchard Town mother has to struggle with snowsuits and boots and would often rather stay home than face the task of dressing and undressing children and walking or driving through the snow and ice. She is afraid to leave her children at home alone, even for short periods of time, lest faulty heating equipment set fire to the house. During the winter months the radio broadcasts almost daily the names of small children who have burned to death in their homes. The seasonal contrast in the routine of living is greater in Orchard Town than in any of the other societies.

Chart II *Climatic Conditions for the Six Societies*[a]

SOCIETY	NYANSONGO	JUXTLA-HUACA	KHALAPUR	ORCHARD TOWN	TARONG	TAIRA
Weather Station	Eldoret	Mexico City	New Delhi	Boston	Aparri	Naha
Observed Period	1930–1945	not given	1866–1943	1870–1949	1928–1937	1891–1935
Temperature						
Hottest month	March	April	June	July	April	July
Absolute high	85°	90°	115°	104°	101°	96°
Daily Range	79–50°	77–51°	102–83°	80–63°	90–73°	89–77°
Coldest month	December	January	January	February	December	February
Absolute low	37°	27°	31°	−18°	59°	41°
Daily Range	76–49°	66–42°	70–44°	37–21°	81–70°	67–55°
Precipitation						
Average yearly fall	40.5 in.	29.4 in.	25.2 in.	40.8 in.	89.5 in.	82.8 in.
Number of months with more than 14 days of rain	3	5	0	0	3	0
Number of months with fewer than 7 days of rain	5	4	10	0	2	0

[a] The material for this table is taken from a report of the Meteorological Office of the British Air Ministry, 1960. The weather stations with the nearest latitude and altitude to the field site were selected.

The sharpest contrast in the weather occurs in Khalapur, where the long periods of heat and drought make the rains in June, July, and August dramatic. Although the actual number of rainy days, even during these months is few (average eight days), the winds that accompany the rains and the intense heat which precedes them in April and May make the seasonal variation striking.

In the other societies it rains frequently throughout the year. But a rainy day ordinarily confines children to their houses only in Orchard Town where precipitation during two-thirds of the year may be accompanied by cold weather. Orchard Town children tend to associate rain with being forced to stay indoors. The rainy season in Juxtlahuaca, which lasts from June through September, can be cold and unpleasant. It rains over 20 days in each of these months and 27 days in two of them (July and August), and the temperature during the same period often falls below 50 degrees. The rainfall, however, is usually a drizzle and does not seem to upset the daily routine so much as the infrequent downpours in Khalapur.

Ecology and economy affect the life of children and their parents in another important way—they partly determine the arrangement of dwellings. The number of people who live in a household, the number of generations which interact daily, the distance between households, and the nature and amount of shared work and play space are factors that influence both the training of a child and his daily experiences.

Chart III shows the composition of households in the six societies. It can be seen that half of the households in Taira, Okinawa include at least one grandparent. It is customary for one son, preferably the oldest, to stay on after his marriage to care for his parents. In Khalapur, India, the majority of the households consist of a man and a woman and their married sons and children or married brothers and their children. In Nyansongo, Kenya, half of the men are polygynists and their wives have separate huts.

Chart III also indicates the average number of adult males, females, and children per household, the extended courtyards in Khalapur having the most people, Orchard Town the fewest. Note that the houses in Nyansongo may have only a woman if her husband is a polygynist who rotates between the huts of his wives. The households have, however, on an average as many children as the extended families in Khalapur. In sum, Nyansongo women have more children than any of the other women in the sample.

Chart IV gives the frequency of the groups whose houses face on an area which the occupants use in common. For the Nyansongo it indicates the people who share a homestead (the people included in these

Chart III Household Composition

	TAIRA	TARONG	KHALAPUR	JUXTLAHUACA	ORCHARD TOWN	NYANSONGO
Nuclear Husband, wife and child. May include siblings of husband or wife	11	19	8	18	23	6
Stem Nuclear family plus 1 or 2 parents of husband or wife	12	3	3	3	1	0
Stem plus Married Brother or married cousins. May include parents' siblings	0	0	7	0	0	0
Extended Lineal Nuclear family plus married children and/or married brothers and/or cousins and their children	1	2	6	0	0	0
Polygynous One wife and her children per house	0	0	0	0	0	8
Other	0	0	0	1	0	2
Average number of adult males	1.3	1.4	2.6	1.3	1.0	.87
Average number of adult females	1.8	1.7	2.4	1.2	1.0	1.0
Average number of children	3.5	3.5	5.7	4.0	2.8	5.8

Chart IV *Courtyard Composition of Groups Larger than the Household Sharing Intimate Space*

	TAIRA	TARONG	KHALAPUR	JUXTLAHUACA	ORCHARD TOWN	NYANSONGO
Households Do not share a yard with another household	23	5	21	5	21	4[a]
Stem Share a yard with one or both parents of husband or wife (who have their own house)	1	3	0	3	3	0
Extended Share a yard with parents of husband or wife and/or aunt or uncle plus married brothers and/or sisters and/or married cousins of husband or wife	0	12	0	6	0	1
Collateral Share a yard with brothers and/or sisters of husband or wife	0	3	0	6	0	0
Collateral Extended Share a yard with married brothers and/or sisters and married children and/or married nephews and nieces of husband and/or wife	0	0	3[b]	2	0	0
Non-kin Share a yard with non-kin	0	1	0	0	0	0
Polygynous Co-wives share a yard	0	0	0	0	0	6
Extended Polygynous Share a yard with married brothers of husband plus husband's parents and/or husband's mothers co-wives and married half brothers	0	0	0	0	0	5
Average number of adult males	1.4	3.2	2.9	2.9	1.1	2.1
Average number of adult females	1.8	4.3	2.6	3.0	1.2	3.2
Average number of children	3.9	7.9	5.9	6.7	2.8	7.1
Total	7.1	15.4	11.4	12.6	5.1	12.4

[a] Includes one polygynous homestead where huts of two wives are far apart and there is tension between the wives.
[b] Includes married first cousins and their children.

units interact daily in an intimate fashion). In Juxtlahuaca the houses face on a private courtyard; in Tarong they surround a yard. Tarong has the greatest number of people who interact on this level of intimacy, and Juxtlahuaca and Nyansongo units are similar in size. Taira and Orchard Town have, on an average, two fewer adults per unit.

As mentioned earlier, the household and dwelling units partly determine the amount of adult help a mother has in raising her children. Our theoretical paradigm suggests, then, that the combined factors of a mother's economic role and the people with whom she lives influence her patterns of child rearing. The first test of hypotheses related to this paradigm are presented in *Mothers of Six Cultures* by Leigh Minturn and William Lambert (1964). Further tests of the hypotheses will appear in a forthcoming volume on the behavior of the children.

The salience of the father in infancy and childhood is another variable that affects the personality development of the society. For a discussion of the relative salience of the father and hypothesized consequent effects on aggressive behavior, see Beatrice Whiting's "Sex Identity and Crimes of Violence: a Comparative study."

Six of the volumes in this series are monographs of each of the six societies. The outline for each is organized around the conceptual system just presented. There are two main parts: one, a description of the adult world into which the child is born—*the ethnographic background*; the second, an account of how the child is trained—*child training*. In Part I, each account starts with a description of the environment and the local setting, including the village plan, the houses, and their interior arrangements. Then the daily routine of living and the economic pursuits of men and women are described. A chapter on social structure follows. In other words, these chapters describe the maintenance system that set the stage for child rearing. The selection of material for the remainder of Part I is also theoretically determined and includes descriptions of either adult behavior or the cultural products that seem to be the best indices of adult personality.

To explain the selection of behavior and cultural products, we must return to the discussion of the dimensions of personality selected for study by the senior investigators. As noted, the hypotheses to be tested focused on aggression, dependency, and the internalization of various mechanisms of behavior control. William Lambert and the Cornell group, because of previous research, were most interested in aggression, Irvin Child in dependency, and John Whiting and the Laboratory of Human Development in the development of internal controls that have been variously labeled as guilt, conscience, and superego.

It was the conviction of the researchers that the areas of study had to be limited and clearly defined if standardized material was to be collected. Chapter 1 of the *Field Guide for the Study of Socialization* is a description of the "systems" of behavior which were chosen for study and the hypotheses which the investigators hoped to test. Although it is impossible to include a detailed description of the theory in this introduction, it is necessary to present at least a summary of the behavior systems and the nature of the hypotheses.*

The nine behavioral systems include succorance, nurturance, self-reliance, achievement, responsibility, obedience, dominance, sociability, and aggression. In the most general terms, succorance is defined as asking others for help; nurturance, as giving help or emotional support; self-reliance, as doing things for oneself; achievement, as striving to meet internal standards of excellence; responsibility, as performing one's expected role duties; obedience, as attempting to meet the demands of others; dominance, as attempting to change the behavior of others; sociability, as making friendly approaches to other individuals; aggression, as hurting others. It was assumed that each of these systems of behavior would exist in some recognizable form and degree in every society and could best be identified by people's responses to specific universal situations. For example, whether an individual who encountered difficulty asked for help or solved the problem himself would indicate the relative strength of his succorance or, in contrast, his self-reliance. A measure of nurturance would be the frequency of the spontaneous giving of help, the reaction to requests for help, or the perception that others need help.

Returning to the monographs, our descriptions of the adult culture of each society include material which we consider relevant to these nine behavior systems.

A chapter on social control is included in each monograph to give information about the frequency of brawls, fights, crimes, and other conflicts and to describe the techniques which the society has devised either for preventing such conflicts from occurring or for stopping existing conflict. This material gives comparative indices of the expressed aggression of the adults and the existence and type of internalized controls. It will be noted, for example, that the incidence of rape is high in Nyansongo, that litigation is frequent in Khalapur and Nyansongo, and that there are few cases of physical violence in either Taira or Juxtlahuaca.

* For a full discussion of behavior systems see Child (1954).

The chapter on medical practices and theories of disease is included because variations in such belief systems were found to be useful indices of personality in the cross-cultural study by Whiting and Child (1953) and in later studies by Whiting (1959). Similarly, the analysis of man's relation to the supernatural was fruitfully analyzed by Spiro and D'Andrade (1958), Whiting (1959), and Lambert, Triandis, and Wolf (1959). Mourning behavior and death ceremonies have also been studied cross-culturally (Friendly, 1956).

We hoped that an analysis of the use of leisure time might be made along dimensions relevant to the nine behavior systems. The man who prefers to be alone in his spare time would be rated less sociable than one who always seeks the company of others. The amount of teasing or playful wrestling in leisure settings, or even the amount of pleasure derived from cockfights, might be used to rate the degree of preoccupation with aggression. The amount of time spent practicing skills might indicate the need for achievement. Whether or not men seek the company of women, men and women, or only men is of interest in assessing personality. Similarly, we might rate a man's personality in terms of his preference for smoking, eating, talking, drinking, dancing, or playing games. The nature of popular games can be analyzed along lines suggested by Roberts, Bush, and Arth (1957).

Part II of the ethnographies is chronologically organized, beginning with pregnancy and childbirth and continuing through preadolescence. The time required to observe this age span made it impractical to systematically study the lives of the adolescent children. The only exception to this is the monograph on the Nyansongo group in Kenya. The LeVines were especially interested in the effect of initiation ceremonies on the Nyansongo boys and girls. For this reason, they selected three age groups for study: the 3-to-7-year-olds, the 7-to-10-year-olds, and the post-initiation boys and girls. The Nydeggers included a brief chapter on adolescence in their monograph on Tarong. The other field teams did not feel that they had enough knowledge to include such a description.

The age span covered in the individual chapters of the six descriptions of socialization differs; each division is made on the basis of the age groups and the transitions recognized by the members of the society. Thus in Khalapur, India, where socialization is not broken by clearly defined stages, there are only three chapters. In Taira, Okinawa, on the other hand, there are named stages and sharp transitions, and the Maretzkis have followed this pattern in describing socialization. Weaning from the breast and back is an abrupt change in an Okinawan child's life. The transition from kindergarten to school age is also clear and dramatic. Before reaching school age a child is "senseless" according to the mothers and cannot be properly trained.

Within these chapters an attempt has been made to cover the treatment of the nine behavior systems by the parent or parent surrogate and to study the child's response to socialization. Obviously, some of the behavior systems are not relevant in infancy. In general, the early chapters in the socialization section concentrate on the handling of succorance, the mother's early contact with the child, the number of other individuals who share in the early care of the child, and their responsiveness to the demands of the infant. Among the hypotheses advanced in the *Field Guide for the Study of Socialization,* several concern the consequence of indulgence in infancy. As stated: "Indulgence in infancy, a large number of nurturing agents, and mild transition from infantile indulgence into childhood will produce (1) a trustful attitude toward others, (2) general optimism, and (3) sociability." It is also stated that training with respect to succorance will tend to influence sociability.

We hope that, on the basis of the information presented in the chapters on infancy, the reader can compare the degree of indulgence in infancy and the number of nurturing agents. A comparison of weaning from the breast and from complete dependence on caretakers should make it possible to evaluate the severity of the transition. For the consequent measures, we may turn either to the description of the behavior of older children or to the behavior and belief systems of adults. Is it true that the Mixtecan child of Juxtlahuaca is comparatively more friendly and sociable in later life than the Nyansongan? In infancy, the Mixtecan is constantly held or carried close to the mother's body, and she responds relatively quickly to the infant's demands. The Nyansongon child is tended for periods of time by a less consistently responsive 5-to-8-year-old child. In adult life, are Mixtecans more optimistic and trustful than the Nyansongans?

With the onset of weaning, other behavior systems become important. Training for self-reliance and the associated punishment for succorance are universal problems, but the degree to which this new behavior is expected of 3-year-olds varies from one society to another. The Orchard Town 3-year-old is feeding and dressing himself, whereas the Khalapur Rājpūt child of the same age may still be dressed and fed by his mother. Similarly, as mentioned earlier, the abruptness of the shift in expected behavior varies. The handling of aggression against parents, siblings, and peers at this age-level is also a universal problem which all parents and socializers must face. Probably closely associated with this behavior system is training for obedience and respect.

The *Field Guide for the Study of Socialization* contains many hypotheses about the antecedents of aggressive behavior in children and adults and stresses the techniques used by parents in the handling of aggression as well as their behavior as models. Specifically, one hypothesis is that permissiveness on the part of parents for teasing behavior should be reflected in the increase of observable unprovoked aggressive behavior on the part of children and adults. Is it indeed true that the Tarongan child who is "playfully" teased by his parents and other adults from early childhood instigates aggressive behavior more frequently than a Rājpūt child whose parents do not "playfully" tease him?

A second hypothesis concerning the handling of aggression states that children will be less likely to retaliate against aggression if parents and socializing agents punish any expression of anger. Again, the Khalapur Rājpūt child whose mother dislikes all expression of emotion, even excessive joy, and the Mixtecan child of Juxtlahuaca who is taught that he will become sick and die if he eats while he is angry should be less aggressive when provoked than the children of Orchard Town.* It will be noted that a distinction is made between unprovoked and provoked aggression. A further distinction is made for instrumental aggression, when a person tends to select aggressive means for attaining his goals. Comparisons between the handling of aggression in childhood may also be used to explore hypotheses about the conditions that lead to the displacement of aggression to others, the use of fantasy to express anger, or the projection of one's own desires to hurt others. For an understanding of consequent measures, the reader may turn to theories of diseases and the nature of the supernatural. Theory predicts that the societies which punish aggression most severely project their anger into the supernatural world and believe in dangerous and malevolent beings or attribute superhuman evil capacity to humans and believe in sorcery or witchcraft. To date, the best socialization variable for predicting the belief in witches and sorcerers is a combination of polygyny and the severe punishment for sex and aggression (Whiting, 1959). Among our societies, the Nyansongans are the most ridden with belief in superhuman individuals. Their treatment of aggression is therefore of particular interest. It is also of interest to

---

* For further discussion of the hypotheses regarding aggression, see the *Field Guide for the Study of Socialization,* Chapter 1.

speculate whether there is some relation between the Tarongan parents' treatment of aggression and teasing behavior and their belief in whimsical spirits who must be avoided and not annoyed.

Each monograph on socialization also includes an extended section on techniques used by the socializing agent. Our theory stresses the importance of rewards and punishments for the specific types of acts included in the nine behavioral systems. We are interested in the differential effect of various types of rewards and punishments and the conditions under which they are administered. Rewards may be material, such as food or money, or immaterial, as love and acceptance or praise and prestige. Privileges may also be given as rewards. All types of rewards may be given to commend good behavior or to incite desired behavior. Punishments depend on two types of sanctions, injury or abandonment; these may have as referents several types of agents—parents or authority figures, peers, the self, or supernatural agents.

These rewards and punishments may be given for different reasons. The locus of evaluation may be a specific response of the child, some consequence of his action, or the child himself as a person. In other words, a child may be praised because he does a chore well, because he has helped his mother by doing the chore, or because he is a good boy.

Rewards and punishments may also be intrinsic to the environment. For example, in a terrain where there are delicious wild berries, being able to locate, pick, and eat the berries without aid from adults may reward self-reliance. Herding large animals may reward dominance. Hot, humid weather may discourage physical exertion.

The nature and strength of internal controls—mechanisms which keep an individual from breaking the rules of a society—are thought to be related to techniques and agents of socialization as well as to the strength of a child's identification with both parents (Whiting and Child, 1953; Whiting, 1960; Burton and Whiting, 1961; Bacon, Child, and Barry, 1963). To determine the strength of these internal controls, we hoped to observe the differences in children's behavior in the presence and absence of socializing agents. On a societal level, we predicted that when a boy's identification with the same sex parent is weak, there will be a higher incidence of crime (see B. Whiting, in press).

We expected to find that authority figures would be important sanction agents in the adult culture when there was marked differentiation of authority within the nuclear family, when discipline was carried out by or in the name of the head of the house, and when responsibility and obedience training were emphasized. We expected peers to be important agents when there was little differentiation of authority within the family, when the right of discipline was not stressed, and when self-reliance training was emphasized. If these hypotheses are correct, we would expect consequent differences in the social control systems.

For most of the societies, the age period from 6 to 10 emphasizes responsibility training. A comparison of the chores assigned to boys and girls during this period, of the rewards and punishments for good or bad performance or omission, is an index of the training in this behavior system. The age at which different types of chores are assigned gives a clue to the age at which a society considers a child to have "sense," to be capable of reason, and it indicates the beliefs about the nature of the learning process. It will be observed, for example, that the Khalapur Rājpūts believe that children learn primarily by observing; hence there is little direct instruction. One type of responsibility is training children to care for younger siblings, cousins, and neighbors. This training may start very early, as in Taira and Nyansongo, or may be late and unimportant, as in Orchard Town.

The size and composition of play groups and the attitudes of parents about friendliness are described for each age level. It was hypothesized that sociability would be related both to training in nurturance and to the treatment of succorance, but initial comparisons of children's observed behavior indicate that nurturance is probably more closely related to training for responsibility and dominance than to friendliness.

In planning the research, the senior investigators were also interested in discovering age and sex differences in behavior which might be universal (Barry, Bacon, and Child, 1957). Is it true, in spite of radically different treatment in infancy and early childhood in the six societies, that boys and adult men are always more aggressive physically than girls and women and that girls and women are always more affectionate than men? Are there regularities in behavior that hold across cultures? Does succorance always decrease with age and dominance always increase? We have tested these and other hypotheses using the behavioral measures derived from the systematic observation of the sample children (see *Field Guide for the Study of Socialization*, Chapter 1). The results will be published in the forthcoming volume on the *Behavior of Children in Six Cultures*. Preliminary findings do reveal universal sex-age difference. Although these questions cannot be answered from a comparison of the six societies alone, consistent age and sex differences should be followed up by further research.

Mothers in Six Cultures by Leigh Minturn and William Lambert (1964) presents the first perusal of many of the hypotheses just given.

The authors based their analysis on factor scores derived from ratings made on the mothers' answers to the standard interview on child-training practices (see *Field Guide for the Study of Socialization,* Chapter 5). For example, the mother's economic responsibility outside the house, the amount of help she received in caring for her infants and children, and the number of other adult women and their kin relationship are studied in relation to her use of praise or physical punishment, to her concern with training her children to be responsible and to help with daily chores, and to her attitudes toward her child's expression of aggression toward other children and toward herself. The authors discuss the rank order of the societies on these variables and the rank order correlation between these and other variables. They also consider the effect of ecological and demographic variables on the mother's deviation from the norms of her group.

The reader will be aware that in spite of the research design, the data are not always comparable; in the different areas studied, some monographs have better coverage than others. These variations result not only from the personalities, interests, and training of the field-workers but also from the nature of the culture of the society they chose to study.

Although these monographs concentrate on the material that the researchers felt was theoretically relevant, it is hoped that readers with different conceptual systems and different hypotheses concerning human behavior will find it possible to peruse the data with relevant comparisons in mind. Those who were concerned with the project have developed new insights and new hypotheses. Some of these can be explored, but for many the relevant data are not detailed enough and further studies must be conducted. We believe that the need for further studies is inevitable in the social sciences and that progress comes from being willing to state hypotheses, test them, derive new theories, and plan new research to test these.

We believe that the detailed comparison of six societies is useful for generating hypotheses about human behavior. To test hypotheses adequately, the social scientist must study predicted variation among individuals within societies as well as across a larger sample of societies.

In conclusion, we should like to acknowledge our indebtedness to many people and institutions for their advice and help. The opportunity to do the study was provided by the generous support of the Social Science Research Council and of the Behaviorial Science Division of the Ford Foundation, and by a United States Public Health Grant, M-1096.

Various faculty members at the three universities helped in designing and planning the research. A list of these and other contributors will be found at the beginning of this chapter, but we wish to express special gratitude to Robert R. Sears, Pauline Sears, Eleanor E. Maccoby, and Alfred L. Baldwin, who have continued to give valuable advice to the project.

While in the field, each of the teams was assisted by graduates of local universities and schools who acted not only as interpreters but also as informants and friends. The aid that these students gave was invaluable. We wish to thank Nariyuki Agarie, Gurdeep Jaspal, Simeon Nyaechae, John Okiamba, Felix Ombasa, Laurence Sagini, Sri Shyam Narain Singh, Taurino Singson, Muriel Eva Verbitsky Hunt, and Kiyoshi Yogi.

We are deeply grateful to all the staff and students of the Laboratory of Human Development of Harvard University who read and helped edit the monographs. Marilyn Johnson, Celia Kalberg, Dorothy Tao, and Susan Horton were particularly devoted assistants. We wish to express our appreciation to numerous other people for reading and commenting on some or all the monographs, especially Masanori Higa, Geraldine Kohlenberg, and Morris Opler.

We are especially indebted to the families in Nyansongo, Khalapur, Taira, Juxtlahuaca, Tarong, and Orchard Town, who were not only cooperative informants, but also helpful friends. We hope that the children we studied will become proud members of the adult world into which they were born and that these volumes will contribute to mutual understanding so that they may live in a friendlier world.

Beatrice B. Whiting

Harvard University
September, 1965

BIBLIOGRAPHY

Air Ministry, Meteorological Office. *Tables of Temperature, Relative Humidity and Precipitation for the World*. London: Her Majesty's Stationery Office, 1960.

Bacon, Margaret K., Child, Irvin L., and Barry, Herbert III. A cross-cultural study of correlates of crime. *Journal of Abnormal and Social Psychology*, 1963, **66**, 291–300.

Barry, Herbert III, Bacon, Margaret K., and Child, Irvin L. A cross-cultural survey of some sex differences in socialization. *Journal of Abnormal and Social Psychology*, 1957, **55**, 327–332.

———, Child, Irvin L., and Bacon, Margaret K. Relation of child training to subsistence economy. *American Anthropologist*, 1959, **61**, 51–63.

Burton, Roger V. and Whiting, John W. M. The absent father and cross-sex identity. *Merrill-Palmer Quarterly*, 1961, **7**, 85–95.

Child, Irvin L. Socialization. In Gardner Lindzey (Ed.), *Handbook of Social Psychology,* vol. II. Cambridge, Mass.: Addison-Wesley, 1954.

Friendly, Joan P. A cross-cultural study of ascetic mourning behavior. Unpublished honors thesis, Radcliffe College, 1956.

Lambert, William W. Interpersonal Behavior. In P. H. Mussen (Ed.), *Handbook of Research Methods in Child Development,* Chapter 20, pp. 854–917. Wiley, New York: 1960.

————, Triandis, Leigh M., and Wolf, Margery. Some correlates of beliefs in the malevolence and benevolence of supernatural beings: a cross-cultural study. *Journal of Abnormal and Social Psychology,* 1959, **58**, 162–169.

Minturn, Leigh, Lambert, William W., et al., *Mothers of Six Cultures: antecedents of child rearing.* New York: Wiley, 1964.

Roberts, John M., Bush, R. R., and Arth, M. Dimensions of mastery in games. Stanford, Calif.: Ford Center for Advanced Study in the Behavioral Sciences, 1957 (mimeographed).

Sears, R. R., Whiting, John W. M., Nowlis, V., and Sears, P. S. Some child-rearing antecedents of aggression and dependency in young children. *Genetic Psychology Monograph,* 1953, **47**, 135–234.

Spiro, Melford E. and D'Andrade, Roy G. A cross-cultural study of some supernatural beliefs. *American Anthropologist,* 1958, **60**, 456–466.

Triandis, L. M. and Lambert, W. W. Sources of frustration and targets of aggression: a cross-cultural study. *Journal of Abnormal and Social Psychology,* 1961, **62**, 3, 640–648.

Whiting, Beatrice B. Sex identity conflict and physical violence: a comparative study. *American Anthropologist,* in press.

Whiting, John W. M. Sorcery, sin and the superego: a cross-cultural study of some mechanisms of social control. In *Nebraska Symposium on Motivation,* pp. 174–195. Lincoln: University of Nebraska Press, 1959.

————, Resource mediation and learning by identification. In I. Iscoe and H. Stevenson (Eds.), *Personality Development in Children.* Austin: University of Texas Press, 1960.

————, and Child, Irvin L. *Child Training and Personality: a cross-cultural study.* New Haven, Conn.: Yale University Press, 1953.

————, Chasdi, Eleanor M., Antonovsky, Helen F., and Ayres, Barbara C. The learning of values. In E. Z. Vogt (Ed.), *The Peoples of Rimrock,* Cambridge, Mass.: Harvard University Press, in press.

————, et al. *Field Manual for the Cross-Cultural Study of Child Rearing.* Social Science Research Council, New York, 1953.

————, et al. *Field Guide for a Study of Socialization.* Six Cultures Series, vol. 1. New York: Wiley, 1966.

About the Authors

Leigh Minturn, now Leigh Triandis, is an associate professor of psychology at the University of Illinois. She received her doctorate in social psychology from the Social Relations Department of Radcliffe College and Harvard University. When she participated in the project she was a research associate of the Psychology Department of Cornell University. Unmarried at the time, she arranged to work at one of the field stations of the Cornell India Project, a project under the direction of Morris Opler of the Anthropology and Sociology Department of Cornell. This arrangement enabled her to take advantage of the housing and facilities of the field station and to utilize material gathered by the other investigators.

The material on mothers and children was collected and written up by Leigh Minturn. Dr. Minturn also collected systematic data on the religious observances of the Rājpūt women. She was assisted in her field work by Gurdeep Jaspal, who acted as her interpreter and helped to record the behavior observations of the children. Gurdeep Jaspal graduated from Women's Christian College in Dehra Dun and received her master's degree in sociology from Lucknow University. As co-worker and interpreter, she assisted not only in the interpretation of language but also in an understanding of Rājpūt culture.

Most of the material for the ethnographic background of Khalapur in the first section of the monograph was collected by John Hitchcock, who is joint author of the first section. John Hitchcock, an associate professor of anthropology at the University of California, Los Angeles, has worked in India and Nepal. He received his doctorate in anthropology from Cornell University and, in addition to articles on India and Nepal, has written *The Magars of Banyan Hill*. During the time the research for the *Six Cultures* volume was in progress, he was the director of the Khalapur station and was working on a study of political life.

John Hitchcock was assisted by Sri Shyam Narain Singh, who served as co-worker and interpreter. He holds a master's degree in economics from Lucknow University as well as a law degree. His unstinting assistance, sense of humor, and affection for the Rājpūts of Khalapur were of uncalculable value. Patricia J. Hitchcock also helped her husband in collecting data and greatly lightened the burdens of administration. She was assisted by Kamla Singh, who received her master's degree in sociology from Agra University.

John Gumperz gave valuable linguistic assistance to the project. S. C. Dube and Mrs. Leela Dube helped by making available field notes on aspects of Khalapur life not studied by either of the authors. Morris Opler facilitated the writing of the monograph by generously allowing Leigh Minturn to use his India Project files, for additional ethnographic material.

Both authors wish to express their deepest appreciation and affection to the people of Khalapur, and particularly to the Rājpūts of Khalapur, who are the subject of this monograph. We wish to thank them for their kindness, patience, and hospitality. This is their story; we sincerely hope that we have told it well.

Contents

Part I

BY JOHN T. HITCHCOCK AND LEIGH MINTURN

The Ethnographic Background

✴
✴
✴
✴
✴
✴

Chapter 1

The Setting

South of the Himalayas, the great mountain chain which forms a natural boundary between India and countries to the north, lies a vast alluvial plain. It is watered by the broad, slow-moving Ganges and its tributaries. The region is very fertile and its western half—most of it now a part of the state of Uttar Pradesh—was the cradle of Indian classical civilization. Khalapur, one of the many thousands of villages in Uttar Pradesh, lies between the Ganges and its large tributary river Jumna. The village is about 90 miles north of Delhi and is so close to the Himalayas that the foothills and snow-covered peaks are visible on clear days (see map 1).

The climate is monsoonal, and a hot, wet summer is followed by a comfortably warm winter and a very hot, dry spring. In April or early May, after the winter crops have been harvested, a scorching wind

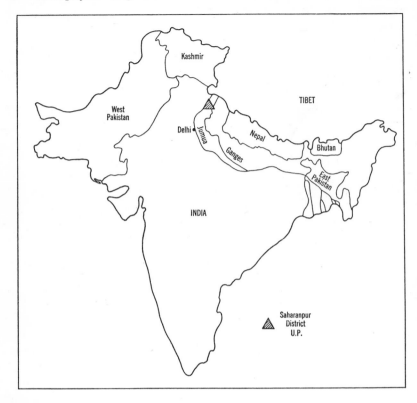

Map 1.

from the western desert begins to blow. It is ladened with dust picked up from the barren fields. The atmosphere becomes yellow and opaque and dust is everywhere. Small twisters sometimes whirl across the plain, and occasional dust storms blacken the sky and lower the visibility to a few hundred yards. In the heat of the day, temperatures rise to 110° F or higher.

Violent thunder and hail storms often precede the summer monsoon by a month or more. These harbingers of the longer and steadier rains are called the "little monsoon" and sometimes cause severe damage to any grain which is still standing in the fields. The heavy rain-bearing clouds of the true monsoon arrive toward the end of June, and from then until the end of September almost all of the 40-inch average yearly rainfall occurs. The usual pattern is rain for a day or two, followed by a few days of sunshine, with each succeeding day becoming increasingly humid and hot, so that the renewal of rain is a welcome relief. Throughout the monsoon insects are abundant, and toward the last of the period the incidence of malaria shows a marked rise.

With the retreat of the monsoon in September, temperatures gradually fall. By November and December nights are cool, and occasionally there may be a light frost. There is some rainfall during the winter, and during these wet periods the weather can be uncomfortably damp and chilly. On the whole, however, the winter months are moderate, clear, and very pleasant.

Culturally the region where Khalapur is located shows a strong Muslim tinge. It was part of Hindu kingdoms and empires until the thirteenth century, but after this, like much of North India, it fell under the sway of Islamic invaders from western Asia. Muslim rule reached a climax during the sixteenth and seventeenth centuries when most of North and Central India was united under the Islamic dynasty which produced Akbar, the great contemporary of Queen Elizabeth of England. Although Muslim power in North India suffered a gradual decline in the eighteenth century, descendants of Akbar continued to occupy their Delhi throne until 1858, about 50 years after the British had become the real power in this section of India. Like most villages in the area, Khalapur shows many evidences of this prolonged Muslim and west Asian contact. The custom of purdah, or seclusion of women, which the high status village families observed probably was taken over from the Muslims. A Hindu temple was recently built in Khalapur, but prior to this the most prominent religious structure was a large domed memorial to a Muslim saint. Hindustani, the language of the villagers, is a blend derived from Sanskrit, Arabic, and Persian. Prior to the adoption of a different script after independence, the schoolchildren learned a Persian form of writing, and most official records also were maintained in this script. Nearly 400, or approximately 8% of Khalapur's population, are followers of Islam, and their number includes some of the landowning families.

The center of Muslim and west Asian influence in the neighborhood of Khalapur is Bhudana, a town of some 25,000. Once an important seat of Muslim provincial rule, it lies about 4 miles northeast of the village and today houses a world-famous center of Islamic learning.

The headquarters city of Khalapur's administrative district is Saharanpur, a large manufacturing and railway center. Villagers sometimes are required to travel there in their dealings with the government, but most often they go to Bhudana, which besides being an important religious center is also the headquarters town for the district subdivision (*tahsil*) in which Khalapur is situated. Here the villagers find such government facilities as law courts, a land-revenue collection office, a dispensary, and a police station. A hard-surfaced road and a major railway pass north and south through Bhudana. Going north by bus or rail one can travel to Saharanpur (some 36 miles distant) and to other major cities of northern Uttar Pradesh and the Punjab. Traveling south 12 miles one comes to Muzaffarnagar, the headquarters city of the adjoining district, and four or five hours later to Delhi. Many people from Khalapur travel frequently within a radius of 100 miles. Although there are many women who have not seen large cities, most of the men have visited a number of them.

Two decades ago a sugar mill was constructed in Bhudana, and at the same time another was built on the railway about 8 miles to the south. Both mills process and purchase cane grown in the village and together have brought a considerable increase in prosperity to the landowners of the area. Another factor of great economic importance is the Ganges Canal. A branch flows near Bhudana, and two distributaries carry water to Khalapur and make it possible to irrigate almost two thirds of the village land.

Approaching Khalapur along the Bhudana road, one passes lines of creaking bullock carts carrying loads of sugar cane stalks to the Bhudana mill. The drivers sit on the yoke and urge on the straining bullocks by making loud popping noises with their tongues. The carts are accompanied by clouds of dust. Occasionally a returning cart bumps past, with a jingling from bells on the necks of its trotting bullocks. It may carry small purchases made in the Bhudana bazaars or sometimes a veiled wife who has been met at the station after a visit to her parents. The few cyclists, most of them with a cloth market bag dangling from their handle bars, hug the narrow, unrutted strip along the edge of the road.

The road enters the fields of Khalapur long before one can see the village. The fields are separated by earth ridges or irrigation ditches, and in many of them one can see farmers at work. Some are guiding a light wooden plow behind their team of bullocks, shouting at them, goading them with a stick, or twisting their tails. In a cane field a man is cutting down the tall, reddish stalks of the standing crop while another strips off the leaves and tops. A number of men move through the fields with huge loads of fodder on their heads. They have bundled cane leaves, grass, or grain into large cloths which they balance with a bamboo staff carried across their shoulders. The burdened farmers are following the network of paths leading through the fields to the village. They move smoothly, with the characteristic hip-swinging jog of persons who carry heavy loads on their heads.

About half a mile from the village, the road passes beside a large mango grove. Monkeys chatter from the dark green leaves. A group of women with heads and faces covered by their white saris walk in the shadows. They carry brass trays and have come to make offerings at a small, conical shrine erected to honor a male ancestor of their family.

After leaving the grove, the road passes between a group of white-plastered buildings. They house, respectively, the cooperative seed store, the Cornell Project, and the new high school. The high school is large and impressive. It was begun about four years ago, soon after India became independent, and some buildings are still in the process of construction. There are classrooms, a boys' dormitory, an office, a kitchen, a diesel-driven irrigation well, and a fenced plant nursery.

A few hundred yards straight ahead, the village itself can be seen. It is a very large village, with a population of slightly over 5000. Its houses are partly hidden in the many trees which have been planted to provide shade. The closest buildings are strung out for a quarter of a mile along the edge of a stream. They are of all sizes and shapes and closely packed together. Greyish, sun-baked adobe alternates with white-washed brick. The tall, curving spire of the Hindu temple rises above the trees. Behind it in the center of the village one can glimpse some of the taller buildings. They rest on an extensive mound, built up from the brick, broken pottery, and tumbled-down adobe that have accumulated during the many centuries people have been living on the site.

Where the Bhudana road enters the village, the brook widens to form a fair-sized pond. Some years ago those who entered the village here had to wade, but now there is a brick and masonry bridge built by the sugar mill. It is wide enough for bullock carts to cross. Yet even with the new bridge, when the rains have been heavy, one sometimes has to wade, for the brook floods its banks and covers the approaches. The pond is used for watering cattle and on hot days farmers or their sons bring the family buffaloes there to be splashed and cooled. In a field just beside the bridge, there is a clump of trees where herd boys often play hookey while their cattle rest in the shade.

The village neighborhood nearest the bridge is the one in which this study was made. The men's houses of some families face the brook and are separated from it only by a small field and a road. Houses and cattle compounds of other families form the easternmost end of the village and in this direction straggle out from the densely packed site into a sandy, barren field. The neighborhood is marked off from adjoining portions of the village site by tortuous lanes and footpaths.

Although Khalapur's jumble of cattle compounds, angled-mud and brick walls, new houses, tumbled-down houses, and narrow, muddy lanes appear patternless, in the minds of the villagers the site where their houses are situated has many clear divisions. There are seven subdivisions, called *paṭṭī* (see map 2). These divisions hark back to a system of revenue collection no longer in use. There is also division into smaller neighborhoods, some reflecting recent revenue divisions, others the boundaries made by lanes and paths. In some of these neighborhoods. washermen, goldsmiths, leatherworkers, sweepers, or Brāhmaṇ priests predominate. In the neighborhood in which this research was done (see map 3) the people all are members of the Rājpūt landowning class. Only after long acquaintance would an order growing out of caste and kinship begin to emerge.

People who are not well acquainted with Indian society think of the caste system as a fivefold division consisting of Brāhmaṇs, or priests; Kṣatriya, or warrior-rulers; Vaiśya, or merchants; Śūdra, or artisans, servants, and laborers; and Untouchables, or persons who are regarded, somewhat paradoxically, as being entirely outside the system. If such divisions ever really existed and served as a means of organizing so-

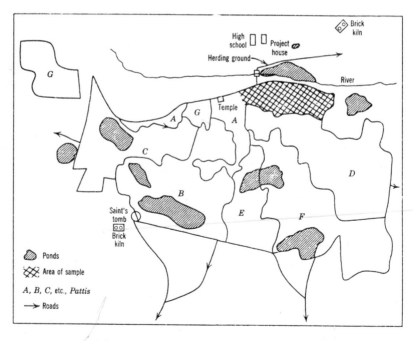

Map 2. Living site of village of Khalapur showing paṭṭī *divisions.*

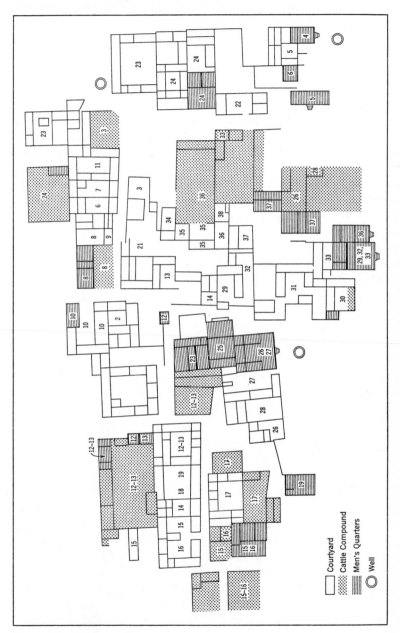

Map 3. Neighborhood of study.

Courtyard
Cattle Compound
Men's Quarters
Well

7

ciety, it was many centuries ago in ancient India. Today the basic unit of the caste system is a social grouping called the *jāti*. A *jāti* is a group one joins by being born into it and it is the group from which one takes a husband or wife. There are many thousands of *jāti*. They vary greatly in the size of their membership, as well as in the size of the area where these members are concentrated.

The *jāti* do have some connection with the fivefold divisions thought to have existed in ancient India. These divisions were ranked, and the first three—the priests, warrior-rulers, and traders—had the highest status. Only the members of these three orders were permitted to hear the sacred Sanskritic texts. Since they went through a period of training believed to give greater spiritual insight, they were known as the "twice-born," and as a mark of their status they wore the "sacred thread," a circlet of string draped over one shoulder. Today most *jāti* in India associate themselves with one or another of the five ancient divisions, and many claim descent from an illustrious personage believed to have been a member of the "twice-born" orders. For this reason the idea of the five ancient classes serves as a kind of organizing device which might help a stranger to a locality in making a rough order of many unfamiliar *jāti* encountered there. The idea is not always helpful, however, for many of the lines are blurred. In a given region or village there are those who claim they belong to one class while their neighbors claim they actually belong to another, lower class. In Khalapur the goldsmiths claim they are Kṣatriya. The landlords, whose claims are better founded, laugh at their pretensions and say they are Śūdra. Many Khalapur villagers are also uncertain whether to call the washerman Śūdra or Untouchable, and there is also some doubt about whether a family which claims to be Brāhmaṇ actually should be accorded this status.

Jāti generally are associated with a particular occupation. This is to be understood as a general tendency, however, for there are always many exceptions. In Khalapur there is a *jāti* whose traditional occupation is leather working, but none of its members will skin dead cows or make leather articles. Everywhere in India agriculture is an occupation in which members of any *jāti* are apt to be engaged either full or part time. In Khalapur most Brāhmaṇ families depend for the major portion of their living on farming, and there are some Brahmans who seldom or never perform priestly duties. There is a leather worker who is a clerk, an Untouchable who is a shopkeeper, a barber who is a minor government official, and another who has become a tailor. The list could be extended, but these examples are sufficient to show that the relation between *jāti* and occupation, while viable in a very general way, is one that in any particular case is very likely to break down. This is especially true in the many villages like Khalapur where new occupations are being introduced as old ones become unprofitable.

Members of a *jāti* usually are found in a number of neighboring villages. Some *jāti* have little political solidarity; others are fairly cohesive and may be represented by strong legislative and judicial councils. *Jāti* are characterized by shared customs regarding such matters as religious belief, dress, and food, and often these customs serve to differentiate them clearly from other *jāti* in the locality.

Relations between the members of different *jāti* are subject to a number of rules which operate in contexts having to do with sex, touch, eating, drinking, and smoking. Most of these rules give expression to the idea that some *jāti* are capable of polluting others. The Brahman, who has the highest ritual status, can be polluted by various forms of contact with others but is not himself polluting. That is why Brahmans are in demand as cooks or as water dispensers. In general, *jāti* having the same or nearly equal ritual status can eat and drink together without fear of pollution. More and more restrictions apply as the ritual distance between *jāti* increases. The rules are complex and variable. A few from Khalapur will serve as illustration.

When Rājpūt landowners of the village are sitting together, they all smoke, using the same hookah stem, although they suck the smoke through their fists so that their lips never touch it. If a Brahman were to join them, he either would be offered a separate pipe, or every time it was his turn to smoke, a different stem would be inserted in the hookah base. He would also be offered the place of honor, at the head of the cot, and Rājpūts would move away to make room for him. If the Brahman were orthodox and his Rājpūt host wished to give him some cooked food, he would offer him only food that had been cooked in clarified butter or *ghī*. Food boiled in water would be unsuitable. If a goldsmith came to join the group, he would be offered a place on one of the cots; but a water carrier or potter would be expected to squat on the ground some distance away from all the others. This is the situation in only one social context, however. If a Brāhmaṇ and an Untouchable were working together in the fields, as they often must, the rules of distance and even of touch would not be observed, at least by the younger men. The Brāhman and the Untouchable would tug together on the rope used to lash the load of sugar cane to the bullock cart. The Untouchable also would help hoist a load of fodder to the Brāhmaṇ's head and in doing so would touch the portion of the Brāhmaṇ's clothing in which it was wrapped. In neither case would the Brāhmaṇ feel he had been polluted.

The relations between *jāti* have never been static and are always in the process of redefinition. Upward mobility, although a slow process, always has been possible. In each region the path of mobility is defined by the customs of those who are highest in the ritual hierarchy. If the local Brāhmaṇs refrain from eating meat and drinking wine, then a *jāti* that adopts these customs lays claim to a higher status. If it is a small group within a *jāti*, its members strengthen their claim if they refuse to intermarry with those who refuse to make the change. In time the new group will become a separate *jāti* and will feel somewhat superior to the group of which they were formerly a part. Another path to higher status, and one which also has brought about a proliferation of *jāti*, is the idea that some occupations are polluting. Making wine or working in leather are occupations which preclude rise in ritual status. Groups that give up these traditional occupations in time separate themselves from those that do not. The nonleather working *jāti* in Khalapur is a case in point.

The twin concepts of *dharma* and *karma* are of basic importance in the ideology of the caste system. The concept of *dharma* has a wealth of connotation but a core meaning is "a way of life appropriate to one's status." Quite simply it means that a potter should be a good potter and should follow the rules governing relations between himself and other members of his *jāti*, and of other *jāti*. By doing this he wins for himself, by the workings of *karma*, a better station in his next reincarnation. He is a potter in this life because of deeds he performed or failed to perform in his last. Besides accounting for one's status, the concept of *karma* accounts for the good or ill fortune one may suffer during the course of one's life. Although the full meaning of these terms is untranslateable *dharma* connotes duty and *karma* connotes fate. Both ideas have religious sanction.

Landowners, who were the subject of this study, belong to a *jāti* claiming descent from the ancient warrior-rulers, or Kṣatriya. Throughout Indian history there have been groups of kinsmen who at various times and places have achieved political power. Generally these kinsmen were organized as patrilineal clans, that is, they were groups of men, all of whom believed that they could trace their descent, if they went back far enough in the male line, to a single man who was the progenitor of them all. The children of these men, both boys and girls, were also members of the clan. The wives, however, were not, for it was the rule that they had to come from a different clan. A powerful clan generally validated its claim to the status of Kṣatriya by securing a genealogy. In the genealogy the descent of all members of the clan was traced back to one or another of the semidivine Ksatriya heroes whose lives and deeds were recorded in the ancient Sanskritic epic literature. And when members sought wives, they picked them from among clans that had established similar claim.

As a matter of historical fact, it is probable that many of the clans which achieved this status are descended from invading tribes that entered India from Central Asia prior to the arrival of the Muslims. Later, during the period of Muslim invasions, many of these clans, now calling themselves Rājpūts, or "sons of princes," fled to Rājputāna, a dry and forbidding mountainous area to the southwest of Khalapur. The kingdoms they established there were in existence throughout the Muslim period and continued as seats of Rājpūt courtly splendor until India became independent. These kingdoms were a center for resistance to Muslim rule, and the heroism and derring-do of Rājpūt groups and individuals today are an important part of folk tradition throughout India.

Some Rājpūt clans, or portions of them, after offering fierce resistance to various Muslim armies—tales of these exploits are also part of widespread folk tradition—drifted north or south into the mountainous regions of Central India or the Himalayas, and some may have gone as far as Nepal. Many of them remained in North India. Most were landholders, and many were persons of considerable local influence. Muslim rule varied in extent and efficiency, and sometimes a group of Rājpūt clansmen were able to set up petty kingdoms in opposition to the reigning power. There were also Rājpūts who took important posts in the Muslim central administration or who ruled provinces as subordinate chiefs.

It is impossible to say with any certainty from which area the Rājpūt clan to which the landowners of Khalapur belong came. According to their own traditions, they moved into North India from Central India sometime during the early centuries of Muslim rule. Their numbers swelled, and as opportunity arose they took up land in northwest India, in the region where the Ganges and Jumna debouch onto the plains. Calculations based on their genealogy suggest that Khalapur, as part of a general southward movement, was taken by a clansman and his sons sometime during the fifteenth century. The descendants of this man, with their wives and children, now number over 2000. No other caste group in Khalapur is as large by half, and the few other caste groups claiming equal length of residence in the village say they came as retainers of the founding family. Today the Rājpūts hold over 90% of the land and regard the village as theirs by right of conquest and 400 years of possession.

Following the usual pattern, the Khalapur Rājpūts and the other members of the clan to which they belong—many of whom have a similar position in a large number of surrounding villages—validate their claim to Kṣatriya status by means of a written genealogy. This is kept by a professional genealogist whose family has served in such a capacity for generations. His home is in Rājputāna, so that he forms a link with the heartland of Rājpūt tradition. He journeys once a year to visit various clan villages and keeps a careful record of births and deaths in the male line. His charts trace the male line back through a succession of historical and mythical figures to Rāma, the divine hero of the epic poem Rāmāyaṇa.

Things the Rājpūts say about themselves show how they tend to create their self-image in terms of their putative and, to a degree, their actual past. For instance, during a conversation in the village it was remarked that a highly placed official was a good administrator. "And why not?" replied a Rājpūt man. "He is a Rājpūt. He belongs to a ᵣuling race, and they have been doing this work since time immemorial."

Because the Rājpūts do consider themselves potential rulers and warriors, their self-image causes many of them to have markedly ambivalent feelings about their present occupation of farming. It is proper that they should own the land but not proper that they should have to farm it themselves. It is regarded as demeaning to become so heavily involved in farm work that one does not have ample leisure.

The fact that many Rājpūts now are more heavily engaged in the actual day to day routine of field work than they believe they should be is the result of the interplay of many factors over the course of centuries. To meet Rājpūt status requirements, the ideal farm is one where there is enough land so that it can support the family owning it as well as the tenants and field workers who will work it. The founder of Khalapur must have had such a farm. As time went on, however, a number of developments made it more difficult for all of his descendants to maintain a similar economic base. It is a rule among the Rājpūts in this section of India that all the sons have a right to an equal portion of the parental estate. It can easily be seen that seven or eight grandsons who partition the estate are going to be less well off than their grandfather as far as the size of holding is concerned. One way the constantly increasing pressure on the land was taken care of was by putting more and more untilled land under the plow. Another was to move off and capture or found another village. But there was a limit to both processes, and in time many Rājpūts were much more like small farmers than they were like landlords.

The pressures bringing this state of affairs about were eased some-what by the fact that up until the latter part of the nineteenth cen-tury the predominant economic pattern was subsistence farming, with a heavy emphasis on herding. There were common lands on which cows and buffaloes could graze and many Khalapur farms apparently were large enough to support tenants and laborers, as well as the land-lord family, if all the latter wanted was grain enough to eat, and suf-ficient reserve to carry it through a bad season.

By the end of the nineteenth century the pattern of farming had changed. The British established more peaceful conditions, and the railways connected the farms of Khalapur and other villages with local and world markets. It became easier and more profitable to sell grain and, later, sugar cane for money. And there were desirable things to use the money for—chaff cutters, which greatly eased the burden of farming, kerosene lanterns, water pumps, mill-made cloth, and many other items of the new economy. Farming not only became more profitable but also such developments as the Ganges irrigation system made it more secure. This, and many other factors which made life a little easier, increased the population. Hence, at the same time that land was becoming more valuable and difficult to obtain, there was also a much greater population pressure being exerted on it.

Among the things that happened in Khalapur as a result of these de-velopments was that the common grazing lands, with the support of newly instituted British legal machinery, were parceled out among individual Rājpūt families. Some families began to work their lands hard in order to obtain a surplus of grain, which they sold for money or to other farmers who had had bad luck or who were not as in-dustrious. When those who had borrowed grain defaulted, legal ma-chinery and its supporting police power were brought into play, and the debtors forfeited a number of rights in their land. They thus be-came tenants to Rājpūts who were better able than they to take ad-vantage of the changing times. As a result, just prior to independence, a few Rājpūt families in Khalapur—and this pattern was repeated in many other North Indian villages—held a high proportion of the land. They were true landlords. Many other Rājpūts, on the other hand, were either small farmers or were small farmers and also tenants of other Rājpūts. After independence a law was passed in Uttar Pradesh (U.P. Zamindari Abolition and Land Reforms Act, 1952) which re-duced the holdings of the larger landlords. Furthermore, tenancy was made illegal. Since there were few farmers left who were wealthy enough to hire all the labor needed to work their farms—a fact which was partly the result of increasing labor costs—many had to begin doing much more actual field work. In the sample studied, there was one Rājpūt farmer who had to learn to plow when he was over 40.

It may be said, in summary, that with regard to field work many Rājpūts in Khalapur and elsewhere in the region, during much of their history at least, seem to have been able to maintain a kind of genteel poverty. In the late nineteenth and early twentieth centuries this became easier for a few and more difficult for many; and today it is difficult for almost all.

In view of their self-image it is understandable that Rājpūts who now are having to do farm work, especially plowing—which is felt to be particularly inappropriate—have a desire to justify and explain the situation. Such justification sometimes takes the form of a mythico-historical tale, as when a Rājpūt told how the Muslim conquerors gave small parcels of their land back to the Rājpūts so "that the regular contact with cows and bullocks would make them patient and calm and they would become like the earth they plowed, all broken and scattered." "Rājpūts," he added, "should be given their own work and that work is not beating the hind end of a bullock."

In line with their image of themselves as warriors, the Rājpūts think they are larger, stronger, and more virile than other caste groups in the village. When one Rājpūt father heard that a primary school teacher was taking the students outside the village to participate in an athletic event, he said, "I am not going to let my son participate. Rājpūt boys do not have to participate in athletics. They are already stronger than other castes."

When discussing the new universal adult franchise, another man complained, "These are critical times because now we have to fight (the members of other castes) with the vote. Formerly it meant something that we were bigger and stronger men."

It is a traditional Rājpūt value to be touchy on points of honor and unafraid to pursue a quarrel to the point of violence when prestige is at stake. This behavior still characterizes the Khalapur Rājpūt. During the course of the study there was a killing as a result of a Rājpūt quarrel, and a number of fights with staffs occurred. The Rājpūt is not, however, quick to take his revenge. He may plot for years to avenge an insult to himself or his family. Outward hostility should not be shown while retribution is being planned lest the enemy be forewarned. As one Rājpūt put it, "We like to wait until our enemy reaches the edge of the pond and then we push him in."

Throughout the nineteenth century the Rājpūts of Khalapur and their kinsmen in nearby villages were a problem to the British because of their cattle thieving, their marauding for grain (especially when crops were poor), and their unremitting resistance to revenue collectors. The police and some government officials still speak of Khalapur as a criminal village, and some of the village Rājpūts still do augment their incomes through cattle theft.

The past century, however, marked a considerable lessening of both thieving from outside the village and feuding within it. With regard to the former, this is partly because the times no longer called for such activity. The increased irrigation and communication facilities greatly decreased the incidence of crop failure and famine. And with regard to the latter, more adequate police protection, the establishment of courts, and the founding of schools tended to mitigate the reliance of sheer force as a method of settling disputes. Also significant is the fact that the village has been strongly affected during the past few decades by two reforming leaders.

In the twenties and thirties a young Rājpūt named Pṛthvi Singh inaugurated a period of cooperative endeavor during which many projects and reforms were carried out. Under the leadership of this man, a temple and a school for teaching Sanskrit and religion were built. It was a time, the villagers say, "when the cart was running nicely." The major stimulus accounting for the success of this leader was the Arya Samaj movement, which both molded Pṛthvi Singh and prepared the people to accept his programs. This movement, which was a revivalistic and reform movement within Hinduism, was strongly ascetic in emphasis.

Many of its teachings, although present in Hinduism, ran counter to Rājpūt values, and one of the effects of Pṛthvi Singh's teachings was to strengthen values which previously had not been emphasized so strongly within his group. The Ārya Samāj opposed meat eating, drinking, opium eating, and smoking, and many Rājpūt men gave up these practices. Despite Pṛthvi Singh's influence, most Rājpūts now smoke, many drink and eat meat, and some eat opium. But it is partly a reflection of his strengthening of the ascetic; Brāhmanical strand in Hinduism that many feel they must justify indulgence in terms of their warrior heritage.

Although Pṛthvi Singh sometimes was authoritarian and used force when crossed, his conciliatory methods, concern for the village as a whole, and a desire to minimize external and internal conflict are the traits for which he is most remembered. He gave the villagers—and the Rājpūts in particular—a new conception of their own potentialities and in many ways laid the foundations on which the reform leader who is now the village's key figure was able to build.

This second leader, though a Rājpūt, comes from outside the village. He was able to channel the enthusiasm for India's independence into support for building the new high school, of which he is now the principal. He also is the medium through which the influence of the Congress Party, the party of Nehru and Gandhi, reaches the village.

At present, then, the Rājpūts are a people whose values are undergoing change. One still finds allegiance to old Rājpūt values, and there are many powerful men in the village who exemplify them. These values, however, have been countered to some extent by more peaceful conditions and by outside movements from which two very influential leaders derived much of their authority.

If answering quickly and without thinking, a Rājpūt will say that Rājpūts everywhere are members of the same *jāti*. Difficulties arise, however, as soon as there is a problem of marriage. To limit the discussion just to the region around Khalapur, there are some groups of kinsmen calling themselves Rājpūt whom the Rājpūts of Khalapur regard as upstarts. Occasionally a Rājpūt from the village has taken a wife from one of these groups, but it has always led to much criticism and, in the past, often to a refusal to share the hookah with the remiss caste brother. These groups as yet have not been able to validate their claims to true Kṣatriya status. There are other groups who are accorded the status of Kṣatriya, but who are not wholly acceptable as marriage partners because the Kṣatriya hero from whom they claim descent is regarded as slightly inferior. But in actual fact this objection seems to be of much less importance than the former objection, and, practically speaking, the *jāti* of the Rājputs of Khalapur includes their own clan and the members of any recognized Kṣatriya clan close enough for intermarriage. These considerations localize the *jāti* of the Khalapur Rājpūts in an area with a radius of about 100 miles, an area which includes some ten or more acceptable clans.

Almost all North Indian villages are composed of persons belonging to a number of *jāti*. In Khalapur some 30 are represented. They vary among themselves in the extent and definition of their social organization. The Rājpūts in Khalapur, for example, are clearly and explicitly a portion of one of the clans in their *jāti*. They always have lived in the village, and only a few outsiders have ever been able to obtain any of the land. The members of other *jāti* in the village, with the exception of the Brāhmaṇs and perhaps a few others, have moved to the village recently, taking the place of others who have left. Few own land and hence do not have one of the basic prerequisites of high status. They know their *jāti*, but their relation to other kinsmen within it, or to illustrious mythical ancestors, is not recorded or defined with any precision, partly perhaps because they have never owned much land. We will speak of all *jāti* segments in Khalapur as "caste groups" regardless of their varying types of social organization.

The Rājpūts and the other caste groups of Khalapur form a complex web of economic interdependence. Each Rājpūt family is dependent for services on families belonging to nine other caste groups, and these families in turn are dependent on the Rājpūt families they serve for most of their food. Water carriers and sweepers come to a Rājpūt house every day, the former to bring the daily water supply—a task of special importance, for wives cannot leave the courtyard—and the latter to clean the latrines or carry off refuse, a job which only an Untouchable can do. Every family, in addition, is served by a carpenter, blacksmith, barber, potter, washerman, and leatherworker. Carpenters and blacksmiths make and repair agricultural implements; barbers shave, cut hair and fingernails, and play a key role on ceremonial occasions; potters make a large variety of clay pots and other utensils, including the jugs in which water is carried and stored; the washerman washes clothing and bedding; sweepers make cow dung cakes and carry away refuse, and the women also act as midwives. The leatherworker removes dead cattle and supplies his clientele with a few simple leather articles, such as a whiplash and parts of the bullocks' harnesses.

Each family also has a Brāhmaṇ priest who assists on ceremonial occasions. Some priests, as noted earlier, have given up their traditional role and obtain a living from their land. Only a few priests in the village devote all of their time to ritual matters. These are the Brāhmaṇs who know how to read and write and how to conduct the marriage ceremonies. The remainder of the priests divide their time between their farms and the ritual needs of their clientele, the majority of whom are Rājpūts. Today priests are called less often than they were in the past. A major reason for this was the Ārya Samāj movement. It had an antipriest bias and taught that each family head was himself capable of carrying out any religious rites which were necessary. The coming of the schools also weakened the position of the Brāhmaṇs, who in the past were prime repositories of whatever learning was found in Khalapur. These developments have made an increasing number of Rājpūt families reluctant to give the full traditional payment to their Brāhmaṇ priest. The priests, in response to these changes, have shown an increasing tendency to give up their traditional calling. And were it not for the fact that the women are much more conservative religiously than the men, it would seem that the decline in the functional importance of the Brāhman would be even more marked. An index of women's greater conservatism in ritual matters is the fact that, unlike most men, they will bathe and wash their hair if they inadvertently come into contact with an Untouchable.

Part of the payment for services performed by members of these nine caste groups consists of a number of customary benefits provided by each of the families served. These include such things as food on many ceremonial occasions throughout the year and the right to cut fodder and fuel from the fields. The major payment consists of grain. These payments are made twice a year, after each of the two food-grain harvests.

This system of economic interdependence, known in its widest ramifications as the *jajmānī* system, is based on mutual need and lack of economic alternatives. It reflects a subsistence rather than a money economy, and many of the strains to which it now is subject arise both from the growing number of different jobs which are open to villagers and to the increasing use of money. Aside from mutual need, the controls in such an economic system are diffuse and cultural, although on occasion sanctions involving either deprivation or force are involved. Culturally the relations between a Rājpūt family and its servants are colored by a semifeudal ideal. The Rājpūt is supposed to be paternal and benevolent, the servant loyal and deferential. The relation between servant families and Rājpūt families should persist generation after generation, like the relations between nobility and their retainers.

Actual relations, of course, have always been a compromise between allegiance to these ideals and many other competing interests. One finds that Rājpūts who are dissatisfied with a servant will shift to another. This usually is not a severe economic blow, for servants work for many Rājpūt families and for members of other castes as well. There have been instances, too, when a servant left a Rājpūt with whom he was dissatisfied. The system always apparently has shown fluidity of this kind. Animosities sometimes are aroused, however, and then it is the Rājpūt who tends to have the upper hand. A powerful Rājpūt family has been known to drive a disliked servant family from the village. The servant families are not always totally without recourse, especially when less powerful Rājpūt families are involved. A servant may be able to obtain the support of neighboring Rājpūts with whom he is on good terms, or he may be able to secure the intercession of a powerful village leader with a just bias. Some caste groups also have considerable solidarity and, in addition, are purveying a service which the Rājpūts would find it hard to do without. This is true of the sweepers, who on a number of occasions have been able to bring quite a lot of pressure to bear by threatening to "strike." However, a caste group like the water carriers has a much weaker bargaining position. They are a comparatively small group, and now that pumps are being set up in many of the women's houses, a "strike" by them is becoming a less effective weapon. There have been occasions when the interests of all the serving castes were seriously involved, and as a group they were able to present a strong front. By this method on one recent occasion they were able to secure an adjustment of the biannual grain payment.

Some of the caste groups formerly a part of this system either have dropped out entirely or are in the process of dropping out. This is true of the weavers and tailors, and there are other groups, such as the potters, blacksmiths, and carpenters, who are tending to shift to an item by item cash payment basis, and at the same time are tending to work for anyone who will pay them.

The labor of almost all of the caste groups in the village is drawn on at the time of the two yearly harvests. For many of them, the portion of the harvest earned in this way is a vital supplement to what often is a meager yearly income. One of the most important of all caste groups to the Rājpūts is the group of Untouchables who no longer work in leather. They represent about 13% of the total population, and many of them are hired as manual laborers. They plow, make adobe houses and walls, do the difficult spading required when the sugar cane is young, gather fodder and chop it up in the chaff cutter, and perform a number of other services requiring hard manual labor. Occasionally they also obtain a field or two from the Rājpūts on a sharecrop basis.

Members of the many other caste groups in the village work at a variety of occupations. Some do much the same work as the Untouchable laborers. Some, including an Untouchable, run the 30 small shops which supply such items as spices, sweets, cigarettes, needles and thread, vegetables and grain. Some work as herders, a few make grain or popcorn, press oil-bearing seeds, or act as bearers and messengers. There are goldsmiths and shoemakers and some who take wadded cotton and fluff it so that it can be used for restuffing pillows, quilts, and mattresses. There are two doctors, one following traditional Hindu, the other traditional Muslim methods. There are also a postman and a number of school teachers. There is such a variety of occupations, in short, that there is someone in the village to meet almost every need.

Although not part of the village caste system, one of the most interesting aspects of village life are the individuals and groups continually moving in and out, many of them following their traditional *jāti* occupations. There are bangle and cloth sellers, a group of colorful, wandering metalsmiths, and a similar group which makes wooden combs. There are Muslim cattle dealers and a man who cuts and trims the bullocks' tails, keeping the hair for making brushes. There are wandering minstrels and occasionally a troupe to put on one of the traditional folk dramas. There is a man who cleans out ear wax, another who doctors sore eyes. There is an exhibitor of a five-legged cow, and a man who makes a living by pretending to be something he isn't —usually a mailman with a fake telegram or letter.

☘
☘
☘

Chapter 2

Social Organization

In the Rājpūt neighborhood selected for study, the largest and most conspicuous houses are some of the men's quarters. Each of these buildings consists of a platform 4 to 6 feet in height surrounded by a retaining wall of brick. One ascends the platform by a series of steps. The height of these platforms lifts the occupants above the dust of the lane, keeps the cows, buffaloes, pigs, and dogs from intruding, and gives the occupants a good vantage point from which to see what is going on, at the same time lending them a certain eminence. Many of these platforms are shaded by trees. When not working, the men of the family and their friends sit together on these platforms, smoking the hookah.

At the far end of the platform, farthest from the lane, there is an open arcade, or porch, which is roofed. Behind the porch is a larger room with two or more doors, entering onto the porch. On each side of this large central room are smaller rooms used for storage. A chaff cutter often is kept in one of them.

The men of the family sleep in these quarters, and when not in the fields they spend most of their time here. During the rains or in the winter when it is cold, they sleep in the large central room, completely swathed in a cotton sheet and resembling white cocoons. Otherwise they sleep in the same fashion outside on the platform. Prosperous families build their men's quarters of brick. Poorer families have quarters of mud, often consisting of nothing more than a small hut without a platform or any extra rooms. The size and type of construction of these houses are an indication of the wealth and status of the family. Bullocks often are tethered in front, and their number, breed and condition also are a reflection of family status (see figure 1).

The other important part of the Rājpūt dwelling unit is the women's house. Since the Rājpūts have adopted the custom of purdah, the women must be carefully shielded from the gaze of the casual passerby. The women's life, therefore, goes on within enclosed courtyards, which may be located behind the men's quarters, across the street from them, or some distance away. The women's rooms open into the courtyard, never to the outside. These windowless rooms serve as storerooms and as bedrooms when it is cold or rainy (see figures 2 and 3). Most of the time household activities go on in the sunny open courtyard. The principal articles of furniture is the all-purpose string cot, which is used for sleeping, sitting, baby-parking, grain drying, and dish draining. The floor of the courtyard is surfaced with a mixture of water and cow dung renewed every seventh day. When dry, this forms a hard, dustless, water-absorbent surface which is very functional. There is

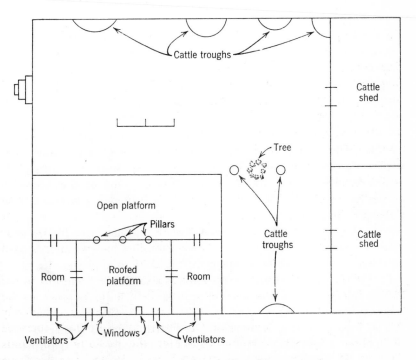

Figure 1. Men's platform and cattle compound.

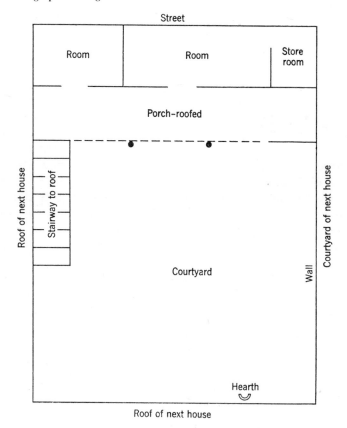

Figure 2. Typical women's house.

usually a drain in one corner of the courtyard through which wash and bath water can funnel out into the street. The drain is sometimes used as a woman's and children's toilet, although some of the women's houses have a small walled-off portion which is used as a latrine and is cleaned daily by the sweeper.

Like the men's quarters, the houses of the women vary in size and materials used in their construction. Most families have women's quarters which, in part at least, are constructed of mud-plastered adobe.

Part of the courtyard may be set aside as a cattle compound for cows and buffaloes. As added protection against theft, bullocks also may be tethered here at night.

The family cooking is done on the hearth, a mud, U-shaped fireplace about a foot square and 6 inches high, usually built against one of the courtyard walls. The cooking pot rests on the mud support, and cow dung or wood is burned beneath it. The hearth is given a new coating of cow-dung paste every morning in order to make it ritually pure for the day's cooking.

All but a few of the village lanes are narrow and wind in and out among the houses in a seemingly endless maze. They are often bordered on each side by the high, windowless walls of the women's houses. A second village thoroughfare is formed by the flat rooftops of the women's houses. Several courtyards may be connected in this way, and staircases, ladders, or footholds in the courtyard walls make these rooftop "lanes" readily accessible. They are often used by the women for interhouse visiting when they do not want to be seen by the men.

The everyday clothing of the villagers is simple. The men wear a *dhoti*, a garment which consists of a length of cotton cloth wound about the waist, pulled between the legs, and tucked in. The upper garment is a cotton shirt. Many of the younger men now wear the "Gandhi cap" made popular by the Congress party, although the more traditional turban is still very common among the older men. When working in the fields, the men often drape their heads in a folded

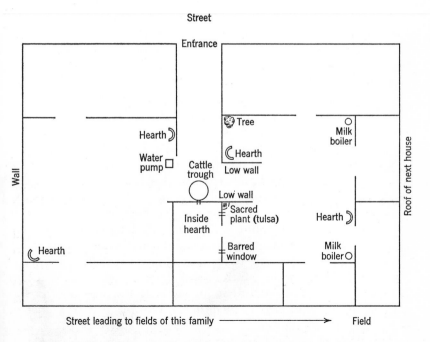

Figure 3. Large double courtyard of two extended families.

square of heavy cotton cloth. This is the cloth used to tie up the bundle of fodder they carry back to the village when they return. Schoolboys often wear cotton pajamas with long tailed shirts, which are not tucked in. Some schoolboys also wear leather oxfords or sneakers, although most men wear leather slippers made in the village. All members of the family go barefoot around the house, and many put shoes on only when they go to town or attend ceremonies. Many men carry a long bamboo staff, which serves for driving cattle, carrying loads, and as a weapon. These staffs are sometimes bound with heavy wire and studded with nailheads. Some even have a metal-spear point. When altered in these ways, they are lethal weapons.

Styles in women's clothing are more varied. They wear saris, loose baggy pants, and sometimes long, full skirts. All three of these are worn with cotton shirts, fashioned like the men's shirts and worn with the shirt tail out. When wearing saris, the women drape the end over their heads; when wearing skirts or pants, they also wear a head cloth, for adult women must keep their heads covered as part of the custom of seclusion. Most of the elder women wear tight, black, cotton pants, a style of clothing which has not gone out of fashion. The women are fond of jewelry and all except widows wear it. The most common type of bracelets are glass bangle bracelets, which fit tightly over the wrist and must be broken to be replaced. Silver and imitation gold bracelets are less common but are also worn, particularly for festive occasions. Gold nose plugs are worn in one nostril. Gold earrings and silver ankle bracelets, hair clips, and belts may also be worn. All married women wear a silver "wedding ring" on the second toe of each foot. The women wear their hair in one braid down the back. The braid is usually lengthened with a string braid. Black eye shadow is the only common makeup on ceremonial occasions. Some of the younger women use lipstick, powder, nailpolish, and a cosmetic spot on their foreheads.

There is no special winter outfit. Sleeveless sweaters may be worn by adults of both sexes during the cold weather. The villagers may also wrap themselves in shawls or in padded cotton bed quilts to keep warm.

Children of both sexes wear simple cotton shirts until they are 4 or 5 years old. Usually this shirt is their only clothing. In cold weather they may wear cotton pants, padded jackets and bonnets, and rubber shoes. Their hair is cut close to the head except for a small lock at the back of the head which distinguishes Hindu men from Muslims throughout their lives. At this young age only the glass bangles and occasional ankle bracelets distinguish the dress of girls from that of boys.

The center of life for Rājpūt women and children is the courtyard, as the men's house platform is for the men and adolescent boys. In the courtyard the women sleep, take care of the children, and cook for the men and boys who come into the house for meals. The women who share a courtyard usually are the wives of brothers, their young children, their unmarried daughters, married sons' wives, and their sons' children, two or three generations related in the male line. Of 36 families studied, 28 were extended families; 9 with two generations, 16 with three generations, and 3 with four generations. Eight of the families consisted of a husband and wife and their children, but in all but one of these cases the nuclear family had split off from a larger household within the last few years or had recently lost a senior parent.

The average number of women and children per courtyard in the extended families is about seven—three of whom are adult women. (Twelve households had two adult women, 5 had three, 5 had one, and 6 had over four.) On the average they feed five or six men and adolescent boys. There are two large double courtyards, one of which has a total of 25 mouths to feed—with six adult women to do the cooking.

There are fewer men's dwellings, for related men from neighboring courtyards may share the same platform. Four brothers, for example, with wives living in three different courtyards shared the same sleeping quarters and spent many leisure hours together there.

After the courtyard and men's house groups, a third important social unit is the joint farm family—the group of males who own and work land in common, plus their wives and children. Although the ideal pattern is for brothers to continue to own and operate the father's farm after death, in practice brothers usually divide the land. The joint farm family, therefore, tends to be a smaller social unit than either of the two groups who share a sleeping area.

Lack of congruence among the membership of these three social units is often the result of quarrels between the wives confined in the same courtyard, a situation leading them to exaggerate small annoyances. The easiest and least disruptive solution of such tension is for the conjugal family to build a separate hearth within the courtyard. Sometimes, however, the courtyard is divided into separate compartments by building a wall down the center, or a completely new women's dwelling unit may be constructed. The men may continue to share the same men's dwelling and may continue to own land in common.

At the beginning of a cycle, a courtyard may consist of a mother and father, a married son and his wife and children. They eat together at a common hearth and share a single women's house. The men and adolescent boys share a single men's dwelling, own land in common, and work together in the fields. Ideally the young sons will marry and continue to live with their parents and raise their children in the common courtyard. The ideal, however, is seldom realized for long.

The first break in the pattern usually comes when a man and his wife decide to have a separate hearth. This step may be taken with overt good nature and willingness on both sides and may be rationalized on the basis of convenience. More frequently, however, as mentioned above, it results from tension and quarrels among the women. It is a weakness of the ideal extended family that fractionating is inevitable but not accepted emotionally.

Although not always regarded as desirable, separate hearths are no real threat to the extended family, for basic patterns of authority and of property allocation and economic cooperation are not broken. The older women still have charge of giving out the daily ration of food. The father runs the farm. Further division, however, is a threat to basic patterns. The division of the courtyard into two sections by building a wall, or the setting up of a new household, entails the division of property: the milk cattle, furniture, and food. Now the mother-in-law no longer has to be approached for the daily ration, and the young wife has a source of pocket money, for she can sell small amounts of grain at the store and spend the money for bangles without permission of her mother-in-law.* At this stage, however, land remains intact.

Further divisions may be more drastic. The land may be divided up among brothers, or brothers and cousins, at the death of the older generation, thus setting up separate joint farm families. The men may still share a dwelling and their wives a courtyard, but the economy of each family is now distinct.

Fathers remain active authority figures until they are very old men. As the sons get older, they take over more and more of the hard work in the fields. The father devotes most of his time to managerial jobs, such as driving the cane to the mill, collecting payments, attending marriages, keeping abreast of village affairs, and making purchases in town, although many continue to help in the fields at peak work seasons like harvest and planting. As they grow older, the sons also take more and more responsibility for their individual families, with the father having a say in how the farm as a whole is managed and guiding

* During the fieldworkers' stay, two major family quarrels occurred which resulted in the division of the courtyard of the women's houses. In one case the personality of one of the wives was the direct cause. In another courtyard, a low wall had been built, and although the children and cousins conversed over it, the adult women were not on speaking terms. This division was the reflection of a fight between an uncle and his nephew.

the group in its political and marriage relations. The father never really retires as long as he is sane and able and the family stays together. Rather, his activities and authority are gradually curtailed.

If brothers stay together at the death of their father, the eldest son usually takes over the father's role. However, if a father thinks that one of his younger sons is more capable than the eldest, he may delegate authority to him, or an older brother may voluntarily relinquish his authority to a younger brother who is more capable or more suited to the role. Some Rājpūt families cannot afford to educate the first son because his services are needed in the fields, but they will usually try to educate a younger son.

The rank of the wives within the courtyard depends on the relative authority of their husbands. The head woman may be very authoritarian in her treatment of her daughters-in-law and sisters-in-law. Probably the greatest conflict arises when an authoritarian sister-in-law takes over at the death of her husband's mother.

Since it is the extended family which is valued most highly, the primary emphasis is placed on the solidarity of this unit, and the nuclear-conjugal family relationship is ideally kept subservient. When quarrels arise, a man is supposed to side with his father and brothers rather than with his wife.

Most of the women who share a courtyard come from clans living in villages to the south and southeast of Khalapur and as brides are strangers to the village, although occasionally they may be related to their sister-in-law or come from the same village. In two cases in our sample, brothers married women who were sisters. Such marriages are considered desirable on the grounds that sisters should be able to live peacefully together. In both of these cases, however, the sisters fought bitterly. In the two other cases sisters married men of the same village subdivision, or *paṭṭī*, but of different lineages.

The life of a woman is surrounded by restrictions imposed by purdah. Women may visit neighbors, particularly if their houses connect with each other and they can go over the roofs unseen by men; but for visits to more distant neighbors they must wait for ceremonial occasions. Although ceremonies are quite frequent, the vast majority of the time must be spent in the courtyard. As a woman grows older, the restrictions of purdah are relaxed. The end of childbearing and the marriage of sons and daughters mark the increase of freedom, especially in the less strict, lower status families. The strictness with which purdah is observed varies not only with social status but also with education. Many young educated people are beginning to question the custom.

In a girl's childhood village, she and the men of her caste group generally belong to the same clan. Any sex relations would be incestuous, for men and women of the same clan regard each other as "brothers" and "sisters."

Even as widows who may not remarry, women usually remain permanent members of their husband's house. A young widow lives in the courtyard under the direction of her mother-in-law much as she did prior to her husband's death, and her husband's kinsmen have the responsibility of looking after her and her children and for arranging the children's marriages.

Some widows complain that they and their children are being cheated by their affinal kinsmen, and occasionally an older widow with maturing children who feels this way will wish to take over the management of her share of the estate. Unless all the husband's close kinsmen are dead, and even then on occasion, this arrangement can lead to tension. There is little difficulty if her sons are responsible and are able to do the field work. But if they are still too young, she must get others to farm the land for her, usually on a sharecrop basis. This means that she herself often must leave the seclusion of purdah and go about the village alone. Even if she is a fairly old woman, this always stimulates gossip, and her affinal relatives are annoyed because it damages the family reputation. More serious than this, however, is their fear that she may allow herself to be duped and lose some of the land. This fear is greatly strengthened if the widow has no sons. Statutory law now permits a daughter to inherit village land, which means in effect that her husband, a member of a different clan, must join the village community or, at the very least, see to the management of some of its land. Regardless of its legality, such a situation is a very serious breach of village customary law, which has always held that no wife, daughter, or daughter's husband could inherit land. This rule was a very important one and still is adhered to with deep emotion. It was a means of excluding persons who were not members of the village land-owning caste group, and in large part it accounts for the fact that this group has been able to maintain almost complete control of the Khalapur land through all the vicissitudes of the past 400 years. Thus it is not surprising that a widow with an only daughter who insisted on managing her own estate and let it out on shares was severely beaten by her husband's kinsmen.

There is much variation in the treatment of widows, and this is a consideration much in the minds of most fathers when they are selecting a husband for their daughters. A number of village families have well-founded reputations for dealing justly with their widows and for taking good care of them and their children. In one family of the sample there was an elderly widow who was treated with great deference and who in the large women's house had become something of a matriarch.

Few widows return to the homes of their parents permanently, although they may often go there on visits. The reason stressed by informants is that the widow's leaving would indicate her husband's family was negligent in their responsibility or too poor to take care of her. If she has sons, the husband's family will wish to have them grow up as part of their kingroup, and they will want the mother to be there to take care of them. There is a strong feeling, too, that a wife's first loyalty is to her husband's house and that it should be lifelong.

When a woman returns to her own village to visit her parents, she does not observe purdah and can go about freely. As a general rule, high-status families in North India do not marry within the same village. The custom partly reflects and is supported by a situation such as is found in Khalapur, where most of the landowners belong to the same clan. Since daughters of the Rājpūt families are regarded by the men of their home villages as "sisters," with whom a union would be incestuous, purdah restrictions are felt to be unnecessary. A young bride usually returns home for a protracted visit after the first months or weeks of marriage and spends about half of the first eight years of her married life in her mother's home, sometimes visiting for a year or more at a time. She is treated as a special guest with no household duties. She spends her time visiting friends, chatting, singing, and playing games. A servant in her mother-in-law's courtyard, in her village of birth she is a vacationing guest. The emotional ties of women to their parental homes are so strong that they persist throughout life, no matter how happy the adjustment to the husband's village may be. Even grandmothers return to their villages and sometimes take their grandchildren home on visits.

Land is the most valuable property which passes from father to son, jewelry the most valuable which passes from mother to daughter. A man cannot sell his wife's jewelry without incurring strong social disapproval, so that this property usually remains in the female line. Much of the extensive dowry which a wife brings to her husband's house is turned over to the mother-in-law who distributes it among the members of the household or includes it in the dowries of her own daughters.

Virtually all the cash assets of the Rājpūt family are obtained through the sale of sugar cane and wheat. Most of this is sold by the men and they keep the accounts. Grain that is not sold at the threshing floor is stored in the women's quarters for family consumption. The surplus of this grain provides the women with a small independent source of income. They use it to barter for items at the village store and sell small quantities for cash, using the money to buy cloth or bangles from the traveling merchants. Women do not usually consult their husbands before making such purchases. The women may also have some control over the cash obtained from the larger sales. Cash is usually stored in the courtyard, for safety's sake, and some men go to their wives when they want money. One woman, whose husband had recently died, said:

> My husband would never buy anything—even if it cost only two pice—without asking me. I had all the money and everything in my hand.

Ordinarily a woman would not refuse money to her husband. We did see one mother refuse to give her son money to buy a new shirt on the grounds that she had recently made him one and that he did not need another. The fact that he was a grown man, married, and the father of two children did not abate her firmness.

The children are not given a regular allowance. It seems to be permissible for them to take grain from the house and use it to buy things at the village shops. Usually they ask their mothers for this, although they may take it without asking. This is not really regarded by the women as stealing. One woman stated that her little girl often took grain without asking her, and she knew about it but said nothing. We observed only one instance of acknowledged theft of this sort. A boy had taken several rupees from his mother without her knowledge, and she was very upset about it. We never heard of children taking anything from their aunts or from other people within the house. It seems to be a characteristic of the Indian household that each member (except for the youngest daughters-in-law, who must ask their mothers-in-law for everything) is fairly autonomous in petty cash matters.

There is relatively little property belonging specifically to the children. They have exclusive use of their own clothes, although these clothes may be the hand-me-downs of an older sibling. Toys are few. Children may possess a cloth ball or toy, a doll, a hoop, a toy cart, but they do not have the great accumulation of toys which causes so many property disputes in American homes. Property ownership is not an important matter for children.

On either side of the courtyard walls live families who are apt to be closely related—members of the same lineage who trace descent from a common male relative. In the area studied there were six lineages represented, 20 of all the families from one lineage, 5 from another (other 4 families of lineage not in sample), 4 from another (other 4 members not in sample), the remaining 4 from three other lineages.

Khalapur as a whole consists of 34 different Rājpūt lineages. With one exception, all are descended through the male line from the Rājpūt founder of the village.

The members of a lineage tend to live in a contiguous area forming a neighborhood closely connected by kinship ties. Ideally the lineage should be close knit, cooperative, and loyal. It is the group to which members should be able to turn for financial assistance and help on ceremonial occasions, as well as for political backing and physical help in quarrels. Some lineages approach this kind of unity. Others are torn by dissention. Over the past two decades, quarreling among the members of one lineage, part of which is in the sample, had led to two deaths, and the opposing factions seldom speak to one another and do not participate in each other's ceremonies.

Each of the seven *paṭṭī* or subdivisions of Khalapur is inhabited by a different number of different castes, but in each the Rājpūts are the most numerous. In four of the *paṭṭī*, the Rājpūt lineages all trace descent from a single man. The descent patterns in the other three are more complex, but generally it is true that Rājpūts in each of the seven are more closely related to one another than they are to the Rājpūts in the others. The fields of the *paṭṭī* members lie for the most part on the side of the village nearest to their *paṭṭī*. The families in this study belonged to the *paṭṭī* with the largest population, including 602 Rājpūts representing ten lineages. The sample consists of 24 of these families forming a neighborhood unit within it.

Marriage invitations are concentrated within the *paṭṭī*, and occasional informal councils are held at the *paṭṭī* level. The voluntary consolidation of land holdings was begun on a *paṭṭī* basis, and *paṭṭī* are the units for a number of Community Development Programs.* Rivalry is often expressed in *paṭṭī* terms, and claims are made that one *paṭṭī* has more prestige or power than another. But although *paṭṭī* are perceived as units, and although their members sometimes cooperate, there are numerous occasions when *paṭṭī* lines are crossed by ties of friendship, neighborliness, political alliance, and other forms of cooperation.

Beyond the *paṭṭī*, for the men especially, the permanent social unit of the most importance is the Rājpūt village caste group. Although this

---

* The Community Development Projects were conceived of and partly implemented by the government of India under the First Year Plan. They were designed to further rural community development in such fields as agriculture, education, public health, and public works. Khalapur is a member of a Community Development Project Block which was inaugurated in the fall of 1953. Its effects had not yet been strongly felt in the village when this study was being made.

group often is divided into opposing units, all the Rājpūts of Khalapur nevertheless have a sense of community. It resides in their knowledge of a shared ancestry and in common loyalty to many traditional forms of behavior. It is symbolized by such tangible evidences of common endeavor as the village itself, the religious school specializing in the teaching of Sanskrit and the traditional Hindu way of life, the Hindu temple, and, most recently, the new high school. It also is seen in their desire for political unity even in the face of frequent failure to achieve it, and in this sphere it is symbolized by the caste group councils which meet to decide on matters of importance to the group as a whole. The village is the stage on which most Rājpūts act out their lives, and the caste group is the audience whose approval or disapproval touches one of the most sensitive of all sources of self-esteem.

Outside Khalapur the Rājpūts share a sense of close kinship with landowning members of their clan in a number of neighboring villages. These ties to surrounding and dominant groups are an important source of psychological security. There is much friendly visiting and ceremonial participation among the Rājpūts of these villages, and occasionally elders from each village meet together to decide on matters of common concern.

Almost every Rājpūt has one or more very close friends outside of his own immediate kin group. Often these friendships have grown up in boyhood and frequently begin in school. A few are said to be rooted in youthful homosexual experience. No ritual marks the entrance into such a relationship, though the institution of ritual sisterhood is found among Rājpūt women. These friendships result, however, in the mutual expectations of loyalty and support characteristic of ritual brotherhood elsewhere in the world. Once established, there is an opportunity to give ritual expression to a relationship of this kind during a portion of the marriage ceremony. One of its hallmarks is the approval with which each party to such a friendship regularly speaks of the other, a trait which is very noticeable in the general prevalence of critical gossip. It also is seen clearly during a serious illness, when the friendship is expressed in deep concern and tender ministrations, such as cradling the sick man's head, or traveling and staying with him if a trip to the hospital is necessary.

These friendships are among agemates, and they cut across neighborhood, *paṭṭī*, and even village lines. One of the best known examples was between two elderly men, one from Khalapur and the other from a Rājpūt village some miles away. The two were so supportive that they were jokingly said to be "the grandfather of each other." Occasionally such friendships even cut across caste group lines, though they never existed, so far as we know, where ritual distance between two men was very great.

Friendship groupings of lesser intensity exist among many of the men who live near one another. These cliques draw their membership from different lineages, *paṭṭī*, and caste groups. Men who belong to them often cooperate in field work, assist in arranging and putting on marriages, and borrow and lend implements to one another. The most conspicuous are groups of elderly men who meet together almost daily in various sections of the village to smoke the hookah and talk. These groupings also tend to be age graded.

Aside from clan members generally and an occasional very close friend, the ties outside the village which are most important for the men are those with relatives by marriage. As is usually the case in societies where great stress is placed on the male line of descent, there are warm and friendly feelings for the men of the mother's family, especially her brother. When a Rājpūt is in such serious trouble that he wishes to leave his family and village, he is very apt to go to his mother's brother. This happened when a young Rājpūt was being subjected to much social pressure because of a romantic attachment between him and a lower caste girl. Easy, friendly relations are also common between a man and his wife's father and brothers. The husband usually accompanies his wife when she goes to visit her parents and returns to pick her up. On both occasions he often stays for a day or more, and most men look forward to these visits. Although the husband is treated with some deference by his wife's people, for they are culturally defined as somewhat lower than he in status—a fact which may account for some of his pleasure—the general tone of the relationship is comradely and without strain.

In village life, formal associations are almost nil. There was a statutory village court prior to independence, and now there is both a court and a legislative and executive council. Neither, however, includes more than a few of the Rājpūt caste group. Some Rājpūts have been active from time to time in local or national political parties. They have attended meetings and campaigned for their candidate in Khalapur and other villages. A few are members of government-sponsored organizations, such as the village cooperative and the sugar cane growers' union. But even when all organizations are taken together, only a small fraction of the Rājpūt population is involved. Social life comprising lineage kinsmen, friends, neighbors, and affinal relatives is by far the more significant aspect of most Rājpūts' lives.

A woman's deepest emotional ties for many years tend to be outside her husband's village with her own parental village. Inside the village a woman's ties are primarily with other women of her husband's family, who are invited to the family ceremonies and who are likely to live nearby. Women also visit neighbors from other lineages, and individual women may make efforts to visit friends from their own village who also have married into the village. Some women form friendships which are ritualized by the ceremonial exchange of a head cloth and the sharing of a meal from a common bowl.

The adult Rājpūt men and women in Khalapur have a dramatically different life and clearly differentiated status and roles. Men control the economic welfare of the family. Although women can own property legally, it is very difficult for them to support themselves and manage their own legal affairs. A woman could only attempt to do this through her sons or brothers. Although women may vote, they cannot attend political meetings or speeches to inform themselves. Men have the power to veto any suggestions made by the women. Women are discouraged from getting more than a rudimentary education (see Chapter 11). Most men wish to keep their wives in purdah, although it is a luxury, since to do this the men must do without their help in the fields and hire servants to help them run the house. The men control even the physical movements of their wives. A man, if angry or inconsiderate, may beat his wife, refuse to try and provide medical care, and may even prevent or cut short her visits to her own home, or refuse to call her back from a visit to her own family.

The subordinate status of women is further emphasized by the custom that women must crouch on the floor and pull their saris over their faces when in the presence of their husband or any man older than their husband. This custom is so pervasive that young women usually cover their faces even in front of older low-caste serving men. This is a sign of respect for the man's status. Covering the face in the presence of one's husband is also a sign of respect for his mother, another of the customs designed to protect the mother-son relationship from being threatened by the son's attachment to his wife. When a man has entered the house for his meal, he will quickly retire into a room or behind the wall of his hearth. The women are then free to move about their business quietly. His meal will usually be served to him by his mother, if she is living, or by an adult sister. Only if some woman of his own family is not present or does not wish to assert her prerogative will his wife be allowed to serve his meal.

Because of this custom, the men always announce their presence with a warning cough before entering the household and when possible send a boy or the youngest male present on errands to the courtyard, since the younger the man, the fewer are the women who must keep purdah from him. When the eldest male enters, the entire court-yard is immobilizd until he has been safely attended. In nuclear families the wife usually does not cover her face before her husband but only because the man usually requests her not to continue this custom.

The symbols of woman's status inferiority are easy to perceive. The ameliorating factor in the status inequality of such a social organiza-tion, however, is the strength of the bonds which exist between mothers and sons and between sisters and brothers. Adult males are taught that they should be respectful and considerate to their mothers and be-cause of their early, prolonged intimate contact with her are influenced by her wishes. The mother feeds her son even after he is married and even has strong influence on his marital life. She runs the family as long as she wishes to assume the responsibility.

Ideally a man and his wife are not allowed to talk to each other in front of the older members of the family. Since the mother-in-law is virtually always present in the courtyard and the young wife cannot leave the courtyard, this means in effect that the young couple may converse only surreptitiously at night.

A husband is not supposed to show any open concern for his wife's welfare; this is the responsibility of his parents. If the wife is sick, the mother-in-law and father-in-law see that she goes to a doctor; if they do not, neither she nor her husband should complain. The villagers report one or two cases where a woman has remained childless for years and, despite the great importance of having children, has not seen a doctor because the husband was too shy to ask his negligent par-ents to take her.

The restrictions, imposed on husband and wife in the presence of others, particularly the mother-in-law, are to avoid jealousy and con-flict and to ensure that the extended family takes precedence in im-portance to the nuclear. The presence of five nuclear courtyards in the sample which have recently separated from the extended family may be an indication of a new trend in the adjustment to this problem or may simply represent an age-old pattern.

After the death of the mother-in-law, a woman can talk to her hus-band in the presence of her sisters-in-law. When her sons marry, she assumes a new and prestigeful role. She is now in charge of the young women and is released by virtue of her relative age from many of the restrictions of purdah. Age in the courtyard brings respect, and every bride can look forward to the day when she assumes this role. There are some women who in spite of purdah and the status inferiority of women become very powerful. In many ways it would seem as if in her young years a woman's relation to her husband is primarily sexual and procreative, and that with age and the death of his mother it may become more one of a companion or even an advisor.

The relationship between a brother and his sister or female cousins also seems warmer and less restrained than the marital one and is considered sacred. A sister, even after marriage, may sit with her face uncovered and converse freely with her male relatives. There are ceremonial days when the strength of this bond is publicly recognized. On Brother's Day sisters fast for the health of their brothers and receive a present of a few rupees from their brothers in return for these good wishes. This festival occurs shortly after the festival honoring a locally worshipped goddess. When the clay figure of the goddess, which has been plastered on the courtyard wall, is removed, a smaller figure of her brother is put up in her place.

✤
✤
✤

Chapter 3

Daily Routine

Life in Khalapur, as in any agricultural village, is paced to the slow and ever-recurring round of the seasons. By day life tends to move according to the sun and at night to the constellations. A man will raise his arm toward the sky and say he will meet you when the sun has risen that far. Or two men in the fields will argue over whether the star Sirius has risen high enough for it to be time to switch the flow of canal water from the field of one to the field of the other. Life also moves in the well-defined patterns of caste and ritual. A man must be asked three times before he will come to a wedding feast, and the last invitation must be delivered by the barber or some member of the family just prior to the beginning of the meal. But for all its measured toil and ritual patterning, one is impressed by the spirit, and sometimes the rough and raw vitality, with which Rājpūt living is suffused. Their greetings and laughter are loud and hearty, their friendship demonstrative. Brāhmaṇs by contrast seem much more distant and restrained. In physical type the Rājpūt men range from the spindly and small, or even washed out and apathetic, to those who show a tendency to be portly. Yet the dominant impression is of men who are robust, muscular, and fairly tall. Some, by any standards, are strikingly handsome. If they seem bigger than other caste groups in the village, no doubt it is partly because of their better diet, though it also has something to do with their confident presence and bearing. One cannot know them for long without sensing, unlikely as most of the props may be, that somehow they have acquired a tinge of the princely and medieval.

The village day begins before dawn when the temple priest blows his horn. This signal calls the sleeping villagers from their cots to start the day's work. How soon the call is answered depends on the morning's division of labor. In the courtyard, the daughter-in-law who is to make breakfast emerges before her sisters-in-law. Grandmother may decide that grain needs to be ground. Perhaps there is a calf to feed or milk to churn. These early morning tasks bring some women from their beds while the daughters and children of the house are still sleeping soundly.

In summer the men must get to the fields early and do the morning's work before the blazing sun drives them to a noonday siesta in the shade. On cold winter mornings they enjoy lingering in the warm quilts, going to work after the chill has lifted and the dust of the roads has become warm for bare feet.

But winter or summer, one by one the villagers arise, and, taking a small brass pot filled with water (the Indian version of toilet paper), they take care of elimination. The younger daughters-in-law use the courtyard's drain or latrine, if there is one; the children may use the streets. For everyone else, the fields are the "facilities." The men may go alone, the older women always in groups; but every gray dawn finds the fields filled with silent, white-cloaked figures performing the first task of the day.

The toilet completed, the women return to the courtyard, wash, and begin the day's work in earnest. Grandmother may go to her churning or grinding, or she may decide to rest and smoke hookah while she waits for breakfast. The hearth must be given its first purifying coat of mud each morning before it can be used. If the family eats breakfast, then the fire must be laid and unleavened bread cooked for all members of the hungry household, and the daughters-in-law whose turn it is to make breakfast have a few busy hours.

Gradually the children emerge from their beds, stumble sleepily into the street or to the drain, and return to wash their faces and huddle, shivering, around the hearth fire waiting for breakfast. If it is winter, they may gather brush and build a bonfire in the courtyard for added warmth. Some people drink only milk to break their fast; others eat a good breakfast. The men finish feeding and milking the cattle before they come into eat. Finally, when the men and children are out of the way, the women have their meal. Eating is a strictly private matter in the village. Each man eats either at his own hearth or men's quarters. Each woman takes her food into her room or into a corner of the court- yard where she can turn her back toward the other women. Children are fed when they demand food and may eat together or separately, depending on whether or not they get hungry at the same time. Since the family does not gather for a meal, the dining hour is not fixed but is a matter of individual convenience.

If an individual wishes to bathe, he uses water from a pot or pail. The women bathe in the courtyards behind screens of cots, placed on edge. The men bathe by the village wells. Both sexes remain clothed while bathing and, when finished, wrap clean dry clothes around them- selves, dropping their wet clothes from underneath the fresh ones with- out ever exposing their bodies.

After breakfast the men leave for the fields or return to their quarters to smoke the hookah and talk. During the morning the women sweep the floor, gin cotton, spin or mend clothes. If there is a daughter to be married, they make things for the dowry. If a festival day is near, they may be busy plastering and whitewashing the house. There is always woman's work to do. The children go to the streets to play. The school- boys collect their books, slates, and pencils, put them in bookbags or tie them in a rag, and start off in the general direction of school, where they will arrive sooner or later. The older boys who are not in school drive the village cattle across the bridge to the grove of trees by the side of the pond. Every morning several hundred cattle leave the village by this bridge, and every evening they return the same way.

By about 10 o'clock in the morning, when the school officially opens, most of the students have arrived. They settle themselves on the open sunny platform, and from then until noon they sit chanting their les- lons, teasing the boys next to them, or just staring into space, to be jolted back to reality by a sharp reprimand from the master. The boys with the cattle have collected and quieted their herds and are playing hockey or *kabaḍḍī* under the shade of the trees. The younger children are playing less organized games in the streets or on a vacant men's quarters. The women start cooking lunch about this time, and in every courtyard a pot bubbles on the hearth. The men are off working in the fields unless it is the slack winter season, when they may be away arranging for a marriage, fighting a court case, or visiting in the vil- lage, discussing local politics.

Around noon, the task of feeding the men of the household demands attention. When work in the fields is light, the men come home to lunch; but if it is harvest or planting time, they prefer to have lunch carried out to them by an older daughter or son. The women pack rice, pulses, and unleavened bread into pots or tiffen carriers, tie them with a cloth, and balance them carefully on the head of a child and send him or her off on the long walk to the fields. The older men may come to the courtyard for their lunch, or it may be brought to them at the men's quarters by a daughter or son. The boys come home from school, and the herders, leaving a few of their number in charge of the cattle, also return for their noon meal. When the women have fed everyone and forced their reluctant sons back to school, or at least out of the house, they again snatch enough time from the day's routine to eat their own lunches.

Now the day is at its hottest. The sun beats down relentlessly. The heat shimmers over the fields and is reflected from the mud walls of the courtyards. Shadows are scanty and everywhere the villagers seek shade. The women huddle with their spinning or mending along the narrow shadow of a wall, shifting as the sun shifts. The men pull their cots under a tree on the men's quarters or under the roof of the rear sleeping quarters. The schoolboys crowd for seats under the trees; the herders abandon their games for conversation; and when they must start their cattle on the long walk to the fields, their pace is slow. In the fields the men leave their plows and squat in groups under a lone tree or rest in a mango grove and eat their lunches. The small children return to their homes or seek the shade of a friendly tree for their play, and their voices are muted. Even the dogs look for a cot to sleep under. In the summer work ceases entirely during the middle of the day. The men work in the fields before the dawn and after dark, and everyone takes a siesta during the middle of the day.

Around 4 o'clock in the afternoon the pace of work quickens again. The children start returning from school; some have chores to do, others return home only to throw down their books and run out to play. The women start preparing the evening meal. In the fields the men get ready to go home. At dusk, around 5 o'clock, the road to the village is once again a crowded thoroughfare. Men and boys carrying loads of fodder on their heads, men driving plows or bullock carts, an occasional youth on a bicycle, and from all directions the lowing, slow-moving cattle—all must filter once again back across the narrow bridge and into the village. This is the time of day so often described by Indian poets, when the dust from the hooves of the returning cattle catches the light of the setting sun and the ground dissolves into a yellow-red haze.

As night falls, the men and boys feed and water the cattle, the women prepare to feed their men again, and the children return from play to try teasing some dinners from busy mothers. The bats emerge from the rafters and become darting black shadows in the dying light. The cattle stamp restlessly and then become gradually quiet as they are fed.

Around 8, the men come into the courtyard for their evening meal. Once again the efforts of the women are concentrated on serving food to their men. Only when the men have left do the women eat their own dinners.

By now the oil or kerosene lanterns are lighted, making small yellow patches in the darkness of the courtyard. The women sit and gossip. If there is a good storyteller in the house, she may tell stories to the children or to the other women. The young daughters-in-law may play games or retire to corners to whisper about their husbands, their joys or disappointments in the home of their in-laws, or to reminisce about their own villages. In the men's quarters the men visit each other, smoke the hookah, and talk of farming or politics. Gradually the children drift off to bed, to be joined later by mother or an older sibling or cousin. One by one, in courtyard and men's quarters, the villagers climb into their cots, cover themselves from head to foot with quilts or sheets, and at last the village sleeps—but never completely. All night a few are stirring. A man slips into the courtyard to call his wife quietly from their children to a separate cot and then returns as silently to the men's quarters, careful not to disturb the occupants of the still cocoons. Another man gets up in the night to check the cattle. A mother stirs in response to the crying of her baby. And if the crops are nearing harvest time, the fields are full of silent sentinels guarding them against the thieves who prowl in darkness. After harvest, farmers plow their fields and the tinkle of bullock bells may be heard far into the night, for the moonlight is bright and cooler than the rays of the sun. In winter the night's stillness may be pierced by the barking of jackals, with an occasional answer from a vigilant watchdog. But these are only periodic interruptions of the silence—intermittent movements in the stillness —for it is night and the village may sleep until the horn of the priest calls it once again from slumber to meet the toil of a new day.

Chapter 4

Basic Economy

The village Rājpūts are landowners and farmers. All families in our sample own their own land and live on the produce of this land. If the family can afford it, they hire low-caste men and women to work in the fields. In such cases the Rājpūt men merely direct their servants, and their own work is slight. But in all except the wealthiest houses, the Rājpūt men do their own farming with the help of their sons and perhaps some servants. When a man's sons are grown, he retires and leaves the work of farming to them. Therefore wealthy men and older men are likely to have plenty of leisure.

The principal crops are wheat and sugar cane, both of which are cash crops, that is, they can be sold for money instead of being consumed or bartered. Cane is sold at the nearby sugar mills and provides the largest income, with wheat coming second. Maize, corn, rice, millet, cotton, hemp, barley, oats, peas, mustard, several kinds of fodder, and various pulses are also grown. Potatoes and other vegetables are both bought and grown.

The plowing is done by hitching the bullocks of the humpbacked Indian cattle to a simple wood and metal plow. During the principal harvests, the crops are transported from the field in bullock carts. The daily loads of fodder and grain are carried back by the men and boys on their heads. Both cows and water buffaloes are kept for milk.

The villagers harvest two major crops a year: the *khārif* crop, gathered in the fall, and the *rabī* crop, gathered in the spring. The fall crop includes maize, rice, several kinds of pulse, cotton, hemp, and some other minor produce. The spring harvest, which is called *rabī*, includes wheat, barley, oats, peas, and mustard. Sugar cane, considered to be a separate crop, is harvested in the late fall and early spring.

The lives of the farmers have a seasonal rhythm patterned around the needs and yields of their land. October and November are two of

41

the busiest months of the year. Most of the *khārif* crop is harvested and the *rabī* crop planted. The men leave for the fields early in the morning and may work long into the night. Some of them actually live in the fields and have their food brought to them there. These months also mark the first of the cane harvest, and carts must be readied for trips to the sugar mills. Toward the middle of November, when the first of the winter rains are hoped for, work begins to slack off.

December, January, and February are comparatively easy months, the only work being occasional irrigation of the *rabī* crops, collection of fodder for the cattle, tillage of the fields in preparation for cane planting, and trips to the sugar mills. During their leisure hours the farmers are to be found sitting on the platforms of their men's quarters, smoking hookahs and visiting. Many marriages take place during the winter months, and the village is noisy with blaring bands. The sale of cane provides the villagers with money for minor luxuries and trips to visit relatives. February is one of the most beautiful times of the year. The mustard and peas are in flower and the wheat has tassled. In the fields and in the village, groups of men are seen sitting around a fire roasting peapods and wheat tassles for a between-meal snack.

By mid-March the tempo of work begins to increase. Some cane fields are still being harvested, others are being plowed, others planted; in still others the thin, dark green shoots of the new cane are being weeded. Some fields are being sown with the millet and cotton of the *khārif* crop, and preparations are being made for the fast approaching *rabī* harvest. On the men's platforms the older men roll strands of hemp between their palms to make the ropes which will soon be needed to tie the harvested crops. Implements are repaired, and arrangements are made for obtaining the necessary extra labor.

Harvesting is a period of intense activity. Rain and hail may fall, and it is important that the ripe crops be gathered promptly. Load after load of grain is hauled to the threshing floor, where it is stacked in high, rectangular piles. For threshing, grain is spread on the ground and bullocks are driven round and round in a circle over it, their plodding feet separating the grain from the stalks. The grain is then winnowed from the chaff, a process hastened by the hot wind which is already beginning to blow. Some of the threshing is done by the women who beat the stalks on the courtyard floor or pound them with sticks.

The period following the *rabī* harvest marks another brief respite from field work and is another season when marriages are held.

The monsoon rains, which begin the middle of July, begin a period when long days must again be spent in the fields. Much of the *khārif* crop is sown at this time, and the paddy fields must be manured. During July the paddy is transplanted, and the wheat fields are plowed again and again between the rains. Toward the end of August, the maize has reached the stage where it must be guarded from thieves and from marauding monkeys and deer. Thatched watchmen's huts are erected in the more distant fields.

In September, as the rains gradually cease, some of the rice and cotton and maize is harvested and the stalks of new cane are now so high that they must be tied together so that they will not blow over. The wheat fields are plowed more frequently, and by October, when the last of the *khārif* crop is being harvested, they are ready for sowing, and the yearly cycle is repeated.

During this yearly cycle there is never a time when there is no work to be done. If for no other reason, daily trips to the fields must be made to bring fodder to the cattle. During the winter months, however, there is comparatively little work. The three periods of peak activity occur during April and early May, when the *rabī* is harvested; during late June and July, when the *khārif* is planted; and from September to November, when the *khārif* is harvested and the *rabī* is planted.

Rājpūt women do not work in the fields, although the young girls and older women may pick cotton and the leaves of pulses, which are used as a vegetable. But once the grain is in the house, it is the job of the women to process it. After the threshing, the grain is dried by spreading it on cots in the courtyard. Each house has a small, metal-lined husking pit in the floor of the courtyard. The dried grain is put in this pit and pounded with a heavy, metal-capped stick. Finally, it is winnowed in hand-winnowing baskets. Ready for use, it is now stored in mud jars or mud-covered baskets (plastered over if it is to be kept for some time), which are kept inside the rooms of the house.

In general, the handling of food occupies a good proportion of the women's time. The principal diet is rice with a potato or vegetable curry, eaten with *rotī* and *ghī*. *Rotī* is the generic term for several kinds of round, unleavened bread (not unlike tortillas). *Ghī* is clarified butter made from curd and is used both for frying and for pouring over food. Both the rice and the curry are cooked over the hearth in large brass pots. The "breads" are first cooked in small, slightly concave pans, then put directly into the side of the hearth to puff, and finally stacked in a dish by the side of the fireplace. Whole spices are ground by placing them on a flat stone or board and crushing and pulverizing them with another stone. Unrefined brown sugar, called *gūr*, is also eaten and used in making various kinds of sweets. In the summertime, the women make vermicelli (thin spaghetti) from wheat flour by rolling it with their hands.

Milk, both from cows and buffaloes, is an important part of the diet. Men usually do the milking unless the cattle compound is within the women's quarters. The milk is boiled in large pots on a special hearth. Most of it goes into the making of *ghi* and curd, although boiled and sweetened milk is sometimes drunk.

Popcorn and sugar cane are popular between-meal snacks for both children and adults. Most of the children are very fond of popcorn, which they take themselves to one of the village shops to be popped. This is eaten without butter or salt. The children also eat quantities of sugar cane, particularly at the beginning of the cane season. We have seen children consume 6 feet of sugar cane during the course of a morning.

An interesting aspect of the division of labor between the sexes is caused by the fact that the women are vegetarians. Those Rājpūt men who like meat must get it and cook it themselves in the men's quarters because their women will neither touch it nor have it in the house. Some of the men keep chickens for eggs and meat.

The principal fuel for cooking is cow-dung cakes. The making of these cakes is one of the tasks usually performed by the low-caste sweeper women who daily clean latrines and sweep out the cattle compound but the Rājpūt women frequently make at least part of their own supply.

After food problems, the other major occupation of the women is the preparation of clothing. The cotton, harvested in September, is ginned by the women on small hand gins—a process which keeps them busy throughout October and into November. After ginning, it is taken to the mill to be fluffed, and then it must be hand rolled into long, loose swatches for spinning. The spinning goes on all through the winter and spring. Rājpūt women do not do their own weaving, however. After the thread comes off the spindle, it is wrapped into skeins on a wooden frame and taken to the weaver. The fabric produced is then used for bedclothes and some of the coarser clothing for men. All finer materials are purchased, and most of them are fashioned into wearing apparel by the women, although some are sewn by the village tailors.

When a girl in the family is going to be married, the women will help to make the various things required for her dowry. These include baskets, papier-mâché bowls, hooked and woven sitting-mats, children's toys, and household decorations made of cloth. This activity begins several months before the marriage.

There is a marked tendency toward sociability in the women's work habits. All the women in one household are likely to do the same kind of work at the same time. For spinning, there may even be a gathering from several households. Chatting is a favorite occupation. Some women smoke the hookah as they talk.

❋

❋

❋

Chapter 5

Politics and Social Control

In the traditional system of social control, each of the caste groups of Khalapur has much autonomy. In the larger groups, the major responsibility for social control rests in the hands of a few elderly and respected men. When problems arise, they meet together in councils called *panchāyats*. Their functions are both legislative and judicial. They adjudicate disputes and in cases involving violations of caste group rules, especially those relating to sex and marriage, they focus public opinion and bring pressures to bear on the culprits. When a change is to be made in caste group rules, such as whether or not the group will continue to perform a particular service, they are the focus for the decision-making process. One or more of these men also act as representatives of the group when it deals with other caste groups in the village or with government officials. Among some caste groups, the lines of political solidarity extend beyond Khalapur and include *jāti* members in other neighboring villages. Occasionally the leading men of the caste groups in each of these villages will come together to discuss an especially difficult dispute or to make a decision of importance to the segment of the *jāti* which they represent.

If the village as a whole presents a picture of semiseparate layering, it is also true that there is considerable segmentation along family lines within each of the caste groups. Each family head is a focus of authority, and there are strong feelings that disputes within the family should be settled by him. These feelings are especially strong among the higher castes. These castes also show a further form of segmentation, reflecting the social and residential cleavage between men and women. A Rājpūt woman who is head of the women's house has considerable authority of a legislative and judicial nature, although it is exercised in a very limited sphere.

The focus of social control within the Rājpūt caste group is a number of men who are called "prominent (literally 'big') men." It is a relatively easy matter to identify them. As one informant said, "You can get the answer from any child you see playing about." In the subdivision of the village where we did the most intensive research, there is general agreement among the adults on the names of ten men.

All ten of these men are married and middle-aged. Thoroughly acquainted with the customs and procedures of a generally conservative group, they also are said to be "strong." The major sources of their strength are ownership of land enough to give them relatively moderate to great wealth (all have farms larger than the farms of about half the other Rājpūts of the *paṭṭī*) and the support of a number of friends and closely related kinsmen, especially sons. Because of their manpower and wealth they have leisure necessary for performing the duties of a prominent man. Their wealth also enables them to command valued symbols of status. As a group they arrange good marriages for their children, with large dowries, big feasts, and affinal relatives who themselves are people of status. Most have large, brick men's houses, and although seven are illiterate, all but two have educated sons.

The prominent men function as opinion formers, advice givers and wielders of verbal sanctions. Some of them move about the village from men's sitting place to men's sitting place, finding out what is going on and discussing the latest developments. Others very rarely move about in the village. They are usually to be found sitting at their own place, and those who wish to see them gather there.

On important ceremonial occasions, such as marriages, two or three of the prominent men of the village are invited to attend. They lend the sanction of the caste brotherhood to the proceedings, and they form an authoritative panel which can decide on moot points of ceremonial procedure which sometimes arise. When a large sum of money changes hands during the ceremony, it is handed to them, and they count it aloud, thus making the transaction public and figuratively stamping it with the seal of their authority. On these occasions one of the prominent men is asked to make the customary gifts to the family servants. As an elder who is versed in the customs governing intercaste relations, he certifies to the correctness of the payments, protects the reputation of the man who gives them, and forestalls bickering.

Perhaps the most important role of the prominent men is sitting on the decision-making and adjudicatory councils, or *panchāyats*. The size of a *panchāyat* varies from two or three prominent men, plus other interested persons, to a group of 50 or more, which may include prominent men from other villages. Only one intervillage *panchāyat* was held during the course of the research. A man who had promised to marry his daughter and (in a very unusual transaction) had taken a sum of money in return for permitting the marriage had refused to honor his promise. The *panchāyat* was able to bring sufficient pressure on him to make him change his mind.

Decisions which affect the Khalapur Rājpūt caste group as a whole are made by *panchāyats* consisting of most of the prominent men. If all are not present, those who are must be able to "speak for" the others if the decision is to be binding. *Panchāyats* at this level are held to consider such matters as a candidate for village office or changes in the marriage ceremonial. Some *panchāyats* are called on a *paṭṭī* basis, and in these meetings all elderly heads of Rājpūt families in the area usually are present even though some may not be prominent men.

The most common form of *panchāyat* is the small council of three or more elders. Such *panchāyats* do not represent any particular geographical unit. They are called when there is a dispute between two men. The aggrieved person selects the prominent men he wishes to hear the case, and the meeting is held at his men's house. His only obligation is to supply plenty of tobacco for the hookahs. The defendant also is asked to appear, and the council listens to both sides. The familial tone of these small *panchāyats* encourages truthful statements as well as discussion of other and perhaps more basic sources of hostility. Truth is also encouraged because the prominent men usually are aware of the facts, and sometimes a man is asked to take an oath in which he asks the deity to bring him bad fortune if he is lying. During the course of the research, small *panchāyats* were held to consider the following matters: disputes over rights to land, water and trees; petty theft, both of articles of clothing and of crops; a decision on whether a man should accept land offered him in the village of an affinal relative (where he, as an outsider to the landowning kin group, would have been unwelcome); and a Rājpūt's use of physical violence against a stranger. Decisions often are made in the form of a compromise. In some cases, such as those having to do with crop stealing, the primary motive of the accuser may be to shame the wrongdoer, and an apology will be accepted.

Although the informal systems of social control tend to operate autonomously, there sometimes are occasions when caste group lines are crossed. This frequently occurs in neighborhoods that consist of both Rājpūt and lower caste families. Rājpūt prominent men are asked to mediate in disputes between Rājpūts and their lower caste neighbors. They also are called on when disputes among members of lower caste groups can't be settled by their own elders.

The operation of the informal system of social control is illuminated by considering some of the different types of disputes or kinds of conflicting interests it must handle. One area of conflict involves the Rājpūts and other caste groups in the village. When such conflicts do occur, the scales are tipped heavily in favor of the Rājpūts because they are so much more powerful than any other group. The primary basis for their power is economic, but there are other important contributing factors. Traditionally the land on which non-Rājpūt families built their houses was regarded as the property of the Rājpūts. Recently the legal basis for Rājpūt claims to ownership of this land has been destroyed by the government. The feeling that they are the rightful owners tends to persist, however, and the threat of eviction still is an effective weapon in their hands. The Rājpūts also are in a position to threaten to prevent lower castes from using the fields for latrine purposes or for gathering fodder. Their ascendancy is further enhanced by sheer numbers and by beliefs associated with the caste system.

The superior power of the Rājpūts was shown when an Untouchable group, in an attempt to raise their status, refused to perform their traditional task of removing dead cattle. The Rājpūts were concerned because they were inconvenienced, and, more important, they saw the move as a threat to the social order. By threatening the various kinds of deprivation mentioned above, they quickly were able to bring the group back into line.

In matters which do not involve serious conflicts of interest, the Rājpūts are more ready to meet demands or to make compromises. When the volume of a traditional measure was officially decreased, the hereditary service castes, who are paid in kind and according to units of this measure, were adversely affected. They were able to obtain an adjustment in a large *panchāyat* which included their caste group leaders and Rājpūt prominent men. Under some circumstances an individual Rājpūt can be made to bend a little before lower caste pressures. When a member of the Untouchable sweeper caste group was beaten because he allowed his pigs to damage a Rājpūt's potatoes, his caste group—which has unusual solidarity and provides services the Rājpūts are very reluctant to do without—was able to obtain at least the semblance of an apology from the Rājpūt concerned. In effecting the outcome, however, an important role was played by a number of

Rājpūt prominent men who lived nearby and would have been adversely affected by a sweeper "strike."

Within the Rājpūt caste group, conflicts of interest may be roughly grouped according to the relative strength of those who are involved. There are many conflicts involving members of Rājpūt families who have neither large farms nor large followings. The occasions for conflict between members of these families are the same as those between stronger families, but the aim and outcome often are different. In conflicts between weaker families, the ostensible cause generally is the real cause. The poor young man steals crops because he is short of fodder for his animals or because his family is short of grain. Or he steals from a men's house platform because the purchase of clothing or tobacco represents a fairly serious drain on his resources.

Disputes between poorer and weaker men usually do not involve violence, though occasionally, as a result of repeated provocation, a man may lose his temper and attack another, especially if he catches him red-handed and the two start arguing. A more frequent recourse is to call a *panchāyat* of prominent men. These *panchāyats* often obtain satisfaction for the man who has been wronged. Since the person who has committed the misdemeanor is weaker than the prominent man handling the case, he fears the sanctions they may apply. If they threaten to go to court against him, for example, he knows they have a good chance of winning. He also knows that they or their supporters can harass him in various ways by "speaking against" him or by creating other difficulties, such as taking some of his crop or depriving him of water. He knows that these forms of chastisement lie behind the appeals which are made to a concern for his own reputation or the reputation of his neighborhood, *paṭṭī*, caste group, or village.

When a conflict results from a wrong done by a strong family to a much weaker one, the system of informal control generally is ineffective. Once when a young Rājpūt, Dharam, stole another's wheat and when the latter, who had only a few close kinsmen and a small farm, approached a prominent man for help in organizing a *panchāyat*, the elder gave him this advice:

You don't have a shoe in your hand * and aren't in a position to do anyone any harm. If I organize a panchayat, Dharam might do something else to you. If you take the matter to court, you won't be able to get witnesses. Dharam comes from the largest lineage in the village. You'd better keep quiet and not get him down on you.

* Beating someone on the head with a shoe is a stylized form of insult, since the head is sacred and leather is impure.

As a rule, however, strong families do not engage in petty theft of this kind. If they do, as happened in this case, it generally is the act of some younger member of the family, not of an older and more responsible person or the family head. The fact that the family head does not take action against his own son, grandson, or nephew is an example of how emphasis on family solidarity often interferes with processes of social control which are supposed to uphold values associated with the larger social unit—the whole Rājpūt caste brotherhood or the village.

In conflicts involving two or more strong Rājpūt families, the meaning of the difficulty generally is different from what it is when two weaker families are involved. There are some conflicts between strong families in which the ostensible issues actually are the basic issues. This was the case, for example, when a strong Rājpūt family used chicanery in an attempt to attain title to a valuable piece of vacant village land. In many other conflicts, however, the ostensible is not what is of primary importance. In such quarrels the end sought is not so much material benefit—a few square feet of property, for instance —as the immaterial gains deriving from a demonstration of power which is relatively greater than one's rival.

In every generation situations arise in which a few previously weak families acquire leaders who are not only able but also proper Rājpūts in the sense that they respond to values calling on them to establish a strong family and to become prominent men. In addition, some of them also have been given an allocation of men and land on which they can build a domain. One way in which such a family can make its influence felt is by acquiring the recognized symbols of status, such as housing and good marriages. The head of the family will also seek to demonstrate in little ways that he and the kin group he leads are persons to be reckoned with. This does not mean that the process is consistently rational and planned. From what has been said above, it is clear that village life is full of many small points of potential conflict. The family of strength can and does demonstrate on a number of occasions that it can defend its own interests. It may have been deprived of some of its land in a prior generation. In this generation it wins the land back in a court case. A few demonstrations of capable leadership and the ability to attain its ends in competition with other families—plus the appropriate symbols of status—move the family toward a position of prominence and attract other weaker families into its political orbit. Its head becomes a prominent man, and the family, together with its alliances, is recognized as a significant power cluster in village affairs.

A prominent man cannot afford to alienate his own kinsmen and friends. If he does, at least to any very serious extent, he is no longer a prominent man. He no longer is "strong." This is why it is usually impossible to obtain his support in cases involving these individuals. Even when a number of prominent men agree that steps should be taken against a person who is supported by only one or two other prominent men, they will be reluctant to proceed because they know that even this much opposition has power enough to cause them trouble. They are not like judges backed by an obedient police force and proceeding against a single deviant individual. For this reason it is difficult to take effective action against strong families. There are stories of strong families that drove others from the village. The ousted families were not able to return until death had changed the composition of the family that opposed them. Apparently murder cases in the early nineteenth century (when not occurring within the family itself, in which case usually nothing was done) brought forceful retaliation by kinsmen and friends. Today such cases are generally handled by the police and the state courts. In the past, according to our possibly partial evidence, the only form of deviance which a strong family could not get away with was an act which threatened the purity of the bloodline. A generation ago a man who impregnated a village "sister" and then attempted to kidnap and sell her to a man in a distant province was outcasted and driven from the village. It seems very probable that today similar strong action for a like offense would be taken. However, there has been a weakening of some of the rules in this sensitive area. A generation ago a man who married a widow or who married a girl from a clan whose claims to true Kṣatriya status were suspect would have been denied hookah privileges with the rest of the caste group. Today it is not possible to obtain the consensus necessary to deny the hookah to men who are deviant in this way. There are at least two younger Rājpūts who have married into clans generally agreed to be of low status. There are murmurs of criticism but nothing more. There was some attempt to deprive a man of hookah privileges who some years ago married a girl who was technically a widow, but only a few of the Rājpūts would agree to carry out the sanction.

The informal system of social control among the Rājpūts is further strained by another process characteristic of village political life. This process seems to be triggered in part by Rājpūt values, which stress pride, sensitivity to slight, and arrogance toward anyone conceived of as a potential rival. A man who becomes strong enough to throw his weight around, so long as he knows he cannot be met by superior opposing force, often will do so. There is also a belief that a Rājpūt family should take revenge for a wrong, and it is felt that an appeal to the informal system of social control is a sign of weakness in a strong family. Apparently, too, a family which acquires a relatively good holding, and especially a number of sons—and is, in addition, a family which has not been prominent—experiences what may be best described as a kind of power intoxication. It is difficult to describe in other terms the act of a family which took possession of some land under circumstances so provocative that they could not help but realize that the step would be met by forceful retaliation, with a good chance of a stick fight that would lead to a killing. As a result of the interplay of factors such as these, there are strong families which become involved in feudlike assertions and counterassertions which may go on for many years. Occasionally there is something of genuine material consequence at issue, but more often the occasions of their quarreling would, under different circumstances, be of little moment. What is really at issue is the relative power of the two families and their supporters. This type of conflict can lead to violence, especially if the competing groups come into contact with one another when they have been drinking. This happened during the course of the research, and during the ensuing fracas a man was killed, a man who ironically and unfortunately had never been a prime figure in either of the two contesting groups.

Paralleling the informal political structure in Khalapur there is a formal political structure. It is the creation of the state government. Before independence, there was a formal, government-sponsored village court presided over by one of the prominent men. Shortly after independence, as a result of changes in the state law, this court was given enhanced powers, and a number of procedural changes were made. It was hoped that these changes would make it more effective in settling minor cases cheaply, expeditiously, and justly.

The village court has handled much petty litigation and in many ways is serving a useful function. It often serves as a backstop for failures of the informal system, which generally is tried first, and a number of cases which otherwise might have gone to the town courts, with resulting expense and prolonged hostile competition, have been successfully adjudicated.

The court has often failed, however, and much of the difficulty can be understood in terms of the picture presented above. Since the court operates in Khalapur, most of the judges are Rājpūt prominent men, and they are subject to the usual sort of pressures. Technically they are government officials. But the concept of "office" and duty to an "office" is not highly developed. To the Rājpūts, the judges are primarily kinsmen and members of their own caste group. Thus when caste group interests are involved, it is difficult for the judges to make just decisions. The police are distant and their ministrations often undependable. There is nothing similar to a bar association or any other kind of group which can provide support at all comparable to the support provided by judge's kinsmen and village alliance. The difficulties are enhanced by the fact that there often is a conflict between statutory law, as set forth in the laws of the land, and village customary law. A just decision according to one concept is unjust according to the other. As a result of these factors, the village court tends to operate successfully or unsuccessfully in much the same way, and for much the same reasons, as the informal system of social control. The prevailing attitude, which both gives it its due and recognizes its failings, was well summarized by a Rājpūt when he said of the court: "It is better to have a broken down bullock in the cattle compound than no bullock at all."

At the same time as the new village court, a new legislative and executive council was created. This body was revolutionary in that members were to be elected on the basis of village-wide adult franchise. There were provisions also to ensure representation for the Untouchables, and the body was given the power to tax, to spend money on village improvements, and to allot certain village lands.

The new council also has run into difficulties, and the villagers for the most part regard it with the same misgivings as they do the court. A basic difficulty stems from the fact that the council rests on a new conception of what village government should be. The idea that all village caste groups should have an equal voice in village government and the idea of making decisions by ballot and by majority vote run strongly counter to long-established custom. In addition, the elective system has enabled the lower caste groups to pose a threat to the long-standing Rājpūt hegemony, since in combination they can outvote them.

Very broadly speaking, it can be said that the new council, during the time of the research, mainly represented the interests of a Rājpūt power cluster. Partly for this reason and partly because the villagers did not really understand the nature of the new governmental instrument, it was doing more to create dissension than to rally the support of the various caste groups of the village or to guide them, with a degree of harmony, toward a more democratic and effective village administration.

Outside the village the agencies of social control of most importance to the Rājpūts are the police and the courts of justice. The police officials with whom the Rājpūts have most contact are stationed in Bhudana. Higher police officials have their offices in Saharanpur. For

Khalapur, the lowest echelon of the state judiciary is the courts of Bhudana. Cases which are appealed from these courts go to Saharanpur and may eventually go to still higher courts located in cities outside the district.

The police are regarded with suspicion and dislike. This attitude is partly due to Khalapur's history. Its residents frequently violated statutory law, and the police were the representatives of authority with whom they were most often at odds. Aversion to the police was also heightened when a detachment was stationed in the village during the latter part of the nineteenth century in order to prevent the Rājpūt practice of female infanticide. In the pursuance of their duties the police necessarily had to violate purdah restrictions, and this caused much resentment. The villagers generally maintain that police contacts more often involve bribery, extortion, and brutality than retribution for wrong-doing.

The negative attitude toward other government officials is much less strong than in the case of the police, and many higher officials of the district and state are regarded with respect. Since independence, the villagers feel that officials at the higher levels are much more accessible. One Rājpūt said that if he wished, he could go right to Nehru.

It cannot be gainsaid that the processes of village government and social control are subject to much strain, nor that this is especially true among the Rājpūts. A more precise estimate of the degree of strain is apparent in answers to a query about the court cases that men in the sample of families used for this study recall being involved in, either directly or as witnesses. Thirty-eight men, ranging in age from about 25 to 65, were asked to mention any court cases they had participated in during the course of their lives. Eliminating duplication, 59 separate cases were mentioned. The main figures involved, with few exceptions, were Rājpūts in the *paṭṭī* where the neighborhood studied is located. Assuming the oldest man was involved in his first case when he was 25, the period covered is 40 years. Over half the cases involved disputes concerning the possession of land or the allocation of income derived from it. About a quarter involved theft, and the remainder concerned such matters as loans of money, water rights, and assault. Seventeen of the cases had taken a violent turn, and in three of them men had been killed. These data, of course, underestimate the number of disputes. Some court cases in which the men are known to have played a part are not mentioned, and a large number of disputes never reached the courts.

A noticeable feature of the lives of Khalapur Rājpūts is suspicion. With the exception of their close kinsmen and friends, men tend to be uneasy about the motives of other Rājpūts in the village. In part this seems to be a concomitant of the fact that family retaliatory power is an important factor in social control. If the other family can get away with something, it is felt they may do so. This is one reason why a high-status family tries to free one of its men from the burdens of farm work so that he can keep his finger on the village political pulse. It also stems in part from the fact that taking revenge is looked on as normal, even obligatory, and that preparations for taking it are concealed. After so many generations of living together, with the amount of jockeying for status and power that goes on, there are few families that cannot think of a number of others whose members may be waiting for a chance to make a move against them.

The women are more openly quarrelsome than the men. Tempers have no chance to "cool off" in the close quarters of the courtyard, and minor irritations build up into open hostility. A woman with whom this matter was discussed agreed that the women fought so much because they could not leave the courtyard. She said that if they could take a walk for an hour, most of the quarrels would not occur. Quarrels often begin over some minor matter. Two women may disagree over the cooking or the children, and the bickering begins. In an extended family, the other women usually take sides, and eventually all the women are lined up against each other. Neighboring women, hearing the rumpus, come to add their voices' worth to the quarrel so that finally the courtyard is filled with angry women. Such an extensive performance, however, does not occur frequently. The women vary considerably in how often they quarrel. We were told that in some houses the women fight daily, in some once a week, and in some not for months at a time.

In any case the quarrels between sisters-in-law are usually not of long duration. Seclusion has the effect of terminating as well as precipitating disagreements. Tempers may flare, but if the women of a courtyard cannot get along with each other, they have no one else to turn to for company. After a quarrel, women may not speak to each other for several days or even one or two weeks, but a wise mother-in-law or loneliness coupled with the restrictions of purdah may help resolve the hostility. An extremely angry woman may show her vexation by going to bed and refusing to eat. When this happens, some woman from the house or a neighboring house may act as peacemaker. In some cases quarrels between sisters-in-law result in permanent unfriendliness. As discussed earlier, the women may insist that their husbands divide the courtyard by building a wall.

The women, like the men, sometimes engage in aggressive gossip and joking when they are not on good terms with each other. When the women are really angry, they are more likely to voice their charge directly, calling witnesses if necessary.

If women are habitually on bad terms with the women of other houses, they stop visiting each other. Often the women's visiting habits follow the patterns of the men's quarrels, that is, they do not visit the families with whom the men are on bad terms. However, women's quarrels are seldom championed by the men. The village women in general believe that the men fight less frequently but more seriously than they themselves do—a belief in which we concur. As one woman said:

The men do not fight, but if they do, it is dangerous. They will start abusing one another and then start fighting with staffs. Like on Holī—the men had a fight and that man was killed. The fights that go on from generation to generation are the fights of men and not of women.

❦
❦
❦

Chapter 6

Marriage

Because the life of women is so curtailed by the custom of purdah, it is not surprising that they look forward with pleasure to any ceremony which allows them to leave the courtyard and associate with other men and women. Among the most exciting of these occasions is the marriage ceremony.

The weeks or months during which marriages are celebrated are the most festive of the ceremonial year. During these seasons almost every day marks the arrival or departure of a wedding party. Some arrive in crowded, honking buses, but most make the journey as far as Bhudana by train and then travel to and from the village in long lines of bullock carts. The platforms of many of the men's quarters are filled with guests, and groups of village women dressed in brilliant saris hurry through the lanes on the way to houses where ceremonies are in progress. Throughout the marriage season the village rings with the

trumpets and trombones of wedding bands and the blare of popular
Indian movie songs which are played over amplifying units hired in
one of the nearby towns.

There are certain times of year when no marriages are ever held,
for these periods are inauspicious. Auspicious times during the balance
of the year depend on astrological calculations, and, as a rule, marriages
take place in November and part of December and in May and June
after the harvest. Most families prefer the latter period because food
stocks have been replenished and the warm weather makes it easier to
provide for large numbers of guests, since they can sleep in the open
and without heavy bedding.

A family must arrange marriages for all of its daughters. A failure
to do so is unheard of in the village and would be met with severe
censure. There is not the same social pressure to see that all of the sons
are married, but a family will make every effort to get wives for them,
especially the eldest. Girls are generally married at 16 or 17. The marriage of a boy may be delayed until he is 18 or 20, especially if he is a
student.

When a girl is old enough to be married, her family must begin the
search for a suitable groom. Marriage negotiations are sometimes conducted by the girl's father, particularly if he is the head of the house.
But it is more usual for the father to obtain the help of elderly relatives.
Information about eligible boys is often obtained when a member of
the family, or a relative, goes to another village to attend a marriage.

The range of choice is limited by a number of factors. Since some
Rājpūt clans are more highly regarded than others, the negotiators
will try to make an alliance with a family belonging to a clan of high
standing. Another limiting factor is the location of the groom's village
in relation to Khalapur. Traditionally wives have come from the south,
and daughters have been given in marriage to the north and northwest. Distance is also a consideration, and few marriages are made in
villages which lie beyond a radius of about 100 miles. Most Rājpūt
villages very close to Khalapur are eliminated because the Rājpūts in
them are clan brothers.

Within these limitations, the selection of a suitable groom requires
a delicate balancing of many factors. The reputation of the groom, his
age, health, looks, and schooling are important. The relative social and
economic standing of the two families must be weighed. It is desirable,
if possible, for the girl's family to make an alliance with a family having
a somewhat higher status than hers, since this enhances their prestige
in their own village and ensures that the bride will not be discontent
with her husband's social standing. But aspirations of this kind must

be trimmed according to the amount of dowry which her family can afford and, finally and most important, by a decision as to whether the girl would be well taken care of, both as a wife and a widow.

When a decision has been reached and a boy's family has agreed to the match, a ceremony is held at the men's quarters of the boy's family. The negotiators who represent the family of the girl present a sum of money to the groom-to-be, plus small token payments to the members of his family and some of his family servants. Since the status of a wife's family is always subordinate to the status of the groom's, this aspect of the new relationship is shown by the very respectful and deferential way in which the elderly representative of the bride-to-be's family presents the gift of money to the groom-to-be. It is also clearly symbolized by the eating pattern. Since members of a girl's family are not supposed to take food in the village of her husband, when food is served at the end of the ceremony by the family of the groom-to-be, the representatives of the bride-to-be's family refrain from eating. This is an indication that the preliminary marriage agreement has been sealed.

An auspicious date for the marriage is determined by astrological calculations made by a Brāhmaṇ in the village of the bride, and the groom's family is informed of the date by letter carried by the bride's barber.

As the date approaches, both the family of the groom and the family of the bride have much to do. The head of the groom's family must see that arrangements are made for the ceremony and feasting which will take place before the groom sets out for the bride's village. Those who are to attend the groom as members of his marriage party must be informed and arrangements made for their transportation.

By far the greatest burden of a marriage is borne by the family of the bride. The money for the dowry represents the savings of many years, and often a family must go into debt in order to provide a sufficient amount. (About a century ago the necessity of marrying all of the daughters in the family, plus the heavy financial burden which their dowry represented, led to the practice of female infanticide among the Rājpūts, although it was also caused, according to some informants, by the reluctance of the male members of the bride's family to assume a subordinate status in relation to the members of the groom's family.) The dowry also includes expensive jewelry, kitchen utensils, and large amounts of clothing and bedding. Some of these articles will have been collected well in advance, since mothers often start putting things aside for their daughters' dowries soon after they are born, and when they are older, the daughters themselves make many of the articles which will be included in their dowries. But much of the bedding and clothing and some of the kitchen utensils and jewelry often remain to be purchased. Arrangements must also be made for housing and feeding the groom's marriage party and for feeding guests from the village and family servants.

A number of preliminary ceremonies center about the bride and the groom separately, but the most important ceremonies take place when the groom and his party have come to the village of the bride, where they remain for three days of ritual and feasting. On the third day the groom and his party leave the village, taking the bride with them. The new bride seldom stays at her husband's village for more than a month or two. The date of her return to her parents' home is decided during the marriage ceremonies, and at the appointed time her brother or some other male member of her family comes to get her. She may remain in her parents' village for as long as three years, but she usually stays no longer than a year. When she again returns to her husband's home, she takes a large number of gifts for the members of her in-laws' family. She does not return to her own village until the birth of her first child.

Although children do not participate directly in the marriage preparations and ceremonies, they have ample chance to view the proceedings from first to last. For months before the marriage, the conversation of the women centers around the event. In the bride's family the women are busy making baskets, bowls, and mats. The children see the preparations and mounting excitement. At the various ceremonies leading up to the wedding and at the wedding itself, the children, in restless, giggling groups, hover in the background, watching with eager interest.

The marriage proceedings are particularly significant for children in that they provide a clear and dramatic picture of the drastic changes in a girl's life following her marriage. During the ceremony which marks the sending of a letter to the groom's house to set the date of the wedding, the girl, hidden in some dark corner of the house, weeps, by herself. This weeping is not a ritual mourning but a genuine expression of grief.

When a new bride enters her husband's house, she is put "on display" every afternoon for several days. All the women of the family's lineage are invited to see her and her dowry. The bride, her sari pulled over her head and face, sits huddled on the courtyard floor. One by one the visiting women lift her veil and peer at her face, while the bride, with lowered eyelids, struggles to turn away. Having seen the bride and perhaps commented on her looks, the visitor turns to an inspection of the dowry. The mother-in-law displays the various items and tells her visitors how many utensils and pieces of clothing the bride has brought to the house. Each woman is comparing the dowry to those of other families, and the older women may verbalize these comparisons and make slighting remarks about the quantity and quality of the goods, or they may praise the dowry to the detriment of some other family who has recently acquired a bride. By the middle of the afternoon, the courtyard is full of women busily talking to each other and catching up on the latest news. No one speaks to the bride, and it would be shameless for her to join the conversation. She must not even be caught looking at any of the visitors. Although she may peek through her sari while it is over her face, she does not lift it, and she must keep her eyes lowered when anyone lifts her veil to look at her. The children, both those of the family and those who have come with their mothers, watch the proceedings, and occasionally a little girl, with a troubled expression on her young face, stands thoughtfully viewing the silent figure huddled in the midst of the chattering women.

A daughter-in-law must cover her face in front of her mother-in-law, older daughters-in-law, and husband's sisters until the birth of her first child. Actually this custom is seldom strictly observed in practice, since it interferes with work, but when visitors are present, a young daughter-in-law will usually pull her sari over her forehead and sit at a lower level than her in-laws.

The bride's return to her home after two or more months for a prolonged visit suggests that in a sense the first marriage ceremony functions as an initiation ceremony—preparing the young girl for adult female life.

❧
❧
❧

Chapter 7

Religion

Sometime in India's prehistoric past, probably around 1500 B.C., horse riding people from the area of the Iranian plateau began pushing across the Hindu Kush, through the mountain passes, and into the land of the Indus valley and its tributaries. Here they found a highly civilized people who lived in fortified cities, had a written language, used copper and silver, and traded with the peoples of the Middle East. Possibly the first wave of invaders, and surely subsequent waves, spoke Indo-European. The religion of these invaders is contained in a collection of hymns, ritual texts, and philosophical treatises called the Veda. Agreement on the sacredness of these texts plus the system of caste—which is supposed to rest on Vedic authority—are the two most general characteristics of Hinduism. During the course of its long development, however, Hinduism has become a great religious storehouse, encompassing a myriad of gods, sects, beliefs, and customs; and each caste, each region, each village, and even each individual may choose a slightly different set of beliefs and customs from this vast diversity. In Khalapur, as elsewhere, the Rājpūt men and other high-caste men have a quite different religious life from that practiced by their women; the old differ from the young, and each caste emphasizes a slightly different set of ceremonies and customs.

The two most important gods of Hinduism are Śiva and Viṣṇu. These gods are sometimes represented as two members of a trinity of gods, Śiva being the god of destruction, Viṣṇu the god of preservation, and Brahmā the god of creation. Brahmā has never been the focus of as much religious devotion as the other two members of the trinity and is now reputed to have only two temples in all of India.

Śiva is represented throughout much of India in the form of a *lingam*, or phallic-shaped stone, the base of which rests in a stone structure called the *yonī*. The *yonī* is shaped like an oil lamp and represents the female principle. Closely associated with this representation of Śiva is his bull Nandi; a figure of Nandi is often placed beside the *lingam* and *yonī*. These three figures are the central figures in the Śiva temple at Khalapur.

Viṣṇu, in his role of preserver, has appeared on earth in the persons of Kṛṣṇa and Rāma. The exploits of these two god-heroes are recorded in two great epics, the Mahābhārata and the Rāmāyaṇa. In the Mahābhārata Kṛṣṇa helps five brothers recover the kingdom which they have lost to their scheming cousins in a dice game. Rāma, hero of the Rāmāyaṇa, save the world by killing the demon Rāvaṇa, who has stolen Rāma's wife, the beautiful Sītā. This epic has special importance for the Khalapur Rājpūts, since they consider themselves to be descendants of Rāma.

Today Śiva and Viṣṇu, although far from impotent, are regarded as passive, whereas their consorts Pārvatī and Lakṣmī are the active members. This contrast between the quiescent male principle and the active female principle is reflected in attitudes toward men and women. Women are regarded as flighty and less dignified than men, and it is believed that women's sex drive is stronger than that of men. This belief justifies early marriages and supports the stereotype of the immoral widow.

In addition to the major gods, some worship of various animals and natural objects may be traced to the Vedic tradition. In the Veda fire, the sun, and several rivers are addressed as gods, and these entities are still regarded as sacred throughout India. Water has purifying, as well as cleansing, properties, and the daily bathing of high-caste Hindus is practiced as much for spiritual as for sanitary reasons. Bathing in sacred rivers or temple ponds is a regular part of worship at religious festivals, and often water is used in ceremonies for purposes of purification. After cremation, the ashes of the dead are finally consigned to some sacred river or canal. Fire may also be used for purification. Dishes which have become contaminated may be purified by passing them through fire. Fire also figures largely in the wedding ceremony.

The worship of trees is prevalent in Khalapur and, like many other elements in Hinduism, may stem from a non-Vedic, non-Aryan religious strata. There are a number of trees around the village which are associated with spirits. One mango tree is supposed to have been a man at one time and is worshipped each year at the time of a festival known as *Ekādaśi*. A Brāhmaṇ goes to another tree to receive the offering of milk made by those whose cows and buffaloes have recently calved. *Pīpal* trees are considered sacred and are also associated with ghosts, which they sometimes house. The *nīm* tree is considered to have both medicinal and magical properties. Its twigs are used for brushing teeth; its leaves are sometimes used in medicine; and its branches are hung over doorways to protect the family from ghosts. Many courtyards have a small *tulsī* or basil bush growing in them. This bush is thought by some to be a Brāhmaṇ girl who was miraculously changed into a tree to escape the advances of a Muslim man who had kidnapped her. There is a song about the *tulsī* bush which says:

> Where *tulsī* is standing, there Kṛṣṇa took birth.
> Ghosts surround the courtyard where god is absent
>   and *tulsī* is not standing.

Although they did not consider cattle too sacred to slaughter and eat, the Vedic writers held cows in high regard, used them as their standard of exchange, and identified them with earth, nourishment, and motherhood. This symbolism has persisted, and cows are today the most sacred of animals in India; it is the gravest of sins for a Hindu to kill a cow or eat beef. In many cattle compounds one sees old bullocks whose days are long past. They will nevertheless be cared for and fed until they die. All of the five products of a cow—milk, curd, butter, urine, and dung—are considered sacred. For this reason cow dung is used in the construction of religious idols, as a plaster to purify the cooking hearth, and as a poultice for the wounds of cattle. Its sacredness explains why many Rājpūt women make their own dung cakes for fuel.

Some animals are sacred because they have come to be associated with particular Vedic gods or have appeared in post-Vedic legends. Thus monkeys are sacred because of the important part that the monkey god, Hanumān, playing in helping Rāma to recover his wife from the demon Rāvaṇa. The villagers sometimes threw food to the monkeys living in the village mango groves. Snakes, sacred to Śiva, are also worshipped on a special day. This worship, however, is chiefly designed to persuade the snakes to stay away from the houses. When found, snakes are usually killed, particularly when found within the village. A number of other animals are considered to be sacred in various parts of India. In Khalapur, cows, monkeys, and snakes are the only animals regularly worshipped, although some villagers accord sacred status to some other animals, such as peacocks and antelope.

It should be noted that since all forms of life are sacred to some extent, reluctance to kill an animal does not necessarily mean that it has some specially sacred status.

As is well-known, there are Hindus who carry pantheistic doctrine to an extreme, taking elaborate precautions to avoid killing any living thing, even inadvertently. In the village no one takes such an extreme position, but the doctrine forms a part of the belief system of those who are strict vegetarians, and there are many villagers who are reluctant to kill wasps, flies, and even bedbugs.

Although an observer might well conclude, from the large number of spirits, deities, animals, trees, and natural entities that figure in village worship, that Hindus are polytheistic, this is not true, strictly speaking. The religion of the Ṛg Veda is largely polytheistic, but in the last book of the Ṛg Veda there emerges from this pantheon the idea of a single world soul or deity who encompasses all of the various gods, goddesses, and forces of nature. This concept is found fully developed in the Upaniṣads, theological texts written in the sixth century B.C. The philosophers of the Upaniṣads conceived of the material world as an illusion. The only true reality exists in the world soul, Brahman. Man's soul, the Ātman, as well as the souls of animals, plants, and even inanimate objects are merely separate manifestations of this world soul. These writings give the basis for the impersonal monotheism of sophisticated Hindus and provide a theological basis for the Vedic tradition of pantheism.

The Rājpūt men in Khalapur adhere, in greater or lesser degree, to these beliefs, and even the women, although much of their worship is directed to lesser figures, clearly express a belief in a supreme deity.

The strength of Muslim influence in the past may be seen in the small contemporary Muslim Rājpūt community. The Hindu Rājpūts esteem this group and consider its members to be blood relatives, although they do not intermarry with them or share the same hookah. There are strong ties of friendship among a number of individual Muslim and Hindu Rājpūts.

Muslim influence may also be seen in the ritual centering around the Muslim saint's shrine. The spirit of the place is generally invoked by the women in any ceremony designed to protect people or animals from harm. It is believed to have special power to protect children and to cure disease and barrenness.

Rājpūt bridegrooms make an offering at the shrine before leaving the village to obtain their brides, and the women of Rājpūt families make annual offerings at the shrine. The saint's special service to the village is the protection of village crops from locusts and hail storms. When the crops are damaged by hail, as they were in the spring of 1955, many believe the disaster is caused by an offense to his spirit.

The strongest, most recent influence on the religious life of many Rājpūt men is the Ārya Samāj movement. This sect, founded in 1875 by a Brāhman named Dayanand Sarasvati, represents a reform movement within Hinduism. Sarasvati objected to the proliferation of caste groups and worship of the numerous local deities. He advocated a return to the religion of the Veda. Sarasvati claimed that the Veda represented a purely monotheistic religion and, further, that all modern scientific discoveries and theories are stated in these texts in germinal form, claims which may well be disputed by more objective scholars. The community which he set up grew rapidly, and Ārya Samāj teachers began to preach their teacher's ideas in many parts of India. These teachers were very critical of beliefs in minor and local gods and goddesses. They preached against idolatry, maintained that all castes, not just the twice-born castes, had the right to study the sacred texts, and that worship could be performed without entering a temple or utilizing the services of a Brāhman.

It was, however, a less extreme version of this doctrine which was introduced into Khalapur by the Rājpūt leader Pṛthvi Singh. Pṛthvi Singh enlisted support from conservative as well as "liberal" Hindus. He persuaded the Rājpūt men that it was not proper for them to worship at a Muslim saint's tomb, then the only major religious structure in the village, and pressed for the construction of a Hindu temple to Śiva. Thus, although Ārya Samājists destroyed temples in some villages in their efforts to suppress idolatry, they were instrumental in constructing one in Khalapur. With the construction of the new temple, the worship of the saint declined. Men are now taken to the temple rather than to the tomb to take an oath when a *panchāyat* wishes to test the truth of their statements. The people most strongly affected by this new movement were the men of a number of high-status families in the subdivision of the village from which the sample for this study was drawn. The strict Ārya Samājist accepts only a core of the widely shared beliefs which form the background of village Hinduism. Most important for him is the belief in an absolute, impersonal, and all-embracing spirit. He feels that only a few ceremonial forms have true religious significance, and he speaks slightingly of much of the ritual activity which goes on, calling it "women's work." He believes that the all-embracing spirit cannot be moved by offerings and that the only way of approaching Him is through personal prayer.

For the women and many men, the spiritual realm is more complex. The name of Rāma is often mentioned by the women in their prayers, whereas the major gods and goddesses are worshipped chiefly during various calendrical festivals in their honor. At other times the women's worship is primarily directed to various disease goddesses, local spirits, and the family ancestors. The worship of disease goddesses is fairly widespread in India. In Khalapur the goddesses are conceived of as 101 sisters. The few who are actually named are thought to be responsible for such epidemic diseases as smallpox and cholera. In their benevolent mother aspect, they may be worshipped on other occasions, when the women are appealing for general protection and good health.

The two most important local godlings are the Muslim saint and the village's guardian spirit, whose shrine was built when the village was founded. In this area of India every village has a shrine built to consecrate and guard the village site. Both this spirit and the Muslim saint are regarded as protectors of the village. Other shrines in or around the village are associated with spirits whose worship is believed to be efficacious in the prevention or cure of a variety of ills. One of these spirits, for example, is believed to have the power to prevent one from getting thorns in one's feet; another prevents boils. In addition, there are several *satī* shrines in honor of women who destroyed themselves on the death of their husbands.

Besides the worship of these many gods and spirits, the worship of family ancestors plays an important part in the religion of the women.

Indeed, some of the women define their religion as ancestor worship. The ancestors are invoked in virtually all prayers and festivals regardless of what other spirit or deity may be involved. Many women utter the name of Rāma and the male ancestors every morning on arising. Usually the ancestors are worshipped for three generations, that is, for as long, generally, as the person is remembered.

Almost every family in the village has one or more small shrines in the fields built in honor of ancestral spirits. It is believed that the spirits of men who have died unmarried or childless or who have met a violent and untimely death and thus have been taken from life before they were willing to leave it are most likely to remain on earth and cause illness to members of their family or to bother them in the form of snakes or dangerous insects. These spirits often appear in dreams or speak through some person they have possessed. At such times they usually request the construction of a shrine where they may live and where offerings may be made in their memory. When the family members build the shrine, they request the spirit to live there and cease bothering them. Worship at these shrines is generally irregular and is carried out by the women. There is one family in the village, however, whose women make offerings at the ancestral shrine every month.

Because the villagers believe that there is an auspicious and an inauspicious time for beginning certain acts, they stress astrology and the reading of omens. The Brāhmaṇs are the astrologers of the village, and some of those who are literate have books in which there are astrological tables. One of these Brāhmaṇs is always consulted when the date of a marriage is to be set, or when a new house is to be lived in, or a new business enterprise undertaken. The reading of omens does not necessarily require a specialist, for their interpretaton is common knowledge. When a dog shakes his head so that his ears flap, those who see him take off their shoes and shake the dust from their feet. This act symbolizes a fresh start after seeing an inauspicious sight. The calling of a crow indicates that a guest will soon arrive. Most people are reluctant to start out on a visit to anyone immediately after they have sneezed or to make plans when the jackals are howling. There are innumerable omens, so many, in fact, that no one takes all of them seriously.

The idea of a sacred place, such as a temple or a shrine, is combined with the idea of an auspicious time with the result that there are certain days, or hours within the day, when it is most appropriate and efficacious to go to sacred places and perform ritual activities. The crossing of time and place is most conspicuous on the occasion of a *melā*, or religious fair. The most significant *melā* for Khalapur occurs once a year in connection with the worship of the goddess Balsundrī, whose temple is located in Bhudana. The town of Hardwar, where the Ganges leaves the Himalayas and enters the plains, is a major Hindu sacred place not far from Khalapur. A *melā* is held at Hardwar every year, and every 12 years a portion of the river at Hardwar becomes one of the holiest places in all India, and pilgrims come from all over the country in order to bathe there.

The seasons are marked by many festivals, observed primarily by the women. Many honor one of the major gods or goddesses: Daśarā is sacred to Durgā, the Mother Goddess, and commemorates the day that Rāma vanquished the demon Rāvaṇa; Dawālī, the beautiful festival of lights, celebrates both the wedding day of Viṣṇu and Lakṣmī, the goddess of wealth, and the return of Rāma to his capitol after Rāvaṇa's defeat; Śiva's wedding day is celebrated in the festival of Śiv Rātrī, the night of Śiva, the only day of the year when the women worship at the Śiva temple. Gias celebrates the awakening of the gods, who sleep during a portion of the year, whereas Janmāṣṭamī honors Kṛṣṇa's birthday. During the important festival of Khānāgat the Brāhmaṇs serving the family are given food for 16 consecutive days, to honor the male ancestors. There are also two fast days kept by the women, one for the health of their husbands and one for the health of their sons.

Certain patterns of worship are common to most of these festivals. Offerings usually consist of water (which is often used to bathe the image representing the divinity), sweets, bread fried in *ghī,* and tiny earthenware lamps, whose cotton wicks have been soaked in mustard oil and lighted in offering. Many of the calendrical rites involve fasting. Such fasts are usually kept by women, but men may also fast on important occasions. Sometimes the fast requires not eating throughout the day, but often it consists only of abstention from such foods as cereal grains, so that fasts are, in general, mild.

Almost all ceremonies are celebrated by the cooking of special kinds of food, the most common being various sweets, milk preparations, and fried breads. The village women frequently begin their descriptions of ceremonies by saying: "We cook sweets and fried breads on this day."

Another feature of these rites is the giving of presents, usually in the form of food, to the family servants. Providing food enough for servants, as well as for family, and offerings keeps the Rājpūt women busy on these festival days.

In ceremonies, the family is the most important unit, and among the members of the family it is the women who take the most interest and participate most actively. Many ceremonies are carried out without the help of any religious specialist, but there are some which require the presence of a Brāhmaṇ. In many ceremonies where the Brāhmaṇ is present, one of his significant functions is ritual eating. This fact has led some of the women to complain that Brāhmaṇs have invented festivals so that they could be fed.

The Rājpūt men usually do not keep fast days or participate actively in the calendrical festivals. Some of the men most influenced by Ārya Samāj say that they are aware of these festivals only because they receive particularly good food on these days. In some of the festivals, however, the men play a part. They participate in the Janmāṣṭamī celebrations, and a few of the younger men engage in the general horse-play and throwing of colored water that takes place during Holī, the spring Saturnalia. Although Rājpūt men elsewhere in India do homage to their weapons on the festival day of Dasarā, in Khalapur the custom has almost completely died out. Stimulated by the Community Development Project, which provided musical instruments, a small but enthusiastic group of men, including a few of the younger Rājpūts, meets weekly in the newly constructed village council house to sing religious songs. Occasionally some of the older Rājpūt men gather on a men's house platform to hear one of their number read aloud from a book such as the Rāmāyaṇa.

The Hindu expresses his religious beliefs not only in ceremonies and prayers but also in the customs which guide his everyday activities and his relations with other people. The religiously supported concept of *dharma* defines one's duties as a member of a caste, one's duties as a man or woman and a man's duties at different ages during his lifetime. In traditional Hindu thought, the ideal life of a man was divided into four stages. In the first stage he was to be a celibate student. In the second it was his duty to become a father and to raise a family. In this stage it was not sinful to enjoy sexual pleasures, nor was it wrong to be concerned with the accumulation of wealth and the enhancement of the prestige of one's family. The pursuit of these goals became sinful only if such activity became so all-absorbing that it couldn't be given up when the third stage of life was reached. This stage began when a man had arranged for the marriages of his sons and daughters and his children had begun to raise their families. Ideally it was appropriate at this period for a man and his wife to retire to a forest and live there as celibate hermits, devoting themselves to a life of religious contemplation. No men and women of the village carry out this doctrine literally, but it is common for a man to begin to give up the management of his farm after his sons have married, and it is considered unseemly for a woman to conceive after a daughter-in-law has come to live in the house. In the fourth and final stage of life, a man and woman were supposed to give up all worldly possessions other than simple prayer beads, an antelope skin used as a sitting mat, a few items of clothing, and a begging bowl. They were supposed to become wandering hermits, concerned only with the salvation of their souls. No Rājpūts of the village have taken this final step, but the power of the ideal is seen in the genuine respect which is accorded many of the *sādhūs* who pass through the village and occasionally spend some time in one of the village orchards. There are some *sādhūs* who are regarded as insincere and meretricious, and they are accorded no respect. Even so, they are always able to obtain alms in the village.

The four stages of life are differently valued. In accordance with the strong other-worldly emphasis of Hinduism, those who have entered the third stage are accorded more respect, a sentiment which is reinforced by the increment in status which men and women acquire as they grow older. But this does not mean that any of the stages should be omitted. Ideally a man should fulfill the obligations of all four.

The beliefs that the ultimate meaning of existence lies in an attempt to renounce it and transcend it and that the ordinary concerns and claims of daily living are in a sense unreal and a barrier between the soul and its true destiny, are reflected in the high value placed on ascetic practices and in a respect for those who have renounced worldly concerns. A man who gives much of his time to devotional practices is called a *bhagat*. A certain respected elderly Rājpūt is known by this title. He lives a life of simple austerity, performing daily ceremonies, and he says he is attempting to atone for sins committed in his youth.

The concept of *dharma*, and the desire to store up spiritual merit, helps to explain the readiness with which villagers give alms, both to holy men and to beggars, for giving alms is defined as a meritorious act. It is especially commendable to feed a Brāhmaṇ, and it is regarded as wrong for other castes to take food from Brāhmaṇs. A Rājpūt may eat with a Brāhmaṇ friend, but he will usually leave a token payment.

When the philosophers of the Upaniṣads developed the idea of the absolute world soul, or all-encompassing deity, they also developed the idea that the true end of each soul, and thus the ultimate meaning of existence, is reabsorption into the One. Until this reunion is achieved, the soul must progress through a repetitive cycle of birth, death, and rebirth, or reincarnations. All forms of life, from insects and animals to human beings, represent stages of life at varying distances from reunion with God. One obtains release from this cycle only through many meritorious deeds performed in successive lives. Increasing asceticism marks a man's progress toward this goal, and the popular veneration for the wandering holy men stems from their presumed nearness to this final goal. The ordinary person acknowledges that the attachment to earthly desires places him a long way from his final release.

The stage into which each soul is born is the result of *karma*. A Rājpūt man explained this concept by saying that God keeps something which resembles a court file. During the course of a man's life his meritorious deeds and thoughts are entered on this file, together with his sins. The file is first consulted when the man dies. At this time the balance between his good deeds and his bad deeds determines the length of his soul's stay in a "small heaven." This heaven is described as a place where the soul has a "good house, good food, and good clothing, such as it did not have upon earth." The file is consulted a second time when the soul is to be reborn. This time the balance between good deeds and bad determines the status into which the soul is to be reborn.

Variant interpretations of the doctrine of reincarnation were given by the women. For some of them, reincarnation simply meant an endless succession of rebirths without ultimate release. For some, the reward for virtue was rebirth into a higher caste; for others, it was greater comfort in the next life. One girl felt that the highest reward would be rebirth into one's own household. Some thought it was possible to be reborn into the body of an animal; others did not. Some women held that faults and virtues were preserved in successive incarnations; that is, if one was a thief, one would continue to be a thief in the next life. This kind of belief is illustrated in the following story, told to us by a Rājpūt woman:

Once there was a man and his wife who kept fighting with each other. When they were born again, the husband was a donkey and his wife was a crow. The crow kept sitting on the donkey and pecking at it.

Most observers of Indian village life have commented on the prevalence of fatalism. It is commonly said in the village that what will happen to a person is written on his forehead at birth. The doctrine of *karma* sometimes merges with that of fatalism. One man said he was sure Nehru must have committed some sins in a previous life, for in this life he had no sons. But usually the doctrine of fatalism and the doctrine of *karma*, with its implications of freedom of choice and opportunity to improve one's lot, are kept separate, and the villager is not bothered by any logical inconsistency. When he is faced with a situation which surpasses his control in spite of any efforts he may make, the appropriate concept is that of fate. The women frequently refer to fate as an explanation for various misfortunes, perhaps because they have so little autonomy over their actions.

Not only are individuals born and reborn in successive lives, but the entire universe is periodically destroyed and recreated. In each cycle there are four stages, each progressively shorter than its predecessor, and representing also a decline in health, happiness, stature, longevity, and morality. The age of the universe in which we are now living is the *Kali-yuga*, the last and worst of the four. It is believed that this age will be brought to a close when God sends a divine warrior to kill all evildoers and begins the cycle all over again. Since the fourth age is characterized by an extreme disregard of *dharma*, there are many villagers who see the new rights and aspirations of the lower castes as expectable aspects of the deteriorated times. There is a strong tendency to compare the present unfavorably with the past, and there are few who express sanguine hopes for the future. Most Rājpūts, whose superior status has been severely threatened by the reform movements of the new government, feel that they were much better off under British rule, and even those who see a change for the better will hold that any real and lasting improvement in human affairs must await the next recreation of the universe.

The children are not concerned with these more general religious beliefs and attitudes. They hear the religious stories and songs told and sung by the adults and learn the ceremonial largely from observation. There is no formal religious instruction.

The villagers take their religious ceremonies rather casually, and except when a Brāhman is present in the house, the ceremonies are not solemn occasions. The children are almost always present during household ceremonies. Little girls may participate actively to the extent of joining their mothers and aunts in keeping a fast, but this is likely to be in the spirit of fun, and children are never required to fast. There is a sex difference here too: little boys fast less frequently than little girls because men do not fast as often as women, and the children's participation is largely imitative.

They may, however, help with some of the preparations, such as the making of the figure of a goddess, which is plastered on the courtyard wall during one festival. During one festival the children run through the village with flaming rags and at another they set off firecrackers.

There are few instances of special religious status for children. Little girls (i.e., virgins) are compared to goddesses because they are pure. They are often called "goddess," and in some ceremonies young girls are given offerings of candy or money. In ritual feeding, a girl may sometimes substitute for a cow or a Brāhmaṇ. Sons should perform funeral rites for their father, but they are usually adults before this duty falls to them.

❅

❅

❅

Chapter 8

Disease and Medical Practices *

Until the 1920's the death rate in all of Uttar Pradesh was extremely high (Bacon, 1956: 37–43), and the fear of disease must have been great. Although epidemics of plague, cholera, smallpox, and so on, since this time have been largely curtailed and famine is more easily prevented because of improved transportation, disease is still a major problem.

Many types of diseases are recognized by the Rājpūts. Diagnosis is based primarily on symptoms, and treatment varies with the type of disease. If one cure fails, a series of other diagnoses and treatments follows. Disease may be caused by the improper functioning of the human body, the needs of which are described in Hindu and Muslim medical texts, by the ghosts of ancestors, or by goddesses and godlings whose nature or function is to give disease. The ancestors may become displeased because they have not been accorded proper ceremonial respect. The goddesses and godlings may punish men for sins of omission committed in this life or in some previous existence. Since one cannot know one's sins in a former life, the actions of the gods are for all practical purposes unpredictable. The supernatural may also be manipulated by individuals through sorcery or the unwitting possession of an evil eye.

Although certain symptoms may be associated with one type of ex-

---

* A large part of the material in this chapter was taken from the Cornell files. Special help in understanding and interpreting the material was contributed by Jack Planalp's doctoral thesis.

planation rather than another,* there is no consistency of diagnoses, and a series of cures may be tried one after another, each implying a different theory of causation. Although the men and the younger and more educated people tend to lean toward traditional or Western medical theories, the women and less educated men tend to favor supernatural explanations. While a man may be seeking the aid of a doctor in a nearby city, the women at home are anxiously offering prayers and food to the family ancestors or to the goddess held responsible for the sickness. An individual may try various types of cures successively or simultaneously.

There is a tendency, however, to diagnose the illnesses of children as supernatural in origin, evil eye being the greatest threat to infants and the epidemic diseases attributed to the goddesses and godlings as the next most frequent.

The diseases most commonly attributed to the more naturalistic causes include pneumonia, stomach-ache, thread worms, eye trouble, coughs, colds, and diarrhea in adults. These are thought to result from the improper care of the body. Leela Dube, in a paper on Khalapur medicine, points out that the villagers have adopted a simplified version of the traditional theory and that their beliefs about proper diet and the regulation of the body are a simplified version of ancient medical texts which contain elaborate instruction about the ideal daily routine, including exercise and cleanliness of the body as well as instruction about food and drink.

Cures which involve fasting or special diet are based primarily on the theory of the nature of certain foods. As Leela Dube (1956: 5–6) writes:

The villagers distinguish between foods that are "hot," that is, which have heat producing effect and foods that are "cold," that is, which have a cold producing or cooling effect. There are also foods that are intermediate between these two and thus are neither "hot" nor "cold." Some foods are constipative, some are laxative. Another distinction is that of catarrhal, billious and flatulent foods. Some foods are supposed to have all three of these properties, some are considered to have two of them and some others may be believed to have only one. There are many commonly used foods to which villagers attribute none of these properties.

In addition there are certain foods like ghi and nuts which are supposed to be particularly strength-giving. Some foods are regarded as better than others in respect to increasing the blood supply in the body. One distinction is that of dry and wet foods. Dryness accentuates the hot quality of a food while wetness accentuates its cool quality.

* Dr. Woodruff's (1959) study of theories of diseases in southern India suggests that a more intensive study might reveal more consistency of symptom determining diagnoses.

The way in which foods are classified in Indian villages varies from place to place, and in Khalapur there is variation from person to person. But many villagers would include as heat producing such items as onion, potato, cane liquor, tea, mangoes, oils, *ghī*, and buffalo milk. Many also would agree that spinach, lemon, and curd are cold, and cow's milk neutral.

In line with these beliefs about diet, it is interesting to note that a number of the older Rājpūts insist that the health of the younger men has been adversely affected by the new varieties of seed the government is distributing. Although better in yield and appearance, it is felt that the crops lack nutritional value and make the young men weak and unable to compete with their elders in agricultural work. Widespread physical deterioration also is attributed to the use of vegetable oil substitutes for *ghī*.

Besides proper food, the villagers emphasize the importance to health of daily bathing, regular elimination, and sexual moderation or abstinence. Village men frequently refer to excessive sex activity as a cause of minor illness, and the longevity of several men is attributed to complete abstinence in their later years. A young man is expected to keep his wife satisfied and beget sons but should not overindulge. When overindulgence is most likely, sanctions sometimes are applied to prevent him. A groom's older sister may regulate the sexual activity of the newlyweds, and his father or uncle may reprimand him or even recommend that his bride be allowed to visit her own house for a time if he sleeps with her too often. (It should be noted that although sanctions of this kind are phrased in terms of the groom's overindulgence, they also in part reflect concern for the new bride.) Sexual intercourse is thought to make men in particular weak and susceptible to disease because the loss of one drop of semen is considered the equivalent of the loss of 40 drops of blood.

Smallpox, chicken pox, measles, and cholera are generally associated with particular disease goddesses referred to as *mātā* or *mai* ("mother"). These goddesses are thought to be sisters, and although informants disagreed, they are most frequently reported as numbering 101. No woman, however, could give the names of more than five or six. Smallpox is named "mother" (*mātā*) after the goddess, and chicken pox is referred to as "little mother." There are shrines to various of these goddesses in the village and its surrounding fields, which the women visit to make offerings. Since smallpox epidemics usually occur in the summer, it is believed that the goddess enters the village at this season. The presence of the goddess is synonomous with the disease, and it is believed that she resides in or near the sick person. Prevention involves keeping the goddess from entering the house, and treatment involves persuading her to leave. Both for prevention and cure, pots of water are placed on the roof of the house to keep the goddess cool or to persuade her not to enter the house or to reduce her power if she is already present. When the patient is recovering, the family performs a ceremony to remove the goddess politely from the house. Like the disease, the goddess is thought to be unpredictable, coming and going like the wind. It is hoped that offerings at the shrines will please her and persuade her not to manifest herself, although there is a contradiction in the ritual themes, for sometimes it is thought she visits a family because they please her.

Certain symptoms are attributed to possession by ghosts of the dead. Possession may be active or passive, the former causing bad dreams and trances, the latter lingering illness. In the trance, the voice of the ghost may speak and make known its wishes.

All persons become ghosts after death but remain so only until after the death ceremonies. If the death ceremonies are not conducted properly, however, a person will remain a ghost. People who have met unnatural deaths or have died in the prime of life while still having worldly desires are very apt to remain ghosts. There are two categories of such persons: suicides, people who have been murdered or killed by ghosts, or who have been killed in accidents fall in the first; unmarried men, men who have not had sons, and women who die in childbirth are examples of the second.

In general, women are more susceptible to possession by ghosts than men, and certain women are more susceptible than others. Girls on the eve of their marriage are sometimes possessed, but even more frequently young daughters-in-law residing for the first time in a strange household become possessed by some hostile spirit. Such possession makes these young brides temporarily the center of concern and attention despite their low status. The ghost is feared, and his demands, spoken through the patient, must be obeyed. The case is reported of a girl possessed by a ghost who became very aggressive, demanding only candy and abusing both her in-laws and the practitioner, who only succeeded in persuading the ghost to depart after it had made a shrewd bargain.

Menstrual difficulties are often associated by women with ghosting. Men are more apt to attribute menstrual disturbance to heat which rises from the lower part of the woman's body to her brain and makes her think she is troubled by a ghost.*

If a ghost simply "sticks" to a person, he becomes ill. A baby whose

* See Jack Planalp's field notes.

mother had died in childbirth is in great danger, since the ghost of the mother is apt to return and "stick" to the child, causing illness or death.

In general, any malingering, undiagnosed illness is likely to be attributed to ghosts. Such patients are taken to magical practitioners called *sianas* rather than to a doctor for cure. There are several such *sianas* in Khalapur and in neighboring villages who are expert in exorcising ghosts and may also perform sorcery. Their cure is usually to persuade the ghost to possess the patient (to "play on" the person in village parlance) and state its wishes. The practitioner then either persuades the ghost to depart to its proper abode in the ancestor's shrine or transfers the ghost to himself and takes the responsibility for taming it. If the ghost will not leave the patient, the practitioner may become possessed himself or he may use an assistant to reveal the identity of the ghost. Another method of expelling a ghost is to put it in a pot and bury it in some field so that it will stick to some person who passes the burial. Obviously anyone may unwittingly fall prey to a ghost in this fashion; however, daughters-in-law returning from their village to their husbands' home seem to be the most frequent victims.

Illness also may be caused by deliberate or inadvertent sorcery. A barren woman may steal and bury the hair of a child and so kill the child and become pregnant. Certain individuals who are believed to have accidentally eaten feces as babies have power to cast the evil eye. A person may not know that he possesses this power, but the act is willful in the sense that the evil eye is an envious eye. Although children are particularly susceptible to the effects of the evil eye, especially if they are unusually handsome or healthy, any person, animal, or even crop which incites envy may fall victim. A man who has an exceptionally good crop puts a blackened pot in the field to ward off the evil eye, and the owner of a good buffalo or cow which is about to freshen ties colored strings to the horns or legs. Black palm prints are sometimes painted on each side of a doorway to ward off the evil eye, and a black spot is painted on the baby's temple or foot.

Although specific cures are associated with different diagnoses, characteristically many techniques are tried simultaneously and in succession. These include diet, herb medicine, Western medicines and massage, prayers and offerings as well as treatment by people skilled in magic, such as wandering holy men, or *sādhūs*, and *sīanas*. No matter what the theory of causation, treatment for almost all illnesses involves food restrictions, which are designed to restore the balance of bodily functions. During some acute illnesses the patient may abstain from all food for several days. The villagers also treat patients with a large variety of local medicines, some of which are purchased at the bazaar and some of which the villagers make themselves. Various herbs and plants are common ingredients in these medicines, which may also include such diverse substances as powdered pearls, soot, and honey. Massage is an important part of the treatment of many diseases. When a man is sick, his friends will gather at his bedside to keep him company and massage his limbs. Often this massage is for comfort only, but for sprains and muscular pains its purpose is curative as well. Oil is used for some massages and as a poultice for skin diseases, although cow dung seems to be the most popular poultice. Bleeding, both by cupping and leeches, is not so important for most therapy, but it is mentioned as a treatment for ringworms and bruises.

Some *sādhūs* treat sickness as well as cases of ghost sickness and sorcery. Accidents at birth or in later life bestow certain powers. Babies who enter the world feet first develop power to relieve swelling in the groin by stroking the affected parts with their feet, and men who have killed a rare species of brown bird are called on to cure a cattle disease with their touch. One Rājpūt has a method for protecting humans and animals from the effects of mad dog bites, and people travel long distances to seek his services.

There are three doctors in the village, who combine knowledge of traditional Indian medicine with a knowledge of Western theories and practices. They combine traditional treatments with such things as antibiotic injections. In general, villagers do not consult these doctors until they have tried a number of other remedies. They may visit a doctor and a *sādhū* or *siāna* simultaneously.

The differences in medical treatment of men and women is a function not only of the fact that women believe more in supernatural explanations for illness but also of the restrictions imposed by purdah. Men, particularly wealthy men, will go to the government hospital at Bhudana or even to Delhi if they consider themselves seriously ill. Such expert aid is almost never sought for women. Seeing a doctor involves a breach of seclusion which is undertaken with reluctance, and the women seldom get beyond the village doctors who can visit them in the home. It is not uncommon for a man to go to a doctor in behalf of his wife. One man, leaving his sick wife at home, traveled all the way to Delhi to seek aid for her. Even when the doctor does see his women patients, he must make the diagnosis and conduct his treatment without a physical examination, since this would constitute an unpardonable breach of modesty.

Purdah is not, however, the only explanation for the better medical care received by the men, since the same relative lack of concern may be seen for the health of little girls. Of some 90 children in the neighborhood of this study, almost two thirds were boys. Struck by this unbalanced sex ratio, we questioned 36 women about the sex of their children who had died after birth, that is, not including miscarriages and stillborns. The over-all infant mortality rate for both boys and girls was 33%; for boys it was 25%, and for girls 41%. (Sixty-one children were reported to have died.) These women were, therefore, losing almost twice as many girls as boys in childhood. A test for the differences between percentages shows that this difference would occur by chance only once in a hundred times.*

This differential death rate reflects the prevailing preference for sons. The phenomena is not peculiar to Khalapur. There is an excess of male population throughout India. This excess is most pronounced among such high-caste groups of Northwest India as those represented by the Rājpūts of Khalapur. Until the turn of the century, the village Rājpūts practiced female infanticide. This custom died out under governmental pressure. However, with an over-all childhood death rate of one third, lack of prompt or prolonged medical treatment for girls may be responsible for tipping the balance. This is not to say that all girls are neglected—they are not. But the villagers always expect quick results from medical treatment and will change doctors if the cure is not effective. With a girl—particularly if the family is poor—they will become discouraged sooner, and if she fails to recover, may stop treating her. The four sick babies in the neighborhood who were receiving little or no medical aid were all girls.

The interviews with the afore-mentioned 36 mothers indicate that the child mortality rate is highest from birth to 3 years and declines sharply after that age. Seventy-eight per cent of the 46 dead children had died before the age of 3 years. Usually the mother did not know the cause of death, often attributing it vaguely to "a fever." Malaria or diarrhea may account for some of these deaths. Nine children were reported to have died of smallpox. Dysentery, boils in the mouth, stomach infections, and lack of milk on the part of the mother were also reported to have caused some deaths. One child reputedly died of sorcery, one from the evil eye, and one from the effects of having seen a corpse.

We interviewed the mothers of 23 sample children concerning the diseases suffered by the sample children. Their reports are summarized in Table 1.

* For further information on surplus of males, see Subcontractor's Monograph, Cornell-8, HRAF-44, *India: A Sociological Background*, vol. 1.

Table 1 Incidence of Disease

DISEASE	NO. OF CASES	PER CENT OF CHILDREN
Typhoid	5	22
Pneumonia	7	31
Mātā (smallpox or chicken pox)	12	52
Malaria	16	70
Measles	6	26
Sore eyes	19	83
Boils	12	52
Colds	6	26
Infection	4	18

Most children contracted malaria and sore eyes repeatedly, both diseases being more frequent during the summer months. The seriousness of these two ailments varied. Reaction to malaria may be severe or mild. Similarly, for some children, eye infections yielded readily to the local red medicine, which so often appeared on the faces of children, while others had more trouble throwing off the infection and might even develop fever from it.

Although the children contracted a number of diseases, serious accidents were rare. Mothers commonly reported that the children bumped and cut themselves, but none of the children had broken any bones, and only two had received serious injuries—one, a boy, when he fell from a cart into a ditch and injured his knee, and a little girl when her irate father shook her so severely that he either sprained or dislocated her shoulder.

The high rate of disease affects the attitudes of parents toward children. Almost every baby wears a necklace containing charms to ward off illness. Delicate children are objects of concern, and adults sometimes openly express their doubts for their survival. When discussing the future life of a child, a mother would sometimes add ". . . if he lives." One mother who had lost two daughters reported that she was reluctant to become too fond of her 8-year-old daughter or to buy good clothes for her for fear that this child also would be taken from her. Sickness and death are very much a part of the villager's experience, and the fear of them is never far from their minds.

✤
✤
✤

Chapter 9

Death Ceremonies *

Since earth, fire, and water are all sacred elements, a body may be
properly disposed of through any one of these mediums or a combination of them. In practice, all three elements usually enter into the disposal of the dead. Thus, in the procedure used with most adults, the
dying person is first laid on the earth, the body is cremated, and the
ashes are consigned to water. Burial or disposal of the body in a river is
practiced when the deceased is a child or a person who has died of an
epidemic disease. Some sects of *sādhūs* bury their dead.

This differential disposal of the dead can be partially understood
in terms of the Hindu's beliefs about spirits. When a person dies, the
divine and impersonal aspect, the soul, immediately goes to heaven,
but the more personal aspect—the aspect which differentiates one from
the others—lingers in the vicinity of the home. The elaborate ceremonies which follow the cremation of a body are primarily designed
to ensure the safe passage of this personlike shade into the world of
the ancestors. If the ceremonies fail in their purpose, the shade will become a malevolent ghost and haunt the family, causing trouble and
sickness. When the body is buried or consigned to a river, there is no
elaborate ceremonial. These latter forms of disposal are, in effect, "short
cut" methods and as such are reserved for those whose shades are considered to be willing to abandon the pleasures of this world without
elaborate persuasion. Children fall into this category because they have
not yet known and enjoyed worldly pleasures; *sādhūs,* because they
have already voluntarily renounced them.

The reasons for not cremating persons who have died of epidemic

* In writing this section the author has used material from the thesis by Jack
Planalp (1956) as well as the field notes on Khalapur. Dr. Planalp worked
in a village several hundred miles distant from Khalapur but with a similar group.
The main outlines of funeral customs are the same for large numbers of the Indian
population.

diseases probably stem from the belief that these diseases are sacred, representing, as they do, the visitation of a disease goddess. Therefore persons who die in this fashion are already touched by a goddess and do not require further purification by fire. The practice has the obvious practical advantage of allowing for rapid disposal of bodies at a time when many people are dying. The death ceremonies, in a somewhat attenuated form, may be held for such persons after the epidemic has abated. When they are held, a figure of the deceased is fashioned and used to represent the corpse.

When a person is about to die, the area beside the cot on which he is lying is made ritually pure by plastering it with cow dung. The person is then lifted from the cot and laid on the ground. The cot is impure, and it is felt that a person should breathe his last on a spot of sanctified earth.

After death, the body is washed and prepared for cremation. When a married man dies, his wife comes to touch his feet; at the same time her jewelry is removed and her bangles are broken over the feet of the corpse by the wife of the barber. When the body has been sewn in the funeral cloth (which must always be newly purchased), the first of several offerings to the spirit of the dead is made. This consists of a rolled piece of dough made of barley flour and water, which is placed on the dead person's chest. Offerings of the same substance are made on the way to the cremation grounds and during the period of mourning, assuring the re-embodiment of the spirit and hastening its progress to heaven. The bedding and the clothes of the deceased are given to the family sweeper.

When married women of the deceased's lineage receive news of the death, they come to help prepare the body and express their regrets. Together with the women of the household they beat their foreheads, breasts, and thighs and raise their voices in the high-pitched tones of ritual wailing. A family will be criticized by neighbors if the women's wails are not long and loud, and one woman said that when women mourned properly, their bodies should show the bruises of their self-inflicted beatings. The wailing reaches a peak when the men of the family arrive to remove the body to the cremation grounds, usually not more than two or three hours after death. In marked contrast to ritual wailing, grief, when wailing is not required, is expressed in complete silence. As the body of a mother-in-law was carried away, a daughter-in-law beat her head against the courtyard wall and had to be restrained by the other women, but the dead woman's teen-aged, unmarried daughter stood on the sidelines, holding the baby of her wailing aunt, with silent tears coursing down her face.

The body is carried by four male members of the family (preferably sons and grandsons of the deceased) to the cremation grounds, a place just outside the village designated for this purpose. Only men, close relatives and friends, join the funeral procession, which is led by the chief mourner, preferably the eldest son of the deceased. The body is tied to a stretcher which is made of the boughs of the sacred *nīm* tree, usually prepared by the family carpenter. Members of the family carry logs of wood or bundles of straw, and one carries a pot of clarified butter and another a piece of burning cow dung. Other mourners pick up twigs on the way, for no one should go to the cremation grounds empty handed. At a particular spot about half way to the grounds, the body is lowered to the ground, and the men who have been carrying the body take up different positions beside the bier. In the past the chief mourner had his head and moustache shaved at this time, but now the barber merely cuts off a token lock of hair.

After the body has been placed on the pyre, which is made of cow dung and wood, and after the mourners have placed their bits of wood, straw, and twigs on the pyre, the family Brāhman throws *ghī* and sacred and aromatic substances over the corpse. All but one pole of the stretcher on which the body was carried are also placed on the pyre. The chief mourner lights a bundle of straw from the burning cow dung which was carried by one of the mourners and moves quickly around the pyre setting it ablaze. All the mourners squat on the ground, and while the Brāhman recites sacred verses, the chief mourner throws the last of the *ghī* and other sacred substances into the fire. He picks up the remaining pole of the stretcher and makes seven ritual passes from the ground to the head of the corpse, signifying that he has broken its skull. The importance of having sons is due in part to this portion of the cremation ceremony, since, to ensure the safe passage of a man's shade into the world of the ancestors, it should be a son who "breaks" his skull. After making the final ritual pass, the chief mourner flings the pole all the way over the pyre. All the mourners then stand up and walk slowly back to the brook which runs in front of the village.

After ritually cleansing themselves in this stream, the mourners walk to the vicinity of the men's quarters of the deceased. On the way they strip some of the leaves from a *nīm* tree. They squat on the ground near the men's quarters, chew up some of the leaves and spit them onto the ground. The *nīm* leaves provide further ritual cleansing, and the spitting is said to symbolize a complete severance of any connection between the mourners and the dead person.

The family of the deceased observes a number of restrictions for the next 13 days, especially in regard to eating. The chief mourner, who is ritually impure, is subject to more severe restrictions. He must sleep on the ground and is not permitted to sit with other men or smoke the hookah with them. If possible, he should remain quietly in one place, usually a corner of the men's quarters.

On the third day of mourning, the chief mourner, the family Brahman, and sometimes the family barber go to the cremation site and gather the ashes and bones. The ashes are put in the brook or into one of the irrigation canals, both of which are said to connect with the Ganges, but, if possible, the bones are saved to be taken to Hardwar for consignment to the sacred Ganges itself.

During the next nine days the family may make various offerings to the deceased's shade and engage in ritual bathing. Women of the deceased's lineage come to the family's women's quarters every afternoon and sit with the bereaved women in silence, a silence which may occasionally be broken by remarks about the virtues of the deceased and the family women who cared for him. On the 11th and 12th days of mourning, more balls of barley dough are offered.

On the 12th or 13th day after the cremation, male relatives and friends plus affinal relatives come to attend a feast and a ceremony. All the affinal relatives bring cloth, sweets, and money. The gifts from families into which daughters have been married cannot be accepted and are returned to the donors with some additional money, but one of the pieces of cloth given by one of the other affinal relatives is taken, and in a ceremony at which a Brāhmaṇ officiates, it is tied around the head of the chief mourner and worn as a turban. The villagers say that this ritual act symbolizes the transfer of authority from the deceased to the chief mourner. The ceremony also serves to remove the last vestiges of impurity from this man, and after it he can sit with others and share the hookah. Meanwhile the lineage women visit the courtyard for the last time and wail again. The Brāhmaṇ also purifies the house on the 12th or 13th day. After this ceremony, the shade's journey to heaven is considered complete.

Funeral feasts occasionally are elaborate, and many guests are invited, particularly when a respected elder of a prosperous household has died. But most are small and include only a few close friends and relatives. Whenever such feasts are held, the family servants are also fed.

If the deceased is a married man, his wife may go to bathe in the Ganges sometime after the funeral feast. There she gives her old clothes to sweepers and dresses in a new white and borderless sari, which is given to her by her family. She also puts on the silver bangles of a widow, which have been provided by her own family. After bathing, she provides a meal for the attendant Brāhmaṇ. If the deceased is a man of importance, a feast similar in nature to the 13th-day feast may be held a year later on the anniversary of his death.

Children who die before the age of about 12 are usually not cremated. If they have not yet had their hair cut in the ceremony usually held when the child is about 5 years old, they are never cremated. A child between the age of 5 and 12 might be cremated with the attendant ceremonies if his family were wealthy and he was a favored or only son. Such an event, however, would be rare.

Since there are no large rivers near the village, children are usually buried beside one of the village ponds. Rarely is a child's body taken to a river for disposal.

The body is taken from the house by the man of the family. After burial, the wooden handle of the spade is left behind, but the metal part, being too expensive to abandon, is retained. The men who perform the burial wash in a stream or well. To signify cremation, a piece of burning cow dung may be placed in the child's right hand until it scorches the flesh. This practice is also present with river disposal. After a burial, in the evening a piece of burning cow dung in a piece of a broken water jug is placed near the grave. Two small earthenware pots of milk and a small earthenware lamp are also placed there. It is said that these things are placed near the grave to prevent animals from digging up the body.

The family may fast for a time, but this is not required.

⁂
⁂
⁂

Chapter 10

Recreation

Leisure time in the village is usually spent in the company of one's own sex. Men gather in their open courtyards and talk and smoke. The daily family gatherings are probably the most spontaneous and friendly. Men also frequently visit other men's quarters and discuss state and local politics, economics, and gossip. Some of this visiting is in the line of practicality and could not be said to be motivated by carefree sociability. Rājpūt men of an extended family are well advised to be on good terms with as many other Rājpūts in the village as possible. A man who is not your friend is a potential enemy, who may be drawn into the hostile camp in time of a dispute. As one prominent Rājpūt man stated: "It is easy to get court cases going, even false cases, if a family is not social and does not go to meet people in the village. I don't accept a family as a good family unless there is at least one person who can go around the village and meet people. This is one of the most important things."

In line with maintaining friendly relations, the Rājpūts have a definite code of etiquette for hospitality. Although strangers may be viewed with some suspicion, they are treated cordially unless there are serious grounds for doubting them. Men must be offered the hookah and should be offered food. There is an attempt to emulate the gracious manners of the traditional feudal court. One of the defining requirements of a good daughter-in-law is that she be able to cook large meals for guests.

Visiting is one of the most important forms of recreation for the men. There are a few Rājpūts who seldom leave the village, and two have retired almost completely from the village and their families, living a lonely life of seclusion in small shelters in the fields. But these men are exceptional. Most Rājpūt men, young and old, leave the village fairly often to attend the marriages of friends or relatives. Brothers often visit their sisters' families, and when their sisters' children are married, they are expected to be present and to bring gifts. Some of the older men make occasional trips to quite distant pilgrimage spots, and whole families sometimes go by bullock cart to those which are closer. Men often have to go to the city—to deliver cane, to pick up their payment, to buy liquor, meat or tobacco, to make small purchases needed by the women for the household, to purchase jewelry for marriages, to attend court cases, and to visit various government offices. Many of the men have friends in Bhudana, and a few have friends in the more distant larger cities. They look forward to visiting them whenever their business takes them to these centers. Many of the younger men and some of the older will also attend a cinema if time permits. A few of the younger men occasionally visit prostitutes. A few of the men are interested in state and national politics, and they sometimes leave the village to hear the speeches of candidates or to meet them personally.

Traveling singers, players, and astrologers are an appreciated source of amusement and relaxation. A few of the young men have harmoniums. They have learned to accompany themselves as they sing local folk ballads and current cinema favorites. They and their friends will gather for singing, sometimes on a men's house platform and sometimes in small huts in the fields or orchards. The temple attendant has a good voice, and a number of the younger Rājpūts gather to hear him sing and to smoke Indian hemp (*Cannabis indica*) together in a hand-pipe which they pass from person to person. Occasionally an Arya Samaj preacher comes to the village. His preaching consists of homilies, interlarded with jokes and songs in the folk manner. He is accompanied by a harmonium, a drum, and small cymbals. These presentations are popular and always attract a large crowd. The village constantly is being visited by *sādhūs*, and the older ones especially are welcome on the men's house platforms. There is one holy man who comes to the village regularly every spring from a nearby pilgrimage center. He makes his home in a field under a large tree, and many of the Rājpūts stop by for a talk with him as they pass to and from their work. He is much respected, and his remarks on the virtue of asceticism and on the glories of the ancient Hindu way of life are frequently quoted. On one occasion a well-known, retired Rājpūt robber visited friends in the village and attracted a large and appreciative audience.

There is much camaraderie of a more informal nature in the fields, especially among the younger men. One of the characteristic village sounds is their calling to one another across the fields. Those in adjacent plots meet together to rest and warm themselves before a fire and to eat their noonday repast. Lower caste field laborers usually are welcome members of these groups.

There is variety in village recreational life. But all else is peripheral to conversation, a never-palling source of pleasure. Once past school age this form of recreation has an unchallenged place among the men. They talk with animation, gesturing forcefully. A joke, a salty phrase, or a well-aimed riposte are much enjoyed, and even on solemn occasions talk is punctuated with laughter.

Similarly, the women in a courtyard spend most of their daily life talking and gossiping with one another as they work. As Patricia Hitchcock describes it:

The young daughters-in-law of the family visit in one room and then another of the same courtyard. While they talk, they work with their hands—knit, embroider, etc. They tell about what happens in their own homes in their parents's villages. The young daughters-in-law play games before dark with the young children. They play hide and seek, dog and cat, and jacks with stones. The older women sometimes tell stories in the evenings, often about the ancient kings and about ghosts. A literate woman sometimes reads to the group. This may last until 10 or 11 in the evening. Great pleasure is afforded by painting simple designs on the walls for religious ceremonies and marriages. The designs may be original but are all in the same style. Music is popular and the women play drums and dance. One courtyard has a victrola which is very popular.*

The women's conversation covers many subjects. They talk about borrowing and lending grain, about marriages and new brides. They discuss the whereabouts of their husbands, whether they have come home from the fields, the health of the cattle, and other practical problems. They may criticize others, perhaps for stinginess or other deviant behavior at the time of a marriage. Any unusual event is discussed with animation, and, during our stay, the Americans at the Project House were a constant source of conversation. There is also a good deal of joking and gossiping of a sexual nature.

Intercourtyard visiting is frequent among the older women, who may pass through the streets and who have delegated much of their work to their daughters-in-law. Among the younger women, whose households demand the observance of strict purdah, visiting is sometimes possible over the rooftops. Visits to the home village are frequent and looked forward to with happy anticipation.

Religious ceremonies and births and marriages are most welcome interruptions to the daily routine. The religious calendar provides many such days, which involve festive preparations. Although the religious aspects are important, there is joy in both the preparations and the get-togethers. Perhaps the most eagerly anticipated event of the year is a fair or *melā* (a religious fair), held in the spring, when in most families all but the youngest daughters-in-law enjoy a day's release from the confines of the courtyard. At this time some of the haircutting ceremonies take place, and the women make offerings of food or money to the goddess of the local temple to ensure good health for their families. The women come early in the morning and spend the day enjoying the sights and participating in the fun. They shop for sweets, jewelry, cosmetics, and other luxuries as well as more practical items, such as metal trunks. The children, accompanying the women, also have a gala day. They may ride on the crude carrousel or ferris wheel, stare curiously at the *sādhūs* who always frequent the *melās,* or, if lucky, persuade mother to buy them one of the many toys displayed for sale.

One man always accompanies the women to the *melā,* to drive the bullock cart, but, as in other social settings, most of the men part company from their women. Since the *melā* comes in the middle of the busy harvest season, the men usually attend at night, visiting a movie

* See Patricia Hitchcock, field notes.

and the circus or watching the dancing of the female impersonators and the antics of the clowns who provide a side show along one border of the fair grounds.

Although the *melā* is a particularly festive occasion for the women, providing for many their one yearly trip beyond the confines of the village, all religious festivals are times for sociability. Often preceded by fasts in honor of some goddess, they include feasting, with the elaborate preparation of special dishes. The house is decorated with wall painting and other ornamentation. The family servants come to receive food, and there is visiting between courtyards, conversation, singing, and often dancing. The women dress in their best sarīs and sometimes get new clothes for the occasion. They wear their most valuable jewelry and cosmetics. Some women may take offerings to the ancestor shrines or other village shrines. Although some women who are in purdah make these excursions, the younger daughters-in-law give their offerings to an older woman or to an unmarried girl to take for them.

The most unlicensed ceremony takes place on the day after the spring festival of Holī. Many of the usual patterns of respect and avoidance are abandoned. Teen-age boys may throw colors at the new brides, and both boys and girls may enter courtyards and break water pots. Any woman who is outside her courtyard is apt to have dyes thrown at her. The sweepers have a band and dance and sing through the streets. Many of the village men drink heavily.

Weddings with all their preparations and ceremonies are events which are enjoyed by both men and women and involve the largest groups. At such times the entire neighborhood has a chance to visit each other and share in the fun and excitement.

When visiting players come to the village with musical dramas, the men usually attend by themselves. The female impersonators who sing and dance in the dramas are not considered proper entertainment for women.

Chapter 11

Education

Although the Rājpūts belong to a culture with a rich heritage of art, music, and literature, and although they also are one of the elite twice-born castes, a high percentage of the village Rājpūts are illiterate. The traditional role of warrior did not require that a man be literate. More recently, however, education, for men at least, has assumed new importance. With the coming of the sugar mills, the average farmer was brought into everyday contact with business methods in which paper work played a very significant part. If he could not read, someone had to tell him how much cane to plant, how much to cut and when, how much it weighed and was worth, and when to come and get his payment. For some decades, knowledge of the law and court procedure has been an important means of protecting family interests. In the present, literacy is becoming increasingly valued as an avenue to job opportunities in the lower echelons of the government bureaucracy. Although some of the poorest families need the help of at least some of the sons in the fields, almost all families now try to have at least one or two boys educated. The educated boy is usually a younger son, the first son having been recruited as a full-time field hand. Most Rājpūt families can educate all sons if they wish. The inferior status of women has meant that education for them was virtually nonexistent.

The increasing emphasis on education among the Rājpūts can be seen in the statistics of enrollment in the boys' primary school. Of the 200 students enrolled in the school, 167 are Rājpūts. The breakdown on the remaining 33 students is 6 Moslems, 6 Brāhmaṇs, and 21 from the other castes. The large proportion of the Rājpūt boys reflects, of course, both the predominance of Rājpūts in the village population and the greater wealth of the Rājpūt families. Nevertheless, they are clearly more education-minded than other castes in the village, including the Brāhmaṇs, to whom the role of educated teacher traditionally belongs.

A breakdown by age shows that education is a very recent development among the Khalapur Rājpūts. Only 24% of the men in our sample families who are over 40 have had any education. Of the men between 20 and 40 years of age, only 38% are literate, but 70% of the boys and young men between the ages of 6 and 20 have been to school or are currently enrolled in school. Clearly the great increase in education for men has occurred during the last 20 years. Extent of education has also increased since the high school has been built. Before that time anyone wishing to continue beyond the primary grades could only choose between attending the religious school * or seeking further education outside the village. Only four men in our sample had any high school education. One of these is a teacher in Bhudana, a second is a government clerk in Bhudana, the third administers a farm, and the fourth is a member of the legislative and executive branch of the village council.

The rather dramatic increase in the literacy rate of males does not hold for the feminine population. Most men still believe that teaching a girl to read and write will only encourage her to write to her family begging to come home whenever her in-laws displease her. Furthermore, because the educated city women usually have servants and are not in seclusion, the men also believe that an educated girl will not cook and keep house and will become restless in the confinement of the courtyard.

On the other hand, there is gradually developing a body of opinion to the effect that a girl should be able to write home and complain if she is unhappy in her husband's house and that an educated girl, being presumably wiser to the ways of the world, does not need the protection of purdah to ensure her virtue. In any case, the statistics for the women in our sample families show an increase in literacy during the last 20 years, although a very gradual one. Seven per cent of the women over 40, 5% of those between 20 and 40, and 14% of

* The religious school (pāthṭhālā) is situated a short walk outside the village to the south. The school was conceived of by Sucheet Singh and supported by other members of the Ārya Samāj reform movement. At the time of research there were 25 students, all of them members of the three highest castes. There is a principal and two teachers. The boys lead an austere life. Sanskrit is emphasized, but the curriculum includes Hindu, civics, geography, natural science, and mathematics. A high proportion of the students attend this school until they pass the primary stage and then shift to the high school. The school is supported by the income from 20 acres of land; 5% of high-caste doweries in neighboring villages goes to the school; and one stalk of cane is taken from every load of cane brought to the mill from these villages. The Rājpūts of Khalapur contribute 10 pounds of grain per plow.

the girls between 6 and 20 are literate or attending school. The older educated women come from exceptionally wealthy and "cosmopolitan" families.

These statistics probably indicate a slight improvement in the educational level of women. It is impossible to be sure, however, since the women over 20 are primarily wives who have married into the village, whereas the women under 20 are primarily daughters of Khalapur. It is possible, therefore, that the figures reflect merely a higher educational level among the Khalapur women as compared with those of other villages. The educational opportunities for girls are still limited to the five grades of primary school, for the high school is open to boys only. Many parents withdraw their girls from school after the fourth grade. Since they have usually mastered enough knowledge to be able to read and write by the end of the fourth year, the fifth year is often regarded as superfluous. Only 40 girls, mostly Rājpūts, attend the girls' school, as against the 200 students in the boys' primary school.

The boys' school is located on the temple platform and the men's quarters of the village council, which is adjacent to the temple platform. There are a number of rooms behind the platform. Classes are held on the open platform, in the rooms, and on the roof of the building. Most of the younger children sit under a large tree on the temple platform. In the winter, during the coldest months, they bring mats; otherwise they sit on the ground. Situated in another part of the village, the girls' school consists of one large room in an open terrace and garden. The school grounds are enclosed by a high wall. Weather permitting, classes are held outside, and when it is unusually cold, hot, or rainy, they are held inside.

The primary school term runs from the first week of July until the end of May. There are several vacations of a week or more and a number of one- or two-day holidays during the school term. Until September, the school day begins at 7 A.M. The morning session runs until 11 A.M. and the afternoon session from 3:00 until 5:00. From October until March, when the weather is cooler, the morning session runs from 10 in the morning until noon and the afternoon one from 12:30 to 4:00. During the winter months many of the boys come to school at 7 or 8 o'clock so that they may have a longer lunch hour. Supposedly, the hours in the morning before the school opens are to be used for study, but there is only one teacher present as monitor, and frequently the boys' bookbags remain unopened. The boys' school has five masters.

There are two teachers in the girls' school. The headmistress is an intelligent and sensible woman, but the assistant teacher is far less competent. During the months of October and November, when the headmistress was on leave, many of the mothers stopped sending their girls to school because of the incompetence of this younger teacher. The discipline in the girls' school is far better than in the boys' school, and the girls spend most of their time studying.

The curriculum for both primary schools is almost identical. For the first two years the children are taught reading and writing, numbers, multiplication tables and simple arithmetic, and general knowledge. In the second year, art is added to the schedule. The third year sees the addition of history and civics, and in the fourth and fifth grades geography is included in the curriculum. The boys are taught farming in the third, fourth, and fifth grades, and the girls are given some instruction in sewing.

Learning is primarily by rote; the children write either on a regular blackboard-type slate or, more commonly, on a wooden slate which is coated with a whitewashlike substance and then written on in ink. The teacher traces the letters on the slate with a pencil, and the children go over them in ink. They learn their multiplication tables by chanting them in unison.

The fees for the boys' school start at one anna, or about 6¢ a month for the first grade, working up to about 46¢ a month for the fifth grade —not a significant drain on the finances of any but the poorest families. The girls' school, on the other hand, charges no fees at all because, according to the headmistress, the villagers would not pay anything to send their daughters to school.

The villagers' interest in education is practical rather than scholarly; hence their attitude toward academic achievement is very casual. They do not press their children to attend school, get good grades, or encourage them to study. As mentioned earlier, a high percentage of the parents themselves are illiterate, and they cannot successfully help the children with their studies. Moreover, their fatalism and the fact that in extended families such educational decisions may be made by the head man prevent the parents from making extended plans for their children's education. We asked a number of mothers how long they wanted their children to attend school. By far, the most common answer to this question was, "It is in his fate, no matter what I want." Even the most educated father, the only man in our sample who holds a white-collar job rather than farming for a living, says about his son's education, "You can never know about the future, or what is going to happen. A man may have high ambition, but only that is fulfilled which is in nature's wish. It depends on his luck. I may wish that my son will become a collector (the highest official in a district), but it is only that which is in his fate."

Because of this attitude, attendance at school is far from regular. Illness, no matter how mild, is always an accepted excuse for non-attendance. We often found children playing actively in the streets who insisted they were too ill to attend school. Since the mothers are in purdah and the fathers in the fields, there is no one to check on whether or not the child actually goes to school once he leaves the house. The headmaster of the boys' school says that usually about 20% of the students are absent in the morning and about 40% in the afternoon. The younger boys do not attend classes in the afternoon, which accounts for the larger number of absentees at that time. The girls play hookey less from their school, probably because those who are in school are better motivated.

Even when parents do send their children to school, attendance is not regular. Parents may take their children out of school when their services are needed at home, for example, during the harvest season. Furthermore, if children do not want to attend school, they seldom are forced to go. Both boys and girls occasionally complain that the teachers beat them, and some children refuse to attend school for this reason. We saw an older boy who was acting as monitor hit two younger boys and make them cry. And, we also saw one master teaching a class and holding behind his back a rather ominous-looking Indian club, but we never observed the teacher actually hitting a child. Probably such events did occur from time to time and were used by children as excuses for not attending school.

As the boys progress in their education, the lackadaisical attitude changes. There is a marked difference in the behavior of the younger and older boys in the primary school, the older ones being far more studious. The boys who elect to continue through high school must work hard. Their examinations are supervised by the government and held in another town. The students are therefore in a competitive atmosphere, which is not true of the primary schools.

Part II

BY LEIGH MINTURN

Child Training

❧
❧
❧
❧
❧
❧

Chapter 12

Pregnancy and Childbirth

The bearing and raising of children are considered appropriate and natural functions of the middle years of life. Parents have a social and religious obligation to marry their daughters; and girls, unless seriously deformed or mentally aberrant, are always married. Persons who die childless are believed to become ghosts. Since they have not in life fulfilled their role of parent, they are still bound to the world of the living by their desire to finish their incomplete life cycle in that world.

The fact that one important belief in sorcery revolves around the desire for children is further evidence of their importance. It is believed that if a woman is childless, she may steal the birth hair of a baby—for sorcery purposes. She gives this hair to a *sīāna* who puts it in a pot with five different kinds of clothing. He then buries the pot, accompanying the burial with appropriate incantations. When this is done, the child whose hair has been cut dies, and the childless woman becomes pregnant. Reports varied as to the effectiveness of this procedure. One woman said that the child usually did not die but always got sick; another, however, warned us never to go near a childless woman. We found only one woman, Mrs. Rāmchand, who thought that such sorcery had actually been performed on her son. This woman, having only one child, born after 12 years of marriage, was very concerned about his health. Nonetheless, all the women knew of this practice of sorcery and were probably on guard against it.

There are other less violent ways for a childless woman to become fertile. A shrine near the village is believed to be an auspicious place to pray for children, and barren women sometimes make offerings at this shrine. A woman with children may pray for a barren friend on Hōī, the day when she gives offerings for the health of her own sons. Mrs. Rāmchand's sister-in-law had prayed for her during her 12 years of barrenness. On Hōī day, the grateful Mrs. Rāmchand was dyeing a headcloth to give to her sister-in-law. She had promised to give her a yellow headcloth on Hōī for five years, in thanks for her successful intervention.

In the matter of sex, sons are greatly preferred to daughters. Evidence of this preference is demonstrated dramatically at birth, with the elaborate birth ceremonies which are usually held for sons only.* There are several reasons for this preference for boys. The family prestige depends largely on wealth and manpower; boys are potential farm hands and fighters for the family name, and, since the society is patrilineal, they are the bearers of the family continuity. Also, a son is necessary for the performance of certain funeral rites at the pyre of his father. Without a son, a man's salvation is jeopardized. A girl, on the other hand, is always a financial liability. She requires an extensive dowry at the time of marriage, and she is committed to making gifts to her husband's household when she returns to visit him for at least the first few years of their marriage. Furthermore, since a girl must marry into a family of higher status than her own, her male relatives are always subservient to the men of her husband's family. Many of the men do not take kindly to this inferior position.

Until the turn of the century, the prejudice against girls was expressed in the custom of female infanticide.† Today, as we mentioned

---

* These ceremonies are sometimes held in an attenuated form for girls.

† The British outlawed infanticide in 1848. A government officer was sent to the village about 1900 to enforce this law. Because of his necessary violation of purdah restrictions, he was murdered by some outraged men. However, government pressure and Ārya Samāj influence brought an end to infanticide as a widespread custom. although isolated instances of it probably still occur.

in Chapter 8, differential medical treatment still causes twice as many girls as boys to die before reaching maturity.

There does seem to be some compensatory status for girls. When asked whether they would wish for a girl or a boy when pregnant, the women either expressed no preference, saying that it was in the hands of Rāma or that they wished for a boy. But when asked whether they *liked* boys better than girls, the women were as likely as not to express a preference for their own sex. They said they were fonder of girls because girls go away to their husband's homes, while boys stay with their parents. This attitude seems to reflect a sentimentality about girls which is not accorded to boys.

At present most couples prefer to have at least one daughter, since the giving of a daughter in marriage is a virtuous act, which, according to Hindu tradition, every man should perform during his lifetime. But a family with a dearth of sons and an excess of daughters is considered unfortunate indeed.

Although the Indian government sponsors a birth-control program, knowledge of birth control had not yet reached the village women. No contraceptive methods are used in the village, although some of the women asked about American practices. They realized that "medicine" was available for this purpose but were vague about its nature. Education, expense, and the high child-mortality rate are probably the three most important factors standing in the way of an adequately planned parentage program.

Certain methods for abortion are known to the villagers. One elderly lady was reputed to perform abortions, and some informants mentioned the use of a medicine which is inserted in the vagina to dilate the cervix. Abortion was certainly not frequently practiced, however. Probably it was usually practiced only for cases of illegitimacy.

Since sexual immorality, particularly among women, is a great disgrace to the family, and therefore a carefully guarded secret, it is difficult to estimate the frequency of illegitimate births. At best one can state some of the conditions under which they might occur and the probable reaction to such events.

Strict sexual mores and early marriage mitigate against premarital affairs for girls. Since any scandal about an unmarried girl will not only reflect on the family but also greatly decrease her chances for a good marriage, Rājpūt parents react with immediate and violent indignation to any remark against their daughters' virtue. Nevertheless, stories persist that the girls sometimes have affairs with boys from the village when they are working in the fields. An illegitimate baby, born to an unmarried girl during our stay, was delivered by the girl's father, who then killed and buried it. The village women were highly critical of the parents for having raised their daughter so badly but made no comment about the killing of the baby. Furthermore, the village officials took steps to see that the police would not investigate the incident. Murder of such children is evidently accepted as a necessary step for the preservation of the family honor.

The illicit affairs of married Rājpūt women would usually occur either in their own villages or with a relative of the husband who has access to the courtyard at night. A woman who conceived in her own village and was unable to hide this fact would probably be abandoned by her husband and his family. If the pregnancy occurred in the husband's house, he might accept the child as his own rather than face a scandal, particularly if the father were his superior.

Since neither abortion nor contraception are normally used, the only check on pregnancy rate is the post-partum sex taboo. This taboo on intercourse should last for two years after the birth of the baby. The reason given for the custom is that intercourse will make the mother's milk bad and cause the baby to become weak and sickly.

The census material shows that the taboo is not always observed, at least not for the full two-year period. There are a number of families who have children at two-year intervals; an interim of more than two years between children usually indicates that a child, now dead, was born during that period. If one examines only the children of parents who are now over 35 years old, one finds that the modal age between these children is three years, as one would expect if the couple were observing a two-year intercourse taboo between each child. Younger parents, however, are more likely to have children at two-year intervals (see Table 2).

Table 2 Birth Rate as a Function of Age of Parents

	MOTHER OVER 35	MOTHER UNDER 35
Children born 2 years apart or less	6	14
		$P = .03$
Children born 3 years apart or more	13	7

The birth rate is not influenced by whether or not the couple is living in a house with a mother-in-law. Evidently the period of the taboo is being shortened by the younger couples, and mothers-in-law are often no longer able to enforce the restrictions. Certainly, at present, the custom presents no significant check to the birth rate. The average number of living children per family is between four and five, but six and seven living children are not uncommon. Since about one third of the children born die before reaching maturity, we estimate that the average woman, whose husband survives throughout her childbearing years, bears from seven to nine children.

Pregnant women do all of their regular work but are careful not to strain themselves. They have a number of dietary restrictions. Among these are milk, cold rice, a pulse dish, food which is either excessively hot or excessively cold, and spicy foods such as pickles. The reports concerning the length of time that milk should not be drunk varied from after the first four months of pregnancy to the last month of pregnancy. The explanations for this taboo also varied. One woman said that milk made the Fallopian tubes septic; another said that the baby would get too big; and a third explained that milk and the baby were considered to be the same.* Some women report a craving for mud during pregnancy, and some eat mud or clay at this time.† Women are prohibited from having intercourse during pregnancy. No ceremonies are held, since men of the household are not supposed to know that a woman is pregnant, and a ceremony would publicize the fact.

When the labor starts, the mother retires to her room, and the family sends for a midwife. They are often not very prompt about calling the midwife. Since blood is considered to be unclean, the Rājpūt women will not deliver children, clean up after a birth, or change bandages on the mother, and midwifery is traditionally the profession of Untouchable women. In Khalapur the wives were usually of the Bhangī or sweeper caste. Although there is a government-trained midwife resident in the village, most of the sample families would not use her, for she refused to return after the birth to change bandages, a service which the Rājpūts consider as important as aid in the delivery of a baby. Furthermore, the government midwife brings an Untouchable woman to cut the cord and clean up, necessitating the payment of two persons.

While the mother is in labor, a sickle, knife, and plowshare are placed near her bed, and a shoe is turned upside down near the foot of the bed or under it. Many women procure a paper with prayers on it from a village Brāhman, which they look at to aid the delivery.

Only one birth was witnessed during our stay in the village. The

* This information is taken from the field notes of Dr. Leela Dube.
† This craving may be due to calcium deficiency.

baby had arrived and the midwife was cleaning up. The following is an account of this incident:

The midwife was there. The baby was lying beside Mrs. A. It was a boy. Mrs. A.'s mother-in-law and an older woman were helping. Mrs. A. was sitting on her feet in the characteristic Indian squatting position. She had each foot on a brick so that she was somewhat elevated from the floor.* She was sitting just beside her bed, facing it. She was wearing a petticoat, blouse, and head shawl. Behind her was a pile of ashes. A small pile of flour was on the floor a few feet away from her. There were blood and water on the floor around her. Part of the afterbirth was on the floor underneath her. The midwife tore off a piece of cloth from an old piece of clothing and removed the afterbirth with it. She pushed this into the pile of ashes, which she was evidently going to use to sweep up with. Then Mrs. A's mother-in-law held out a pot of water to Mrs. A. and she washed her hands. Then the mother-in-law helped her onto the bed. Mrs. A. removed her petticoat, which was wet and bloody. When she was seated on the bed, the mother-in-law took a piece of cord from out of the cloth braid in her hair and gave it to the midwife. The midwife pulled at it and it broke. She rejected it. The mother-in-law then took off another piece from the end of Mrs. A.'s braid. The midwife tied the baby's cord with this. The other woman handed the midwife the vegetable cutter. (This is a curved knife mounted on a board. The women put one foot on the board to hold it while slicing vegetables.) The midwife cut the umbilical cord with this knife. Then she rubbed the baby with flour. She pinched its breasts and then cleaned the eyes and nose with her finger. The mother lay on the bed and pulled the quilt over her. She was moaning slightly. However, she did not seem to be in much pain, and the baby's head showed only slight deformation. We were informed that it had been an easy birth.

In the room, watching the midwife at work, were seven children, one of them holding a small baby. They were all watching quietly, and none showed the least signs of fear or upset. When Mrs. A lay down on the couch and covered her head, moaning, her son (age 2) got a little frightened and whimpered briefly but did not shed any tears. His grandmother spoke to him and he stopped. A few minutes later he was running around happily in the courtyard.

After finishing with the birth, the midwife buries the afterbirth by a rubbish heap. She bathes the baby and sometimes the mother. She comes daily to the household and cleans the cot, washes the soiled clothes of the mother and baby, throws away the mother's bandages, and cleans the room with cow dung. She also removes the excrement of the mother and the baby. The mother is not allowed to go outside the room to eliminate until the ceremony of Jāsūtan. Until then the midwife must come into the house to remove her excrement. The length of time that a woman is in confinement varies with her age, how she feels, and how many other women there are in the household

---

* Birth sometimes takes place while the mother is in bed. The squatting position is an alternative.

to take over her tasks. She should remain in bed for 10 to 14 days and do no work for 12 days after that. She cannot start cooking until she stops bleeding because until then she is unclean. The mother, except for the Bahari ceremony, does not change her clothes for from 14 to 22 days. At the end of this time she puts on new clothes, and her old clothes are given to the sweepers. During her confinement no one may touch her eating plate and glass, which are also unclean. When the mother's confinement is over, the family cleans the room and purifies the mother's eating utensils by burning coals in them and washing them in Ganges water. After this the midwife cannot enter the house.

On the day that the baby is born, the mother eats sweets, a special corn dish, and a dish of pulse. The mother is fed as much *ghī* as she can consume, and many of the women eat a great deal after their babies are born. She may also be fed a dish which is a mixture of sugar, water, *ghī*, almonds, coconut, and dry ginger powder. This diet is considered to be healthy for the new mother and is continued for 20 days. The mother is not supposed to drink milk for some time after the baby is born. Again the length of time reported for this taboo varied from 15 days to one and one quarter months. The baby is fed sugar and water when it is first born and is given mother's milk from one to three days after its birth. The baby may also be fed a dish consisting of about one cup boiling water, caroway seed, two puffed sugar candies and a pinch of ashes. Before nursing begins, a sister of the husband washes the mother's breasts with Ganges water or milk. For this she receives a present of jewelry. Sometimes the sister-in-law clamors for a particular piece of expensive jewelry. If the child is a boy, particularly a first-born son, her request is usually granted. If no husband's sister is present, another woman acts as a substitute. She receives only a nominal gift.

There are four ceremonies connected with the birth and early childhood of a village baby. The first is the Bahari ceremony, which occurs on the first Sunday of a boy's life. The second is the Chotilī ceremony, when the baby is 5 or 6 days old. The third is the Jāsūtan ceremony, on the baby's tenth day. The fourth is the Mundan hair-cutting ceremony, usually held when the baby is about a year old.

The differential status of boys and girls is apparent from birth. The midwife is paid twice as much for delivering a boy as for delivering a girl. The birth of a girl occasions no public ceremony. One informant, in fact, declared that when a girl is born, the mother hides, although this is an overstatement. When a boy is born, on the other hand, a sweeper is called to beat on a drum before the door of the happy household, announcing to the village the advent of a son. The Brāhmaṇ women are summoned to sing special songs, and the branch of a *nīm* tree is put over the door of the mother's room for good luck and to keep ghosts away. This singing and drumming are repeated every day for ten days. A yellow cord is placed around the waist of male babies.

The first ceremony in a boy's life, the Bahari, may find him anywhere from 1 to 6 days old. The Bahari is usually held only for boys. It takes place in the late afternoon of his first Sunday, and to it are invited all the women from the family lineage and any other close female friends of the family.

Preparations for this ceremony are elaborate. The Brāhmaṇ women who serve the family make abstract designs of cow dung decorated with green and yellow dots. These are "painted" on the courtyard wall on each side of the mother's room and represent all of the gods and goddesses. The Brāhmaṇ women say that these designs are in honor of the ancestors. On the floor in front of the door to the mother's room is placed a square design made out of rice-water paint. This pattern is a sign of respect for the baby and mother.

Since the birth, the mother and child have remained in bed in the mother's room. She is still considered unclean. Now, however, she is bathed, her hair is washed, and she dresses in new clothes. Outside in the street, the sweeper man is drumming; in the courtyard the Brāhmaṇ women sing. Both Brāhmaṇ and low-caste women bring contributions of *dūb* grass, for which they are given money. The grass symbolizes that they wish the family to prosper, as the grass prospers. A low wooden stool is placed beside the design at the mother's door and before it two or three bowls of food and a bowl of water.

When everything is ready, the mother comes out of the room and sits on the low stool, holding her baby. She greets the guests and they bless her. A woman, usually an elderly one, sits beside the mother and gives her water from a bowl. The mother sprinkles this water onto the food, and then the food is given to the Brāhmaṇ women. Each member of the family and each guest offer money and a handful of grain to the "ancestor" designs, and these gifts also are given subsequently to the Brāhmaṇs. Sometimes the wife of the family barber is present and touches the fingernails and toenails of the new baby to indicate that she will cut the child's nails when he gets older. After this brief ceremony, the mother again greets her guests and returns to her room. There she is permitted to break the fast which she has kept all day by eating a paste of sugar and *ghī*. She resumes her soiled clothes and remains in them until she completes her period of seclusion and returns to her normal working life.

The details of this, as well as other ceremonies, vary from time to time. Instead of having the Brāhman women sing the ritual songs, sometimes the guests themselves sing them. The type of grain blessed by the mother differs with the season. The amount given in payment to the servant families may vary somewhat. But the general ceremonial pattern remains the same.

The second ceremony, called the Chotilī, is held on the fifth day of a baby girl's life and on the sixth day of a boy's. For this rite, a red sacred thread is tied around one leg of the mother's cot, and a small figure is made out of cow dung to represent the goddess Bahamatā, maker of children. This goddess is one of the 101 sisters concerned with disease; she receives homage only at the Chotilī ceremony. The family women offer whey, grain, and a tiny oil lamp; they invoke the names of the ancestors, of Mātā the smallpox goddess, and the goddesses Balsundrī and Bahamatā. The family may invoke the names of 5, 7, or 9 such deities, including local gods, goddesses such as the Bhumia and Darga, the Moslem saint, and ancestors. The baby receives its first costume, which may be either a cloth to go around his stomach, a shirt and cap, or both. These clothes are called Chotilī. These are colored for girls and white for boys. Women from other houses in the lineage present gifts of grain to the mother, and the ceremony is over. Afterward, they hide the figure of Bahamatā in a room of the house for good luck.

Jāsūtan, the third festival, occurring ten days after the birth of a boy, terminates the family's rejoicing over a new son. On this day the boy's yellow cord is exchanged for a black one. It is the last day that the sweeper drums and the Brāhman women sing. It is the end of the holiday from spinning, observed by the women of the lineage out of affection for the new son of the house. Apparently in some cases the Chotilī ceremony is performed on Jāsūtan, although it is more common to clothe the child on its fifth or sixth day.

According to some accounts, a wealthy family gives a feast on Jāsūtan for one unmarried girl from each Rājpūt family in the *paṭṭī*. In the sample studied here, there were no families which observed this custom, but the family Brāhmans are fed and sweets distributed to the other houses in the lineage. It was stated that at least one Brāhman must be fed on this day in order to ensure the cleanliness of the kitchen.

A boy is not named on the day of Jāsūtan but may be named any time after this date. Until babies are named, and often during the first year or so of their lives, they are called *lālā* (masculine) or *lālī* (feminine), an affectionate term literally translated as jewel.

Choosing a name is always difficult, particularly for a son. He cannot be given the name of any man in the family or any of the in-law's families, since there will then be some women who will not be able to say this name out of respect to the older man who bears it. The names of older women must also be avoided for girls, although here the rule is not as rigid. Many women liked to give their children a name which included Rām so that one would take the name of Rām whenever one said the name of the child. Names with Dēvī (goddess), Dēv (god), and Rāj (king) in them were also common. Generally a woman has several possible names in mind, and the baby might be called all of them until one is settled on. In some cases the baby is 6 months old before the final name is chosen. Naming a child was, therefore, a casual and informal procedure.

After Jāsūtan, the cow-dung designs placed on each side of the mother's room are taken down and sometimes replaced with hand prints made in rice water, which are good luck symbols.

The first hair-cutting ceremony usually takes place during the child's first year of life. This, like the Chotilī ceremony, is performed for both boys and girls, and there are three occasions on which it may be done. The first and most usual occasion is the spring religious festival for Balsundrī, held in Bhudana. A second possibility is the Shakumbri religious festival, held in the fall in a town about 80 miles distant from the village. Because it is so far away, the villagers do not often get to the *melā* or "fair"; but some manage it and may perform the hair-cutting ceremony at that time. A third and fairly common practice is simply to go to the family shrine and offer the hair to the ancestors. According to report, the ceremony follows the same general pattern wherever it is performed. The birth hair, cut any time from 12 days to a year after the child is born, is offered to the goddess as a gesture of consecration. This hair is material which can be used for sorcery purposes. Offering it to the ancestors or to a goddess, therefore, presumably consecrates the child and protects him from harm.

When the hair-cutting ceremony is performed at the family ancestor's shrine, a Brahman and a barber are called. They go to the shrine with the family. The family barber cuts the child's hair, and it is placed between pieces of unleavened fried bread and left there. We asked what happened to the hair and were told that the dogs eat the bread and the hair blows away. But since the hair has been offered to the ancestors, it cannot be used for sorcery.

Although there was no opportunity to observe a hair-cutting ceremony at the ancestor's shrine, we did see one at the Balsundrī *melā*. This was performed on a little boy from our village. We traveled with them by bullock cart, leaving the village at 4 in the morning and reaching the *melā* grounds about 6:30 A.M. The usual order of proceed-

ings at this *melā* is described in the section on religion. On this particular visit, the hair-cutting ceremony was performed right after the baby's
mother and older sister had washed at the bathing pool inside the
temple wall and changed into clean saris. The mother carried the baby
boy to a barber, who was sitting just beside the temple platform busily
clipping the hair of the numerous babies brought to him. He held the
baby and ran his clippers hastily over its head, leaving tufts of hair
here and there. Then there was a brief bargaining over the price,
which ended with the mother giving the barber 2 annas, half of what
he had asked. Collecting hair and baby, the mother then went to the
door of the temple and threw inside the birth hair and the newly purchased sweets as gifts to Balsundrī. This was the end of the actual
ceremony, and the women went on to perform other customary rites or
worship at the temple before leaving to spend the day shopping at the
fair grounds.

✳
✳
✳

Chapter 13

Infancy

Rājpūts consider their children to be "pure." This means that they are
holy, God resides in them, they have committed no sin and cannot
distinguish between good and evil. Some women say that babies remain in this state of purity until they begin to eat solid food. Some
commented that children are born with their hands shut because they
are sent from God fully equipped and do not want anything from the
world.

The villagers believe that "The fate of a child is written on its forehead at birth." There are days on which it is considered unlucky to be
born, and children born on these days will come to no good end. But,
in general, the villagers consider that the child's fate, while divinely
predetermined, cannot be known.

Because of the high death rate among young children, their health
is a matter of concern and anxiety. Babies are believed to be particu-

larly susceptible to certain kinds of supernatural dangers. Sorcery by means of birth hair has already been discussed. Necklaces of various kinds and protective charms are worn by babies up to the age of a year and a half. An elaborate version of such a necklace worn by a boy whose mother had lost several children contained the following charms:

1. A charm, which had been given to the mother by a *siana*.
2. A paper with charms written on it.
3. A package of tiger's meat to make the boy brave.
4. Four silver ornaments—a moon, a flower, a bow and arrow, and one unidentified ornament—to ward off smallpox.
5. A shell, some red beads, and several cloth packages for which the informant could give no function.

Not all children wear such charms, and only a few wear necklaces as elaborate as the one described. But many small children, particularly boys, wear a simple thread with one or two charms or coins on it.

The evil eye is another danger which threatens children. The evil eye is put on a child by someone who is jealous of him. Handsome people of any age, since they are the objects of jealousy, are susceptible to the evil eye, and all small babies must be protected against it by a black dot on the temple or foot, which is worn continuously during the first few weeks of life and may be worn on occasions for several years. Mothers of handsome children are warned that they should not dress the children well and make them look pretty lest they incite envy. One must never praise a child by saying that it is pretty or exceptionally big and healthy. Such praise may bring bad luck to the child and leave the praiser open to the suspicion of throwing the evil eye. Beliefs about the children's susceptibility to the evil eye varied. Some women were firmly convinced of the reality of this danger, whereas others believed that all illness was determined by the will of God. Some worried only about handsome children, and still others feared for all children.

Another danger to children is ghost sickness. Ghosts may stick to children when they are sleeping and make them ill or may possess them, causing them to laugh, dance, and sing. The family must then take the child to a *siana* who may determine why the child has been bothered by the ghost. He can drive out the ghost but is not able to predict the behavior which the ghost causes. One mother said that she did not let her child go out after dark in the village because of the danger of ghosts.

Finally, all boys wear a black cord around their waists, which sometimes has a charm or two on it. Although some women said that it was worn simply "for fashion," its chief function is to make the vein in the penis grow straight. If the vein does not grow straight, it is believed that the boy will be impotent. Boys wear this cord from infancy on, and some men evidently wear it throughout their lifetime.

Once the birth ceremonies are over, the women return to their usual household routines, and the new baby causes little or no further disturbance to the usual pattern of living. All babies sleep with their mothers for several years. Girls may sleep with their mothers until they are 8 or 9 years old. During the day, when the infant is not in need of food or some other attention, it is placed on a cot with a quilt or sheet entirely covering it, to protect it from insects and envious glances. Babies are often so well hidden by piles of quilts that one cannot detect their presence. Generally, unless the baby cries, no one pays any attention to it, and it lies well covered in the midst of the busy courtyard until it expresses its demands in loud and persistent crying. Children, particularly boys who have been born after several years of barrenness or after the death of several children, may be accorded more attention.

When the baby cries, adult response is usually fairly prompt, but if the mother is busy with a task, like cooking, she cannot leave, and the baby may have to wait. Most mothers said that they would leave their work or try to finish it to pick up a wailing infant, but a few women reported that they might let the baby cry for an hour or so.* We observed three sickly, probably unwanted girls who cried often and were left to cry for extended periods, but these children were definitely exceptions.

Whether or not the mother receives assistance from the other women of the household depends largely on how well they get along with each other. Although the women are generally not unfriendly to any children, each woman cares for her own children exclusively if the women are on bad terms with each other, but if the courtyard is a friendly one, the women help each other out. In such a courtyard the crying child may be picked up by any woman or older child. If the baby continues to cry, it may be passed from one woman to another while each tries her own devices of distraction and consolation. Grandmothers sometimes offer their milkless breasts as pacifiers. If nothing is effec-

* The promptness of response to a crying infant was a point on which the mothers were questioned. Out of 24 mothers, 21 said that it was their practice to pick up a crying baby and try to pacify it in some way. Nine said they would do this at once, 9 said they would pick the child up as soon as possible or in a few minutes, and only 2 said they would delay for any length of time. Eight mothers said they left their work to pick up the baby, 6 said they would carry the baby while they went on working, and 5 said they would finish their work and then pick up the child.

tive, it is assumed that the baby is hungry, and the mother-in-law or aunt will take over the work of the mother so that she can stop to nurse. During the months when the baby is too old to lie quietly on a cot and too young to walk itself, it is, if possible, turned over to an older girl to carry when the mother is busy working. As a rule, this caretaker will be an older sister, but a cousin may take the child if the sisters-in-law are on good terms.

The role of the men in the care of infants is negligible, except for a few elderly men who are too feeble for farm work and have retired from active participation in the village political scene. To such old men are relegated the tasks of rope making, baby tending, and guarding the cattle. Such men may spend the day in the cattle compound or on the men's platform. John Gumperz reports that some spend most of their time making rope and playing with a baby. If there is such an elderly grandfather or great uncle in the family who is willing to take on this role, the baby may be given to him instead of to an older child. However, since it is unusual for villagers to reach such an advanced age, most babies do not have such a doting male as a companion. It is more common for an uncle to take the baby to the men's platform for an hour or so, but when the child begins to cry or fuss, it is quickly returned to the women.

If the mother is very busy and has no one to help carry the baby, she may resort to the use of opium to put the baby to sleep. The women agreed that this was not good for babies and should be used only as a last resort. One busy mother administered two grains of opium a day to a baby that was a few months old. When under the influence of the drug, it was impossible to awaken the baby even by vigorous shaking.

Whether or not the baby is tended and amused by other women, an older child or an elderly male, the mother retains the responsibility for feeding, dressing, and washing her own child. She is the one with whom it sleeps and until it is weaned, no substitute caretaker will carry the infant far from its food supply.

From the time that the mother's breasts are ceremonially washed and she begins to nurse the baby, it is nursed on demand. One informant said that young babies were nursed every 30 to 35 minutes and, when older, three or four times a day. Since the baby sleeps with its mother, night feeding is no problem.

Mother's milk is considered to be the best milk for the child. Some women believe that it is sufficient food for the infant, and no supplementary feeding is required. If the mother has no milk or insufficient milk, supplementary milk is given. Goat's milk, which can be purchased, is supposed to be best for this purpose, cow's milk next best, and buffalo's milk least good. One mother, who did not lactate, fed her child on powdered milk, but this is the only instance we know of where powdered milk was used. Supplementary milk is given either by spoon or from a small brass nursing bottle which is shaped like a round pot and has a small spout in the side for the nipple. These pots are about 2 to 2½ inches in diameter and hold only an ounce or two of milk. Wet nursing is uncommon. We were told that some sisters-in-law would do this, but most women did not like to nurse another woman's child.

Reports as to the age at which supplementary feeding is started varied from six months to two years. Our observations indicated that generally children were regularly given some solid food, a piece of bread or a little candy or rice, at about one year, but that very little solid food is given before this age. Some mothers believe that solid foods fed to a nursing child cause dysentery. If the milk supply is not sufficient at this time, the mothers feed the child some cow's milk. Mothers who think that their milk provides sufficient nourishment may delay longer before giving solid food.

Babies are not diapered; they wear only a short shirt and sometimes a cap or scarf on their heads. When put on a cot, they are laid on a sheet which then serves the purpose of a diaper. When the baby is being held by someone, it is simply held away when it urinates. Sometimes the mother sits the baby on her own feet while it urinates. Since the urine is quickly absorbed into the mud floor of the courtyard and the hot sun dries the moisture in a few minutes, accidents of bladder control on the floor present no problem. At night the mother holds the baby away from the bed if the urination awakens her. Some mothers did complain that their babies wet them frequently because they slept too soundly.

Bowel movements are regarded somewhat less casually. The mother tries to anticipate the baby's bowel movements and holds him over the courtyard drain or a pile of trash in the cattle compound at what she considers to be the appropriate times. When the baby does eliminate on the floor or on someone's clothing, he is quickly removed from the feces and washed. The feces are also cleaned up at once. The women are particularly careful not to let the baby get smeared with his feces or play with them because it is believed that a person who has accidentally eaten feces as a child will have the power of the evil eye. Although the women sometimes show mild disgust at a baby's bowel movement, their reaction is surprisingly mild considering the extreme disgust attached to adult feces, which can be removed only by a sweeper, the lowliest of the Untouchable castes in the village.

Because of the relaxed attitudes of the women, neither feeding nor elimination present a problem for the Rājpūt baby—the same cannot be said, however, for bathing. This is a most distressing experience, which the baby must face daily. Babies, like adults, are given "sponge baths" with water from a bucket or pot. No villager immerses himself in water except when bathing in a river. The mothers ordinarily do not use soap when washing the babies, but they rub the eyes rather vigorously with the heel of the hand and often are not very gentle in their handling of the baby during the bathing process. Babies usually cry and struggle violently while being bathed, and they particularly dislike having their face and eyes washed.*

Although the infants and small children wore nothing but shirts, we saw no evidence of masturbation. Whether or not the babies masturbate while hidden under their covering of quilts we were not, of course, able to observe. Since infants are usually carried when they are not sleeping, they do not have much opportunity to masturbate. The only instances of handling of genitals that we noted occurred with a boy about 1½ years old. One day, while sitting on his mother's lap, he took his penis in his hand and said "penis" several times. His mother laughed and said, "He is showing you his penis." Some time later we saw this child's aunt playfully pull the child's penis while joking with him.

The life of the Rājpūt baby is, aside from the daily bath, bland and free from stress, but it is also free from deliberate creative stimulation. A person in the village is viewed as a member of a group rather than as an individual. According to the religious beliefs, he represents one incarnation of a soul that may have appeared on earth a million times and may appear on earth a million times again in the future and that is but a fragment of the universal world soul. The individual does not, as in Christianity, represent a unique event in the world's history. The sex and health of the child are the important characteristics which will determine its individual future. Assuming that the child will live to maturity, its future life can be predicted with great accuracy. A boy will become a farmer; a girl will be a farmer's wife. A boy born into a wealthy and powerful family may now have more diversity in his choice of occupation. He may become a government worker, perhaps even a governmental official. Such diversity will, of course, increase in the future, but at present such exceptions are still rare. It is to a large extent true that the fate of the child is written on its forehead at birth. Throughout his or her lifetime, the person will function in a group; seldom, if ever, will he be called on to act independently of the group,

* The custom of massaging babies with oil, popular in other parts of India, is not common among Khalapur Rājpūts.

let alone oppose it. Whereas a mother who conceives of her child as a unique individual emphasizes how he differs from other children, the Rājpūt mother, for whom all people are but transient elements in a permanent group structure, insists that "all children are alike."

This attitude is, no doubt, accentuated by the fact that the village mother has had far more experience with children than a mother raised in an isolated nuclear family. She has grown up in a household where the advent of a new baby was a fairly common occurrence. She has seen babies born, seen them nurse, seen them live and grow up, and seen them die. She has probably cared for a younger sibling or cousin herself. Furthermore, she has her own children in the company of older women to whom childbirth is a familiar experience. Therefore babies are neither the objects of interest nor the objects of anxiety that they are in this country. A mother does not fear that her child is sick every time it cries; she knows better. But, by the same token, she is not as delighted with its smile because she also knows that all babies smile. She therefore continues with her usual routine, attends to her infant's needs but does not hover over it or "drop everything" to rush to its side. If there is sufficient help, someone will comfort the child; if there is not sufficient help, she may resort to opium to quiet the child while she gets her work done or she may use some other device to amuse the child.

The elderly men who sometimes care for babies may "play" with them, but usually neither the women nor the girls who go about their own activities with a baby on their hips spend much time interacting with the child. The baby receives attention only when it cries or fusses. When it thus exhibits distress, the mother, another woman, its child nurse, or even a young child of 4 or 5 will attempt to sooth the baby back to quiescence. When it becomes quiet, its distractor leaves it. Adult interaction with babies is generally aimed at producing a cessation of response rather than a stimulation of it.

The concept of educational toys is foreign to the Rājpūt, and there are few toys of any kind. Some infants had plastic rattles or painted wooden animals which their mothers gave them. More commonly the toys were hand-made cloth balls brought by a new bride or returning daughter-in-law. One mother sat her toddler beside a stool with a woven seat. She then scattered grain on the stool, which the baby picked off and ate, grain by grain. When he had finished, he waddled expectantly over to his mother, and the process was repeated.

Because of the belief in the evil eye, a visitor who followed the American custom of admiring the baby, praising its unusual healthiness, good looks, or well-kept appearance would cause panic rather than pride, and a village mother would no more show off her baby to the admiration of a visitor than an American mother would deliberately expose an infant to a contagious disease. Even during the birth ceremonies the baby remains well hidden, wrapped in his mother's arms, and no visitor makes an attempt to see the child.

Thus the baby spends his first two years as a passive observer of the busy courtyard life. He is never alone, never the center of attention. He spends his first months sleeping on a cot, covered with quilts. Later, when he is more wakeful, he moves from cot to hip. His child nurse may carry him out to the streets or to a neighbor's house, but since he is still being nursed, he is not taken far. If his mother leaves the courtyard to attend a ceremony in a relative's house, she will take him with her, but such excursions are rare. It is quite common, however, for the mother to return home to her own village for a visit during this period. Here she is relieved of her household duties and spends her days visiting with her relatives and friends with her baby on her hip. Sometime during these years the child will be taken to a mēlā for his hair-cutting ceremony. This will probably be the child's most extensive excursion during this period.

A baby spends little time crawling. Sometimes, unattended, he may set off across the courtyard on his own, but someone usually grabs him before he gets far. Since the women do most of their work on the floor, the food dishes, grain dishes, and so on are usually lying somewhere. This makes a crawling baby something of a nuisance, although there is little that can hurt him except the hearth fire and an occasional spinning-wheel spindle or knife. If the infant is crawling toward some area where it is not supposed to be, or playing with some object which it is not supposed to have, an adult simply removes either the baby or the object rather than attempting to coax the baby to give up the object or to crawl away. Occasionally the process is not so simple, as the following observation illustrates:

J. (boy aged 6 months) fell into the spindle when Mrs. S. (his mother) was spinning. She picked him up and scolded him; then she gave him to her sister-in-law, Mrs. D. Mrs. D. kept facing him toward the other courtyard and telling him to go there. A lady from the other courtyard called him, but he kept crawling back. Mrs. D. would shake her fist and say, "Should I break your mouth?" Finally she hit him on the back. The baby just smiled. Eventually he cried a little. His mother called him to her, picked him up, and put him in the other courtyard. One of the women in the other courtyard was cleaning a parrot cage. The baby watched her do that, and the women of the other courtyard gave him something to eat.

When the child is ready, he learns to walk; he is not encouraged or rushed in this process by adults. Only once did we see a grandmother and older sister, each holding the hand of a baby who was laboring to take his first steps. One family had a wooden walker, consisting of a cross T-bar on three wheels, with an upright handle built on the cross bar of the T. We were told that the family had bought this for a boy who was slow in learning to walk. This was the only walker we saw in the village, although they were sold at the spring *mēlā*. When the child does learn to walk, he may still be carried when taken outside the house, but he now wanders about the courtyard on his own. He may venture just outside the door to look at the street. A fond father or uncle may take him for a visit on the men's platform, or he may follow an older child to the men's quarters. But he still is not allowed far from the house, and he is still an observer rather than a participant in the busy life around him.

*
*
*

Chapter 14

The Preschool Child

Until the child acquires the use of speech, he is not considered to be teachable, and no demands are made on him to modify his own behavior. A mother may place an infant's palms together in the gesture of "Namaste," the Hindu greeting, or shout at a crawling baby who ventures too near the hearth, but no systematic demands are made on the child until he can walk and say a few words. From this time on he is considered able to respond to directions and may be punished for failing to do so. He is still considered too small, however, to learn from verbal instruction. He can be told to do something that he already knows how to do, but it is believed that young children learn new activities best through observation and imitation rather than instruction. The years from infancy to school are a transition period during which the child moves from observer to participant in the life of the village. This transition is a gradual one with no clear signposts to mark its beginning or its end. The time required for the transition varies from one child to another, depending on how urgently his services are needed by his family, but all make the journey in their own way and in their own time.

As far as sleeping arrangements are concerned, the preschool child is still a baby. He continues to sleep with his mother and may do so for some years. When a new baby arrives, the older child is usually moved to a cot, with another sibling, at least temporarily. However, the child may later return to the mother's bed. It is not uncommon for a mother to sleep with two or even three children.* Children are not encouraged to take naps and seemingly do not sleep during the day except during the hot season, when everyone takes an afternoon rest. Their sleeping hours are much the same as adults', only longer. On cold mornings the mothers encourage children to stay in bed until the fire is well started and breakfast is ready, but too much sleep is considered by some mothers to lead to laziness, even in youngsters, so ordinarily the children are up shortly after the women.

The first systematic demands made on the child are that he stop nursing and that he eliminate in some appropriate place. Both weaning and toilet training usually occur during the second or third year.

The mothers reported three reasons for weaning a child—illness, failure of the milk supply, and pregnancy. Of these, pregnancy is the most usual. A few mothers reported that their children stopped nursing of their own accord. Mothers usually nurse through the first months of pregnancy, but they try to wean a few months before the birth of the new child. Several mothers reported that their milk stopped during pregnancy. Since children are usually born two to three years apart, most children are weaned between the ages of 1 and 4, the mean age being 3. Children whose parents observe the post-partum sex taboo on sexual intercourse for the full two years, are, of course, likely to be weaned later than children whose parents ignore or attenuate the period of the taboo. If the mother does not become pregnant again, she usually nurses the child as long as her milk supply lasts. In such cases the child may be nursed for five or six years.†

* In our sample there were two households in which adult men slept in the women's courtyard. In one of the largest of the courtyards, two cousins about 19 years of age slept with their respective wives, aged 15 and 17. Neither couple had produced offspring yet. The most aberrant case is that reported for a household consisting of two married brothers but not any parents. It was reported that the father, aged 25, slept in the house and shared a cot with his 3-year-old daughter and that the 7-year-old son shared a cot with his mother.

† When interviewed, four mothers said they weaned between the ages of 1 and 2, six said between the ages of 2 and 3; eight said between the ages of 3 and 4, and three mothers said they nursed for five or six years.

Most mothers said they had no trouble weaning their children. A few reported that the children had troubled them for three or four days. One mother said that her child cried off and on for 20 days; this was the most extreme case of emotional upset due to weaning reported to us.

Chillies or *nīm* leaves, which are bitter, may be put on the breast to aid in a difficult weaning, but since the mothers are reluctant to use such punitive measures, they rarely resort to this practice. Two mothers told us that they were using *nīm* leaves to wean their children, but in both cases we saw the children nursing without protest. One mother held the leaves in her hand while nursing but did not use them. A milkless woman, usually a grandmother, may give a child her breast to keep it quiet if the mother is busy, but pacifiers, other than the breast, are not used during weaning. The fact that the children are usually getting supplementary milk and some solid food before weaning is instituted seems to make it a relatively easy adjustment. The children we saw did not show signs of emotional upset, and, according to the mothers' reports, the children rarely tried to resume nursing after the birth of a second child.

As mentioned earlier, most children are given some solid food between six months and a year. The first solid food is bread; later grains of cereal and bits of candy are added to the diet. After weaning, the children eat the same food as adults. If there is a shortage of milk, it is saved for the children. Other foods may be substituted for particular dishes that the children dislike, but the limited diet does not allow for extensive substitutions, and the children quickly learn to accept the adult diet—spices, peppers, and all.

Most mothers reported that their children had learned to eat by themselves before the age of 2. Several reported that they had learned this before one year, but this undoubtedly referred only to bread and bits of cereal. It should not be assumed, however, that because 2 year olds have mastered the skill, they are allowed to feed themselves regular meals. Some mothers continue to feed children their regular meals until they are 3 or 4 years old. One reason for this practice may be that the mothers feel it is quicker and easier to feed the child than to let him eat by himself. Religious beliefs concerning food pollution probably contribute to this prolonged feeding of children. Food which is left on the plate unattended becomes polluted and should not be eaten. For this reason adults cannot be interrupted in the middle of eating. Learning to finish eating all that has been served without interruption is therefore part of the process of acquiring adult eating habits, and one of the "naughty" behaviors which mothers frequently mention is making a mess while eating. Some mothers may prefer to feed their children until they can count on proper eating behavior.

Children are not encouraged to eat if they are not hungry, and we saw no children who were "feeding problems." The only problem of the village children seemed to be to get enough food. One of the things that mothers complained of was that young children nagged them for food before it had been cooked. Since cooking is a slow process, most women try to keep a supply of bread and left-over rice to take the edge off the children's appetites until dinner is prepared. We frequently heard children ask for food and complain that they had not been served enough. Food was also mentioned by the mothers as a reward for good behavior.

When the child can walk, he is led to the courtyard drain, to the cattle compound, or to the street just outside the house to urinate or defecate. Adults may make a "squizzle" sound to encourage urination. Later, when his mother sees him squatting, she encourages him to go by himself to the latrine or the cattle compound—if there is one—inside the courtyard. Most children learn to eliminate in the proper spot during their second year, although some do not go by themselves until the third year. Since adults urinate in public, the children can learn the procedure through imitation, and since children ordinarily wear only shirts, they have no clothes to remove for elimination; thus the learning process is not difficult. During the winter the children sometimes wear pajama trousers. However, if the child is not yet toilet trained, he wears trousers with the crotch cut out—the very opposite of diapering.

We saw one little boy during successive stages of this learning process. On one occasion he went to his mother, saying, "Water, water." His mother promptly carried him to the courtyard drain, where he urinated. A month or so later he was toddling to the drain himself.

For some time after the children have learned to go to the drain in the daytime, they may still wet the bed at night. If the night is cold and rainy, the mother may encourage the child to urinate in the room. A few mothers reported that their children refused to do this and always used the courtyard. The last stage of this learning process is learning to use water to wash after a bowel movement. Mothers do this for babies and young children. By the age of 4 or 5, the children have learned to do this themselves and may sometimes be seen eliminating by a stream and washing themselves. The adult attitudes about human feces and their association with the Untouchable castes are undoubtedly communicated to the child, but no direct punishment of accidents was observed. The training seems to present no real problem for adults or children.

Children are usually bathed by adults until they are 5 or 6 years old, but although personal cleanliness is highly regarded by adults, who bathe daily, it does not seem to be regarded as so important for children of this age range. Babies are kept clean and their nasal discharges are removed. However, once the children are old enough to play around the dusty village streets, they and their clothes are often quite dirty, and I doubt that all mothers bathe their children daily, although they are, however, required to wash their hands before eating. Runny noses and eyes are particularly common at this age, and the children frequently have eye infections which are quickly spread through the lamp-black eye makeup, which is taken from one container and used on all the babies and young children of the family. Luckily the fear that elaborately groomed children will contract the more serious variety of evil eye prevents the regular use of this makeup. It is usually reserved for festival occasions.

At this age, warm-weather clothing is similar for both sexes. All children wear a shirt. In the winter the boys may be bundled into padded jackets and cotton pants or sleveless sweaters. Babies and young children may also wear padded bonnets in cold weather. Mothers seem less particular about warm clothing for girls, who do not wear padded jackets. Little girls may wear adult clothing, a sari or pajama trousers and overblouse or a sleeveless sweater if the day is chilly, or they may simply add a headcloth to their shirt. Some of the wealthier families have black rubbers for children to wear on cold days, but most children go barefoot the year round. On winter mornings and evenings when it is really cold, both children and adults wrap themselves in quilts.

The hair of young children is cut close to the head except for a small lock in the back called the *chōtī*, which distinguishes Hindu men from Moslems throughout their lives. The hair of girls is cut during this period because the villagers believe that it will grow thicker if kept cropped for some years; also the short hair makes lice easier to eliminate. Girls also have a *chōtī*, and often a cloth braid, a miniature version of the ones worn by the women, is attached to this tuft of hair. This braid, glass bracelets, and sometimes ankle bracelets are usually the only items of clothing which distinguish the preschool girls from the boys.

The mother has the primary responsibility for feeding, dressing, and washing her own child. If the mother is very busy, an indulgent mother-in-law may feed or bathe a young child, but for the most part, the older women consider that they have reached an age deserving of some leisure, and they expect their daughters-in-law to care for their own young as well as attend to the household tasks. Actually there was a living grandmother in less than half of the families studied.

In theory, disciplining should be carried out by the oldest person present. Within the courtyard this would usually be the grandmother, a grand-aunt, or the wife of the eldest son. In practice, among the women at least, this rule is not strictly observed. It is true that the younger wives are reluctant to discipline the children of their older sisters-in-law, and daughters-in-law would rarely scold the children of the mother-in-law. They do not, in other words, scold the children of women who outrank them unless perhaps the child is bothering them personally. This does not mean, however, that the oldest person present punishes the child because, in general, no woman, not even the mother-in-law, will punish a child if his own mother is near and has also seen it misbehave. If the mother is in another part of the court-yard and the women are on good terms, an older woman may reprimand a child, but serious scoldings are usually administered by the mother, and a woman hardly ever strikes a child that is not her own.

The role of the grandmother in discipline depends on the grand-mother's personality. In general, she is more lenient with the children than the mother and is more likely to scold the mother for being too harsh than she is to scold the children. In extreme cases of incom-patibility, a grandmother may send the mother home, keeping her child and refusing to recall her until pressure is exerted on her by the girl's family. When this happens, the grandmother replaces the mother as major caretaker. If the mother dies, it is the grandmother or great-aunt who is likely to care for the child rather than an aunt. The grand-mother may continue to care for the child even after the father marries again.

The custom of having the oldest person present discipline children is evidently more strictly followed by the men. Several men said that they are shy of scolding their children when their father or uncles are present. A man may feel free to discipline his children in the court-yard but not on the men's platform. The father often remains a fairly stern and remote figure to his children, although this is much less true now than it used to be. Traditionally, as one of the mechanisms to promote the solidarity of the extended family, the father was expected to trust the welfare of his children to his father and brothers. He was the disciplinarian, and they were the defenders. A man, out of respect for the extended family and perhaps because of sexual connotations, was supposed to interact with his nephews rather than his sons. At present this custom, while still considered ideal, is seldom observed.

One elderly man told us that his father had scolded him but never played with him, and he had never held his son, only his nephews. Now, he says, times have changed—the brothers have more tendency to separate, and each man interacts with his own children. At the preschool age, the children of both sexes are usually with women, but as a shadow of things to come, the men begin to exert more control over the boys, while the disciplining of girls falls to the mother. Men are not supposed to reprimand their older daughters; such matters should be carried out by the women, and a few men are reluctant to reprimand their daughters even at this young age. In general, fathers are probably more severe in their punishments of the boys; but a few mothers said that their husbands were the lenient ones.*

Aside from the parents, older brothers and sisters feel free to shout at or even slap an erring child. Within the courtyard an older sibling is more likely to be unofficial second disciplinarian than an aunt. If a child misbehaves outside his home, neighbors usually feel free to shout at him. Such a person is usually a man, since the women stay in the courtyards.†

Regardless of who disciplines the children, the villagers agree, in general, on the methods of discipline. Despite individual differences in the handling of children, and some variance between the discipline of the men and that of the women, there is a clear consensus of opinion which forms the norm of the villager's socialization techniques.

The core of this consensus is the belief that praising children "to their faces" will spoil them and make them disobedient. As one man put it, "If we praise, the child will think we love him too much and then he will not be under our control." Some men were of the opinion that children obeyed men better than they obeyed women because the women "loved them too much." This phrase "loving too much" also occurs in the women's discussions of children, for when asked, "What do you do when your child has done something good?" the women said that they loved him "very much." Despite the belief that praising is wrong, mothers reported that they do praise children, using such phrases as "You have done good work," "You are a queen (king)," or "You look very nice like that." In examining our observations, how-

* When asked, "Who scolds your child when all the adults are present?", 8 mothers said that either they or their husbands did; 3 said everyone in the house; and only 1 said the grandmother. When asked, "Who in the house usually sees that the child behaves well and who forbids him?" 7 mothers named themselves; 4 named themselves and their husbands; 8 said everybody; 2 said the father; no one named either grandparent.

† Thirteen out of 17 mothers said that older siblings punished the children, and 14 out of 24 said that neighbors sometimes punished them.

ever, we find only one recorded instance of a mother praising her child. When her 4-year-old daughter presented her with some dishes she had just washed, this mother said simply, "Oh, you have washed the dishes, good." It may be that some mothers were somewhat reluctant to praise children in front of us, but I doubt that our presence reduced the normal frequency of praise to any great extent. In general, the village women seldom praised their children.*

Although it is bad to praise children "to their faces," it is permissible to praise them when they are not present or to hold them up as examples to other children. In the best of form, one should use only nieces and nephews as role models and leave it to the other members of the family or neighbors to use one's own children as good examples. This technique, perhaps because of the increasing residential segmentation of extended families, is seldom practiced. Very few women are so firm in their friendship that they will hold up each other's children as examples to their own. On the other hand, most women in extended families are probably reluctant to lavish praise on other children for fear of being accused of spoiling them. A careful impartiality in children's disputes, although not always achieved, is by far the safest course. The mother-in-law, similarly, must be careful in her use of praise or she will be accused by the women in other houses of "playing favorites" and causing dissension among her daughters-in-law. The men of the family are subject to similar pressures. Among the men, it is the grandfather who is most likely to love the children "very much." These patriarchs usually confine their attention to the younger children, and the descriptions of their behavior in this connection sound more like doting grandparent behavior than systematic attempts to reinforce certain responses. Certainly, considering the infrequent use of praise by the women and its reputedly less frequent use by the men, one can only conclude that the village child is seldom complimented for specific good behavior.

The use of tangible rewards for good behavior is equally rare. Only 6 out of 24 mothers said that they sometimes gave small presents, usually food, to children when they were good. About one half of the women mentioned that they promised trips to a nearby town or a visit to a relative in return for good behavior. Such trips are made relatively infrequently, however, and do not serve as immediate rewards. Pocket money or a little grain to buy candy is given to children, even young children, but not necessarily as a reward for good behavior. In our

* The reluctance to praise young children may also be related to the belief in the evil eye.

work with the mothers we never saw them give children rewards or special privileges for being good.

In general, then, reinforcement is used sparingly in socialization. The mothers do not often capitalize on the child's love for them by rewarding their actions with praise, nor do they use material objects to encourage good behavior. Instead they rely almost solely on punishment to control children. By far the most common punishment reported in interviewing, and by our observations, is a simple scolding, often consisting of a curse or a derogation. We recorded some 24 scoldings in our observation protocols. Sometimes this scolding is nothing more than a curse, ranging from the mild "Go away," to such terms as "immoral widow," or "sister seducer," or simply "Go to Hell." The stronger curses are more likely to be used by older children than by the women. More commonly the scolder calls the child by a derogatory but not obscene name. "Chamar," or "Bhangī," both Untouchable castes, were commonly hurled insults. "Monkey" is also used. "Let the dog bark" is a phrase indicating that the speaker disdains to notice the culprit's behavior. Such insults point to the absence of the expected caste behavior and threaten loss of status. Ridicule is also used frequently. When interviewed, one half of the mothers said they laughed at their children and make fun of them when they were naughty.

Sometimes other mothers are used as the sanctioning agents in such statements as "They will say the sweeper is crying." "They will say you are a dirty boy." Such derogatory statements come closest to love-oriented techniques, since they threaten the child with loss of support. The source of the support, however, is the social in-group rather than the mother herself. Similarly, some men reported that when they are displeased with their sons, they announce this publicly to the other men of the men's platform. It is probably at such times that a man is likely to praise a nephew and cite him as a good example. The technique might best be called status oriented rather than love oriented, since it capitalizes on fear of lost status and consequent abandonment by the social group rather than fear of loss of love from a particular person.

Other types of scoldings involve the threat of physical punishment. A mother may reprimand her child with a sharp "Stop that! Do you want a beating from me?", or she may go so far as to threaten to cut off the ears of a naughty child.* This threat is so obviously a hoax that few children take it seriously, as can be seen in the following exchange between a mother and her 4-year-old daughter:

* To pull a person's ears is a great insult.

Mother: I will cut off your ears.
Daughter: Oh, I will see how you cut off my ears.
Mother: Really, I am telling you, I will cut off your ears and send them to
             the mill, and they will make flour and we will have bread from that.
Daughter: Don't be silly.

Again, some of the mothers in threatening the child with physical punishment or removal from the group invoked supernatural agents, animals, and, more recently, Americans as the punisher. About one third of the mothers said that they frightened the children most commonly with ghosts, who will take them away and presumably kill them. The terms *hāvā* and *lūlū* are also used to frighten children. These words denote something frightening and may refer to ghosts, animals, such as dogs, wolves, and jackals, or Americans. Some mothers frightened children by telling them that the Americans would give them injections, take them away, beat them, or even eat them. Jackals and wolves were used chiefly to quiet children who fussed at night. During the winter months jackals can be heard barking in the fields at night, a sound that must lend considerable weight to the threats.

Another method used to frighten children is to lock them in a room of the house. The intent is to frighten the child, since the rooms are windowless and completely dark when the door is closed. Thus, locking a child in such a room would be more like locking him in a closet in America, except that the room is bigger than a closet. The mothers considered this a rather severe punishment and used it rather rarely.

A number of women claimed that frightening the children with ghosts and locking them in a room were not effective because they were not frightened. It seems impossible that in a culture where the women, at least, are genuinely afraid of ghosts, the children would not be frightened by them. It is more likely that the strong value placed on bravery by the Rājpūts leads the women to insist that nothing frightens their children. The fact that the men strongly disapprove of the women's practice of frightening the children on the grounds that it makes them timid, and do not use this practice themselves, indicates that it was not ineffective. This disagreement about frightening children seems to be the only sharp divergence between men and women on matters of discipline. It is understandable that the women use supernatural agents to control the children, whereas the men do not. The men are less likely to believe in ghosts, place more emphasis on bravery, and have more authority than the women. It is enough for a man to frighten a child with his own wrath; he does not need the aid of a ghost.

Men sometimes use a mild form of isolation as a punishment. A number of men said that they sometimes sent children to the corner of the men's platform or inside one of the men's cubicles when they were naughty. This would not be nearly so frightening as being shut inside a room of the courtyard. It is more common for the men simply to send the children to the courtyard when they are naughty. The women may send them out to the men's quarters for the same reason. One woman humorously said that children sometimes go back and forth from courtyard to men's quarters all day long. This practice is clearly more a "buck-passing" technique to get rid of obstreperous children than a device for punishment by isolation.

Children are not threatened with the wrath of gods or ancestors for being naughty. Using fear of the gods or fear of the ancestors for such a purpose is evidently considered improper. All of the women interviewed denied doing this, one protesting indignantly that it would be a sin because ancestors are to be respected, and one should not make fun of them.

Although physical punishment is often threatened, it is less often administered, particularly to young children. Almost all mothers reported that they slap their children sometimes, if their scolding is not heeded. Some mothers beat their older children, but many said that a threatening gesture is sufficient. We did not observe many cases of physical punishment, but our presence may well have decreased the frequency of such punishment. The village mother is reluctant to create a scene when company is present. Older children are less inhibited and do occasionally land a blow on a young child. One blow with the hand is usually the extent of the punishment—children were not held and beaten; however, the threat of such a blow as the ultimate sanction is ever present.

None of the mothers punish children by withholding rewards. "What we have, we give; the thing we do not have we cannot give," was the most common answer to this query. The answer reflects, in part, the relative scarcity of tangible rewards at the mothers' disposal. Since money is not regularly given, it cannot be effectively withheld. Mothers who are themselves confined to the house have little to offer by way of special entertainment to children whose social mobility is considerably broader than their own.

A number of mothers interpreted the question about withholding rewards in terms of food, which they said was the only thing the children asked of them. Although fear of upsetting a balanced diet would probably not dissuade the village mother from sending her child to bed without his supper, withholding food was never used as a disciplinary technique because refusal to accept food is a common, culturally patterned way of showing extreme displeasure. Since a person may not accept food from anyone of a caste lower than his own, refusal to accept food from a person may be a serious insult. The ultimate caste sanction, outcasting, consists, in part, of refusing to eat or smoke with the outcasted person. Adults commonly show their displeasure by wrapping themselves in a quilt, retiring to their beds in stony silence, and fasting until someone persuades them to forget their anger. Even older children sometimes walk away in a huff, refusing to speak to someone who has insulted them.

Refusing to speak to a person, like refusing to accept food from him, is a serious breach of etiquette, usually reserved for major disputes among adults. When mothers were really displeased with their children, however, they would sometimes show their anger by refusing to speak to them. About one third of the mothers said that they sometimes stopped speaking to their children. Several of the mothers who did not use this technique explained that the children were too young to understand it. Needless to say, the mother's silence lasted only for a matter of hours, whereas the silence between feuding adults may last for years. The child may have interpreted this silence as withdrawal of love by the mother; yet, because of its cultural significance, it has the implication of a group as well as an individual sanction.

Aside from the periodic shouts of "Don't," the village women do very little to guide their children's behavior. Since children are thought to learn from observation, they feel little need to reason with children, to explain the demands made upon them, or to spend time instructing them. The content of the mother's scoldings does not contain a description of desired behavior. The scoldings are little more than the briefest condemnations. They are never developed into long, explanatory lectures. The few chores required of children are simple enough to be learned through observation, perhaps with the guidance of a few simple instructions.

As we have said, the villagers occasionally use other children or, less frequently, adults as role models to guide children's behavior. This technique is not, however, used frequently and certainly is not employed as a deliberate teaching device. The heroes and heroines of epics and myths probably function, to some extent, as role models for children. Stories are not told to children, but the women sometimes amuse themselves in the evening by telling stories to each other, and some of the men read the religious epics in groups or relate tales of great Rājpūt warriors and rulers. On festival days someone may relate the festival's origin myth. The children, as well as adults, listen to these narratives and hear of the bravery of Arjuna and Pṛthvī Rāj, the wisdom of Rāma and the obedient devotion of his wife, Sītā. However, identification with these epic figures is not evident in the children's play nor in their fantasy responses on interviews or story completion. We conducted a short interview with the children as well as a story completion test. The children always completed the stories briefly and realistically; fantasy figures never entered the story. When asked "Who would you like to be if you could be anyone in the world?" almost all of the children named a family member despite the fact that we gave them a long list of characters, including such figures as bandit, king, queen, god and goddess, from which to choose. The children's only imaginative play is adult role play, in which the boys play at farming and the girls at cooking. Once, just after the *mela*, which had a circus, we found a group of children playing circus, but we never saw them pretend to be kings or warriors. Certainly the adults, particularly the men, identify with their epic heroes. Judging from behavior, however, this identification may not take place in early childhood, probably not until adolescence.

All of the socialization techniques employed by the adults are probably less effective in the modification of the children's behavior than the observation and imitation through which the children gradually absorb the skills, customs, and values of their group. As the villagers say, the children learn from observation. The preschool period might be called the period of observation and imitation for the Rājpūt child. He is considered too young to learn from instruction; very little is expected of him; and he spends most of his day observing the busy scene around him. As a babe in arms he was carried from the house by his child nurse; he saw the children playing; he might be taken into a neighboring courtyard or, more rarely, to a ceremony. Once weaned, housebroken, and walking, his sphere of observation widens. He may spend more time with the men. Sometimes a fond uncle will take a young boy to the fields with him. Two small boys spent most of their time in the fields with the men, but since young children tire easily and are likely to become a nuisance in the fields, most preschool children remain in the village. If the child is a boy, and the mother is alone in the house or very busy, the grandfather may assume a position of major caretaker. Two 3-year-old boys spent much of their time with their grandfathers. Both of these men were too old for active field work, and neither was powerful enough to assume the role of "Big Man" that many of the wealthier and more prestigeful men assume in their declining years. Once the child can walk, the grandmother is more likely to take him with her when she visits a neighbor, and from this time on, the children attend all of the birth ceremonies and weddings of their village even if the mother must remain at home. Children may accompany their mother, aunt, or grandmother on a visit to her parent's village. When not with an adult, the young children tag along after the 5-, 6-, and 7-year-olds, who are themselves too young to be working. Since the courtyards are crowded, they play in the streets, on the empty men's platform, or by the pond in the road and fields just outside the village. Usually the children do not venture more than a quarter of a mile from their homes, and they are seldom far from an adult. The 3- and 4-year-old children are frequently seen standing on the outskirts of a game of tag, "rooting" for an elder brother who is playing shells, smiling vaguely at a group of boys who are "plowing" a field, or following an older brother or sister to the pond with the water buffalo.

As the children grow older, they begin to participate in the games and activities. Children of about 4 to 8 have relatively extensive social contacts. Their daily social interactions are not hemmed in by restrictions that segregation of sexes imposes on the adult social life. Most mothers would probably have prevented their children from playing constantly with lower caste children, but since they do not live in the neighborhood, there was little chance for such friendships to develop, and we did not observe children playing with Untouchables. Children of different lineages play together if their houses happen to be close together, and children move freely from one house to another even though their parents may not have been on speaking terms with the adults of the house for years. Only one woman said that she did not like her children to play with children of women with whom she was not friendly, and her statement was probably made to insult her sister-in-law, with whom she was quarreling and who was present during the interview.

We were impressed by the fact that the women did not take their own quarrels out on the children. Men's quarrels, on the other hand, result in blood feuds which may go on for generations. Probably for this reason men are more concerned with impressing upon their sons that they should know their enemies. Fathers stated that they told their children not to be friendly with people with whom their fathers did not talk but to speak politely to their father's friends.

Strangers from other villages are unpredictable and tentatively suspect, and some fathers warned their children about them.

We tell them that you should not believe people from a different village. You never know what they will do at what time.

For the most part, however, visitors from outside the village, particularly those with whom the children would have contact, are visiting in-laws and guests, toward whom the children are taught courtesy.

If any man from another village comes and the child knows that the friend of his father is here, then if the father is not there, he will give him the hookah, and talk nicely to him. Even if a man comes whom nobody knows, the children will ask him to sit down, and if it is time for meals, then they will give him food.

The difference in training of boys and girls is reflected in the child interviews. When asked how they would react if a strange child tried to be friendly with them, 8 of the 10 girls said they would be friendly, whereas 5 of the 9 boys said they would not be friendly.

The mothers prefer that the children play in groups rather than alone.* When asked if they preferred some playmates to others, the mothers were reluctant to name specific children they did not like but stressed the fact that they did not want their children to play with children who fought. More than half of the mothers stated that they liked their children's friends and, when asked to specify those they would choose as playmates, usually named the playmates we most frequently observed with their children. Mothers summarized their feelings by stating they preferred children who were nice and did not fight or have bad habits.

The adults pay little attention to the activities of children unless there is quarreling or trouble, so that the children's recreation is informal and without adult supervision. A great deal of the play of younger children consists of almost random activity. They chase each other, tease each other, climb on a vacant cart, or play seesaw on a wagon wheel that is lying beside their house.

The children have relatively few toys. Families do possess toys, but they are likely to be *objets d'art* rather than playthings. One family showed us a collection of painted plaster dolls which they had made. The only time we ever saw them was on this one occasion when they were displayed for our benefit. Only once or twice did we see children playing with such plaster figures. A few of the girls have rag dolls, but they very rarely play with them. Some girls have sets of toy cooking utensils with which they play. Two of the children in one of the wealthiest households had toy grain grinders which their grandmother had given to them, and some had toy scales. The boys sometimes have small, wooden bullock carts, some made by the village carpenter, some,

* When asked in the parent interview whether they liked their children to play alone, 18 of the 23 mothers stated that their children should play with others, not alone.

crude affairs which they make themselves. These may be a block of wood with two wheels attached or one solid wheel with a bent piece of sugar cane for an axle. The boys also make bows and arrows for themselves and play with small iron hoops which they roll with a stick.

The adult segregation of the sexes influences their role play. The village boys and girls do not join forces to play house or other fantasy play modeled on adult life. Both sexes, however, have their own type of fantasy play which is modeled on adult work. As mentioned earlier, the little girls play at cooking and the boys at farming. One child in the sample studied was particularly fond of playing at cooking. She had a set of toy dishes, and she would build herself a hearth out of three stones and go through the exact motions of making bread. She used either mud or potsherds for her bread, rubbed "oil" in the frying pan, patted the breads, fried them on the "fire," turned them, put them in the "fire" underneath the pot to let them puff, took them out, flattened them, and stacked them on a dish beside her. It was an exact copy of the motions that an adult woman goes through in making bread. When she finished playing, she washed the dishes and stacked them, and washed the floor in the place where she had cooked. Another bit of imitative play observed with this child was her cooking spinach with water in a small pot. She put it onto the hearth and carefully stirred it. She even blew on the "fire," as do the adult women.

Although the role playing of this girl was unusually detailed and accurate, the making of mud breads is a fairly common play activity of the little girls. Their favorite place for doing this was at the edge of the village pond, where there was plenty of mud at hand for the dough.

When the little boys play at farming, they sometimes make rather elaborate imitations of fields and then irrigate them. More often the play is somewhat simpler, as in the following observation:

A group of boys were playing at sowing. They had long sticks and were pretending to plow. They said, "Let's grow wheat." Some of the boys started scattering dust like seed. They were following boys who were "plowing" the ground with sticks. They said, "Brrr, brrr, brrr," which is what the men say to the cattle. Then they leveled the ground with a stick by rolling it along the ground.

The preschool child is free to play most of the time, since little work is expected of him. He gets little training in responsibility. The first chore that may be assigned to the child is shopping, a necessary task which the women, confined to the courtyard, cannot do. Children are sent, with handfuls of grain clutched in their shirt tails, to the nearest store to buy spices. Sometimes they take grain to be popped. Usually an older child is chosen for this task, but if none is available, a 4- or 5-year-old may be sent. One mother, alone in her courtyard with a 3-year-old son, sent him to shop for spices. This boy also served food to his grandfather, for it is not customary for a woman to serve her father-in-law. The shop is several hundred yards from the neighborhood, and the way lies through the maze of twisted village streets. Such excursions are the longest trips that the young child is likely to make alone. Aside from shopping, little girls may occasionally wash a dish or two, and either girls or boys may bring water if the daily allotment brought by the water carriers runs short. One 5-year-old boy took the cattle to water by himself, but this task is usually left to older children. Children also serve as messengers to the men's platform. All of these chores are irregular and brief. There is little feeling that children should be given work for the purpose of developing a sense of responsibility. Children are asked to work only when their services are needed. Mothers are particularly lenient with girls in this matter, since a girl is considered to be a guest in her own home. The mothers often emphasized that since a girl must work so hard in the house of her husband, she should not have to work in her parents' house.

In some families the eldest son may be singled out for more training in responsibility. There is no clear pattern, however. Some parents said that they gave him special training, since the management of the farm and the authority of the extended household would ultimately fall on his shoulders. They stated that he had some special status even as a child. Younger children are encouraged to obey him, and he in turn is taught that he has the responsibility for other people in the household, that he must be fair to them, take care of them, and be industrious in running the farm. As one informant said:

We advise the eldest son to help his parents when they get old, and give good advice to his younger siblings. We tell the younger brothers to obey the eldest boy. As soon as the oldest son is old enough to be running the fields and finances, the father gives him all the responsibility and retires. The father trains his son until he knows how to do it. We stress obedience to the elders equally for the elder and the younger son.

Other parents stated that the status of the eldest son was not different. There are several possible explanations for the divergence in pattern. The parent may elect to turn over the position of headman to whichever son he considers the most capable. As mentioned above, the eldest son may be the least educated, for his help may be needed in the fields during the school years. A third reason may be the breakdown of the extended family pattern and the frequent division of land after the death of the father.

Self-reliance training is almost as scanty as training in responsibility. Mothers still dress, bathe, and serve food to children of this age; sometimes they still feed them. When the children want something, they ask their mother rather than try to solve the problem by themselves. The extent to which the mothers reinforce this dependency is seen in their often repeated phrase, "What we have, we give." The children may be scolded for nagging for food before it is ready, but this is a condemnation of the unreasonableness of the demand, not of the request itself.

During the preschool period the children learn to determine the appropriate sources of various kinds of aid. Although they are free to play in a neighbor's house, they do not stay for dinner. Food is not casually shared, and a child learns to go to his mother when hungry. Cooked food is served to the children by an adult. However, the children eat grain, sugar cane, and candy between meals. If the family has a common food bin, the children may help themselves from it. If the food stores are divided, they must take cooked food from their parents' hearth and grain from their parents' bin, which is usually inside the wife's room. Within these limits the children are usually free to help themselves to small quantities of grain without asking permission. Similar caution must be observed toward all the aunts' possessions, money, clothes, jewelry, and so on. However, each woman keeps her belongings securely locked in a trunk so that there is little lying around to tempt a child into trouble.

The extent to which the children were capable of insistent demanding was brought home to us almost daily. Although the children do not ordinarily ask anything of the adults of other houses, my interpreter and I were exceptions to this rule. Whereas other adults would quickly discourage any approach of this kind, our role in studying the children required us to be nonpunitive. The children discovered very quickly that they could pester us without being punished. Throughout our stay we were rarely out of earshot of the whining cry, "Give me my photo." Since we took photographs of the children daily, and sent the films to Delhi to be developed, it was impossible to give the children all the pictures that had been taken of them, although we passed out as many as we could. No amount of explanation could silence their demands, nor did the mothers reprimand their children for this persistent begging. Many mothers were, in fact, only slightly less demanding in this regard than their offspring.

In general, the apparent lack of self-reliance in both adults and children is one of the first characteristics that strikes an American observer. The children's interview included two questions about succorance. We asked what the child would do if he or she were having trouble in some task (schoolwork, herding cattle, or fixing a toy). Eleven children said that they would ask for help, and 6 said they would do nothing or abandon the task. Only one 10-year-old boy said he would solve the problem himself.

Children usually seek help from adults rather than peers. As the children grow older and spend more time outside the home, playing in peer groups, succorance becomes a somewhat less notable part of their behavior. In the first place, peers can provide fewer rewards than can adults. Also, children generally are less responsive to succorant behavior. We asked a number of children whether or not they would assist a friend who needed their aid in schoolwork, catching a stray cow, or fixing a toy cart. Ten children said they would help, and 8 said that they would not. When asked what they would do if a friend fell and hurt himself, 10 said they would help or get help, and 8 said they would do nothing.

Although the parents' behavior encourages the children to make frequent requests, parents do not place much emphasis either on training them to comply with the requests of others or on training them to be spontaneously nurturant. Four out of 6 of the mothers of preschool children said that they thought their children should help younger children when they were in trouble. The remaining 2 mothers said that their children were as yet too young to do this. Only a few mothers, however, could remember an incident in which their child had, in fact, helped a younger child, perhaps because the children are more likely to seek aid from an adult than from a child. The fathers were similarly vague on the subject, one father commenting that only good-natured children would help younger children. In practice, the children follow the adult pattern of giving aid only when it is asked and often only if the supplicant is insistent in his demands. Children were not punished for failure to give help unless they refused to give alms to a beggar or food to a servant who had come for her daily pay, nor were they praised for generosity. Therefore the children's nurturant behavior depends largely on their temper of the moment and the quality of their relationship with the person who is in need of assistance. Sometimes they completely ignore the need of their playmates and siblings as in the following instance taken from an observation protocol:

Sr. (boy aged 4) came out of the room with a ball. He knocked down Sa. (brother aged 1½) in the doorway. Sa. was crying slightly and could not get up. Sr. paid no attention.

Girls are more likely to exhibit nurturant behavior toward babies and younger children. For instance:

Sh. (girl aged 5) was eating bread. R. (brother aged 1) was sitting beside her, and she gave him some of her bread, saying, "Take, eat. Do you like it? It is sweet." . . . The baby was crying. She went up to him where he was lying on another cot. She said, "Don't cry, who hit you?" . . . She brought the baby to the grandmother, gave him to her, and sat beside them saying "Brrrrrrrr" to the baby.

As judged by their verbal reports, the mothers place primary emphasis on obedience and the training of passivity, begun in infancy. When asked, "Whom do you call a good boy or a good girl?", they were able to answer the question adequately, although their answers were usually brief. The most frequent answer to this question was that a good child is one who obeys. Several women also said that a good child should study, should not fight, and should respect its elders. However, inasmuch as respecting one's elders includes such behavior as using the proper greeting and kinship terms, and speaking politely, and since obedience is also a sign of respect for elders, the concept of an obedient child is undoubtedly closely linked with that of a respectful child. Since these kinship terms denote respect, the continued insistence that children use them keeps the lines of authority clear and "sets the stage," as it were, for ensuring that children will obey their elders.* According to the interviews, obedience, politeness, and peaceableness were the most emphasized virtues. There were no consistent differences between mothers' descriptions of what was expected of a good boy and what was expected of a good girl. In practice, obedience is stressed somewhat more for girls and bravery for boys; but both sexes are expected to be both obedient and brave, although in the contexts of different tasks.

The mothers were also asked, "Whom do you call a bad child?" or "What sorts of things do you punish your children for?" Stubborn demanding of attention was the most frequently cited negative characteristic. This concept was phrased by the women in a number of different ways, for example, "When he is stubborn," "When he troubles me," "When he cries for nothing," "When he will not listen," "When he will not stop crying," or "When he insists on having food which I cannot give him." Another frequently mentioned fault was fighting or abusing: "Those children who fight and abuse among themselves," "Those children who hurt others." These two were by far the most frequently mentioned causes of punishment. Other faults included less frequently were stealing, getting dirty, spilling food (spilling milk from a pail or

* In several instances, mothers deplored to us the fact that the proper use of kinship terms was becoming less frequent. We even heard children praised—a rare event—for the correct use of kinship terms and we heard mothers commended for requiring this amenity of their children.

spilling food when eating), and not working. These answers clearly indicate that the mothers desire a child who will simply do what he is told, stay out of trouble, and not demand too much.

The Rājpūt children do not strike an observer as being particularly well trained. One reason is because of the pattern that a strong or repeated request is required before a villager, adult or child, will comply, unless the request falls within the limits of some customary obligation, and such formal obligations do not affect the children. Thus it is often necessary for a mother to ask a child several times to do something before the child complies.* Since mothers are usually lenient with small children, they sometimes do not comply at all. The custom of seclusion of the women fosters disobedience to some extent, for the unruly child is safe from pursuit if he simply leaves the courtyard. When we interviewed the children, 14 out of 16 said that they did run away when their mothers scolded them, so it is a common method of avoiding punishment for wrongs committed outside the house, since it is difficult for the women to check on the child's story. Mothers commonly lose their tempers and shout at disobedient children and then "cool off" and forget the matter without having exacted obedience. Consequently it seems that the children learn more about how to weather the mother's emotional storms than they do about obeying her will. On the rare occasions when the grandmother scolds the child, she is little more effective. Since the grandmother is usually more lenient and permissive than the mother, the children know that grandmother is a "softie."

The men, by virtue of their higher status, evidently expect and receive more obedience with less effort than do the women, at least when the children are in their presence. However, even their discipline is by no means perfect. Dr. Gumperz cites an incident where a Rājpūt man sent a boy on an errand. When the boy did not return, he sent another boy to find him. When the search proved unsuccessful, he simply dispatched the second boy to run the errand. He was apparently not upset by the first boy's disobedience.

Another reason why obedience is often more in evidence in preaching than in practice is that the authoritarian hierarchy of village social

* When asked whether they expected their children to obey at once or whether they gave them a little time, 12 mothers said they should obey at once, 3 said it depended on the urgency of the work to be done, and 6 said they give the children some time. When asked, however, if they always followed up any shirking on the part of their children, 15 out of 19 mothers said they sometimes let it go when their children did not carry out orders. The attitudes of the fathers are similar to those of the mothers except that the men make more of a distinction between work which is urgent and work which can wait.

structure requires that people shall be obedient to persons who are above them in status but domineering with persons below them in status. Therefore, within the framework of the social structure, dominance is considered to be a desirable trait. Each mother in the sample was asked whether she thought her child should direct the play of his peers or whether this made the child bossy. Even the mothers of preschool children usually said that being the leader is good and a mark of intelligence. The fathers expressed similar opinions.* Thus, although obedience is emphasized, dominance is tacitly encouraged. Since the mothers almost never clarify their expectations to the children, some of the reluctant obedience to adults may well be due to the fact that the child is not clear about what behavior is required in what circumstances.

The following is an example of the preschool childrens' responses to their mothers' demands.

Mrs. H. is preparing dinner. Her daughter Bw., aged 4, is sitting beisde her trying to open a tin can containing chillies for seasoning. Her son Bb., aged 6, and her nephew M., aged 4, are also present.
Mrs. H. says to her son: Go and give the cattle water.
Bb.: I will go after some time.
Mrs. H.: No, go now.
Bb. leaves, shouting crossly: I won't go all the way to the pond. I will come back from the well.
Mrs. H. to daughter: I will put chillies in the chutney.
Bw.: No. I don't like chillies.
M., male cousin aged 4, takes shell from Bw. She screams and he returns it. Later he takes it again.
Mrs. H. shouts to him, "Don't do that" and he gives it back.
M. to Bw.: You open the tin.
Bw.: No, I won't open it.
Mrs. H. to Bw.: Give me the tin. I will put in the chillies.
Bw.: No, no, no.
Mrs. H.: No, I am keeping your chutney separate.
Bw. continued to play with the tin.
Mrs. H.: Don't do that, you will drop all the chillies.
Bw. let go of the tin and leaned against her mother sulking.
Mrs. H.: Will you eat now?
Bw.: Yes, bring it for me.
Mrs. H.: Will you eat it with chutney?
Bw.: Yes.
Mrs. H. got some water and started feeding her daughter.

The interviews show that training in the inhibition of emotion is also begun during the preschool period. The mothers reported that

* Fifteen mothers thought it was good for their children to dominate, 5 thought this was not good, and 2 mothers said it depended on the situation.

they stop the children when they get too excited, laugh too much, cry, or become angry. Occasionally mothers would even scold or punish children when they cried, even if they hurt themselves, as exemplified in the following:

> We were visiting R.'s house in the evening when M., a 4-year-old girl, fell off the cot and landed on her shoulder. She cried loudly. Her teen-aged sister came over to her and said sharply, "Get up. You did not get hurt. Get up." I put on the flashlight briefly in order to see M. in the darkness, and the sister, in an effort to distract the crying child, pointed to the light and said, "Look, look at that." M. went on crying. Her mother, who was several yards away at the hearth, shouted very crossly, "I will beat you if you don't stop crying. I will throw the big spoon at you." M. continued to cry, although not quite so hard. No one paid any further attention to her. Eventually she stopped.

A number of children corroborated this observation, stating that their mothers punished them for falling and hurting themselves.* Probably the Rājpūt emphasis on bravery is partially responsible for this unsympathetic attitude.

Although parents say that they discourage outbreaks of anger and aggressive behavior, they in fact sometimes ignore or even reward such behavior. The severity with which such behavior is punished depends on the status of the person to whom the aggression is directed. Theoretically aggression directed at adults is a graver offense than aggression directed at peers, which often goes unpunished. On the other hand, small children sometimes become angry with their mothers, aunts, and grandmothers, "scolding" them and, less frequently, hitting them. When this happens, the mothers sometimes scold or hit the child, but sometimes they ignore the outburst. In the extended family, issues are seldom so important as keeping the peace. This is true of quarrels among adults, and the same attitude evidently holds for the misdemeanors of children. When we asked the mothers of all the children, "What do you do when your child gets angry when you or your husband do not let him have something or are angry with him?" 12 of the women said that they would give in to the child at this point and console him or give him what he wanted, 4 said they would discipline him, and 3 said they would ignore him. Five women either repudiated the question or failed to answer it. Half of the mothers, then, report that they give in to their children when the children become angry with them. Insofar as this practice is followed, it probably re-

---

* When asked what they would do if they fell and were hurt, 7 children said they would ask for help, 3 said they would fix the hurt themselves, and 9 said they would ignore it. A number of children mentioned that if they hurt themselves, they would be punished by their mother.

wards the expression of anger and undermines the mother's authority by increasing the frequency of the child's challenges of that authority.

Quarrels among children of approximately the same age are usually ignored by the women until actual blows are struck or until a child cries or complains. When the mother does not know who started the fight, she usually makes no attempt to find out. Women are sometimes reluctant to scold their sister-in-law's children or children from other houses for fear that it will be said that they scold other people's children but never their own. When she finds her child fighting with neighbor children, she will usually scold her own child, perhaps slap him, and give the other children only a mild reprimand or send them home. If her child is fighting with the child of a sister-in-law, the mother's action depends a great deal on her current relations with the sister-in-law, and whether the sister-in-law is above or below her in the family hierarchy.

In general, however, almost all mothers, not only of preschool children but of older children as well, discourage fighting in their own children. When asked what they did if their children got into a fight while playing, 20 of the mothers said they punished their children, and 4 said they determined who was at fault and punished the offender. Three out of 24 mothers said that they sometimes told their children to fight back, but the other 21 said that they never did this, and several were quite shocked at the idea of giving the children such bad advice.

The children engage in a good deal of minor bickering, name calling, snatching of objects, and semiaggressive teasing or "horseplay." More serious quarrels are infrequent, for parents intervene before they reach this point. If a fight occurs outside the house, only a young child who feels he has been unfairly treated by an older playmate will go crying into the house to report to the mother. Older children, knowing they will receive no sympathy, keep their fighting to themselves. Only once did I hear a child try to justify his attack to his mother with the explanation, "She hit me first."

The type of aggression that is most likely to invoke swift retribution from the parents is that which is directed against a young sibling or cousin. This situation applies chiefly to the older children who may become angry at a preschool child, but it can also apply to a 4-year-old hitting a 1- or 2-year-old child. The deciding factor here seems to be one of inequality in physical strength. In such contests the bigger child receives most, if not all, of the blame. If, however, a boy is fighting with a sister who is older than he but not appreciably stronger, both will be scolded. Bullying, then, is strongly discouraged.

Sibling rivalry is conspicuous by its absence. This is not to say that the children do not fight with their brothers and sisters, but they do not show hostility or resentment to a new baby. Only one child displayed open resentment to a newborn sibling. This child was a 2½-year-old boy named Kheer, the first son of a young woman who was visiting her parents' home. The only other child in the house, except for the baby, was a 10-year-old boy. The mother had an unusually large supply of milk and so continued to nurse both children. Once we saw Kheer try to push his baby sister away from the breast and nurse himself. Another time we made the following observation:

S.D. came walking along the road. She was carrying her baby girl. Her son Kheer was following her, crying. She said that he wanted her to carry him also. As he came up behind her, she sat down on the road, and he knocked her off balance. He then hit the baby several times, walked around his mother, and hit her on the back several times. The mother laughed and said, "Are you trying to kill baby?"

Three factors seem to contribute to this striking lack of sibling rivalry.

1. Adults are not overly affectionate with children of any age. Infants are usually not given special attention beyond their physical needs. They are not cuddled or played with. Consequently the older child, never accustomed to being the center of his mother's attention, does not feel displaced in her affections by the new arrival.

2. In an extended family household women are present who can replace the mother in taking care of the older child when her time is demanded by the new baby.

3. In an extended household it is unusual for any child to have the experience of being the first-born child within the household. If he is the son of one of the younger brothers there are some older cousins present. If he is the son of the oldest brother, there are usually uncles and aunts in the household who are still children; since the women marry so young, it is not uncommon for grandmothers to be of child-bearing age or to have preadolescent children.

Because of these circumstances the child is always a secure member of a group, but he is never an important individual. His needs are cared for, his reasonable demands met, but he never monopolizes his mother's time.

It seemed to us significant, in this connection, that Kheer came from a household containing no other young children and that his mother was in her own home and therefore had no household duties. As a result, he got an unusual amount of attention before the birth of his sister. Obviously further research is necessary to test these hypotheses. We present them here merely as a tentative explanation for the striking lack of sibling rivalry.

Temper tantrums seldom occur. Only twice did we see a child lying on the floor and screaming in a real hysterical tantrum. On the first occasion the child, a girl, was ignored; on the second, a 6-year-old boy was taunted by his mother and aunt and an older cousin who shouted at him, "Are you the only child here that you are fussing so?" When very angry, the children, like their mothers, may retire to their beds and refuse to eat. This performance, however, is also rare.

Young children are often not punished for being rude to the low-caste servants. The caste hierarchy can be clearly seen when such incidents occur. Children are also generally not reprimanded for being rough with animals. Almost every household has a dog, and a number of children have puppies. Although not deliberately cruel to them, they are often rough in their treatment. They may pick up the puppy by one leg or throw it. Such behavior is ignored by the adults; indeed, the children are only imitating the adult pattern with regard to most animals. Adults will hit a dog that happens to be in their way, and, as mentioned previously, the men sometimes twist the tails in driving their bullocks until they are broken in several places. Since cows are sacred, they are accorded more respectful treatment.

The following observation is an extreme example of a child's aggression but illustrates the mother's lack of concern.

M. (girl aged 6) picked up a puppy. She twisted it so that one of its paws scratched her face. The puppy had nothing to do with it. She hit the puppy and threw it on the ground. I said to stop before I remembered myself. The puppy hid under the cot. She chased it to the other side of the cot. She grabbed both its paws and dragged it across the courtyard. She hit it again, and the dog finally retreated under a cot in the far corner. A few minutes later she was holding it again. She twisted its leg and it howled. K. (interviewer from project house) hit her and said to stop. She threw the dog on the floor, and it ran out of the house. About ten minutes later she hit it again. This time the mother intervened, but she hit it once more after the mother had told her to stop. The dog again retreated, and she lay on the floor and hit her mother's and K.'s feet. The mother had been present throughout but had not intervened until the last.

No specific ceremonies mark the transition from one age to another. The age of 5 or 6, however, may be marked by the performance of a second hair-cutting ceremony involving a pilgrimage to some shrine to thank a goddess for preserving the child's life. If a woman is particularly concerned about her child's health, especially if she has lost several children, she may vow to a goddess that she will offer her the child's hair and other gifts if the child lives to a certain age. Since sons are more highly valued than daughters, these ceremonies are usually performed for boys. One mother had performed two hair-cutting ceremonies for each of her four boys. She had offered the birth hair of her sons to the Bhudana goddess, and, when each had reached the age of 5, she took them to the Sakumbrī fair to offer their chōtīs, along with bread and sweets to the goddess Sakumbrī. Another mother said that she intended to leave her son's hair uncut until he reached the age of 5 and offer all of it to Sakumbrī. Another mother, concerned over the possible use of her son's hair for sorcery, offered his chōtī to the Bhudana goddess.

The aforementioned ceremonies and the Hōī fast for sons are the only ceremonies specifically concerned with children. The initiation rites of vesting boys with the sacred thread of the twice-born castes have become part of the marriage ceremony for the Khalapur Rājpūts.

✤
✤
✤

Chapter 15

The School Age Child

The changes to be described in this section come about gradually, as does the transition from infancy to the "preschool status." Chronological age is of no interest to the Indian mother, and there are no named age grades. There are no linguistic terms which differentiate children as they mature—one is a child until he becomes an adult.

At about age 5, the child is gradually taught to identify with the members of his or her own sex. Boys and girls, who until this age have been treated very much alike, now begin to face somewhat different experiences. The casual observer will first notice this change in the children's clothing. As mentioned previously, small boys and girls are usually dressed alike, but from the ages of 4 to 6, they begin to wear adult clothing, first on special occasions and then more regularly, so that by the middle of their sixth year most children have completed this external transition.

Girls may wear either saris or the loose trousers, shirt, and head-cloth, and most of the girls have outfits of both kinds. Since the shirt and pants are easier for an active youngster to manage, they are the more usual outfit for the 6- and 7-year-olds. After this age the girls are more likely to be seen in saris. Girls begin to cover their heads as soon as they wear adult-styled clothing, although even preschool age girls sometimes wear a headcloth with their shirts. Adults, however, insist that girls cover their heads in public until they are adolescent.

Along with the change of clothing, the girl's hair is allowed to grow; as soon as it is long enough it is braided, and a cloth braid is added to increase its length. When it is sufficiently long and thick, it is dressed in the elaborate fashion of the adult women: a number of small braids are made from one side of the head to the other; these are then woven into each other at the back of the head and finally meet in the one long braid. This coiffure, once completed, is left untouched for several days. Sometimes, usually between the ages of 5 and 8, the girl's ears and one nasal septum are pierced. Since the gold nose plugs and earrings worn by the women are not usually purchased for a girl until she is about ready to be married, most preadolescent girls wear small twigs in these holes. The ears are usually pierced a year or two before the nose because the women say that the nasal aperture will become enlarged if pierced when the girl is too young.

Boys simply add short or long pajama pants to their shirts. The dhōti, an older style of clothing, is usually not worn by boys, except for special occasions. When children begin wearing adult clothing, they more or less follow adult standards of modesty. Parents vary as to the strictness with which they enforce these rules. One mother shocked her neighbors by allowing her 7- and 9-year-old sons to attend school without trousers; another sometimes allowed a 7-year-old girl to leave the house wearing only a pair of shorts. Both of these incidents, however, drew criticism from neighboring women. At this age children are expected to remain covered, at least outside the house.

A second, more subtle change in the children's lives occurs as the responsibility for their care falls more and more to the parent of the same sex. This shift of caretakers takes place gradually, usually over a period of several years. Its timing and extent depend largely on the size of the family. Children of small or nuclear families, whose services may be needed by both parents, move more freely from men's platform to courtyard then do the children of the larger extended families. Boys may be sent out to the men's quarters to sleep occasionally but may not move out permanently until they are 12.

For girls, who have always spent most of their time with their mothers, the change is not great. They continue to spend their evenings listening to the women tell the stories that transmit the background for the complex ceremonial tradition and emphasize the virtues of a good Indian wife. The chief change for girls comes in their gradual expulsion from the men's platform, where they played so freely when they were younger. They may still play on the platform when the men are away, or loiter for a while when sent on an errand, but it is considered somewhat immodest and disrespectful for them to stay among the men for extended visits. Furthermore, since fathers are not supposed to punish their daughters, and since this prohibition is more carefully observed as the girls grow older, the disciplining of girls falls entirely to the women.

There is no similar prohibition against mothers punishing their sons, and mothers continue to discipline boys but often ineffectively. Many of the older boys were not only disobedient but also rude to their mothers. The boys' increased awareness of the low status of women in village society probably contributes to the ineffectiveness of their mothers' discipline. A rather extreme example of such difficulty is illustrated by the following observation.

Mrs. Singh is attempting to persuade her sons, Bīr, aged 9, and Patrām, aged 7, to leave for school. Bīr is sulkily trying to push his foot into his oxford without untying the lace, which is knotted. Patrām is in the bedroom taking things out of his mother's cupboard.

Having failed to persuade him to untie the lace, Mrs. Singh tries to help Bīr put on his shoe, but he pulls her hair. In retaliation, she hits him and they start wrestling. After considerable struggle, she pins her son to the ground and beats him with a shoe. Bīr hits her back, crying loudly. He grabs a stick to continue the assault, and his mother with some effort tears it from him.

After temporarily vanquishing her eldest son, she turns her attention to Patrām. Discovering him in the bedroom, she beats him, exclaiming, "I will see how you will go to school. You sit there and do not come out of the room at all. If you just step out I will beat you. You are just like daughters-in-law, not to go out at all."

Meanwhile Bīr is sitting on the courtyard floor, crying loudly and defiantly tying one knot after another in his shoelace.

Having effectively reduced Patrām to tears, Mrs. Singh returns to the court, sits down with her 2-year-old daughter Lālī and begins to fondle her, but with the warning, "If you do like this, you will also get a beating." Bīr, balefully eying the favored sister, threatens, "I will bury her." His mother laughs and mocks him, whereupon he returns to his room, wraps himself in a quilt, and lies down on his cot. After a minute he emphasizes his displeasure by getting up and closing the door.

"Go on, close it," says his mother. "Bolt it well and don't come out." At this command, Bīr promptly opens the door and returns to the courtyard. He procures some scissors and begins cutting a piece of cloth on which some grain is drying. "Go ahead, do that, but don't go out," proclaims his mother. Bīr abandons the cloth and begins to cut his hair.

Meanwhile Patrām has left the room where he is supposed to be cloistered and stands sniffling in the courtyard. At this point a 3-year-old girl from the neighboring house wanders in and begins playing with the toy push wheel belonging to Lālī. Lālī looks quite distressed at this encroachment on her property. Bīr, with an evil glint in his eye, takes the wheel from the neighbor girl. She appeals to Mrs. Singh but is crossly told that the wheel does not belong to her. Bīr rolls the toy out of the house and then returns it to the child, looking at Lālī to see what she will do. His maneuver is successful, and she tries to retrieve her wheel, which he promptly reclaims and wheels away. As Lālī returns weeping to her mother, Bīr vents his anger on the neighbor child, hits her, and sends her home crying.

As Mrs. Singh comforts Lālī, telling her not to talk to her brothers, the two boys finally gather up their bookbags, and despite their mother's prohibition on leaving the house, go off. When we asked whether or not they had gone to school, Mrs. Singh said that they had probably gone to play, since they would not go to school after being beaten.

The most striking example of loss of maternal control over a son concerned a 12-year-old boy, Sham, whose father had died when he was 11 months old. His mother had virtually no control over him. His 19-year-old brother, of whom he was somewhat afraid, was the only member of the family who could discipline him. The following interview excerpt will illustrate the difficulty faced by this mother.

Q.: When Sham is naughty, do you ever send him inside the room alone?
A.: Yes. I lock him in the room. Yesterday he ran away and I chased him. He ran in one room and then I chased him there and he ran in the other. Finally he ran out of the house and I could not catch him.
Q.: Do you ever take the name of ghosts, etc., to frighten him?
A.: When he was young I would frighten him with ghosts. I would say, "Don't fight or I will call the ghosts," or "I will call the police." But he is very bold and is not frightened. He would say, "I will beat the police."
Q.: Do you ever frighten Sham by telling him you will send him to another village or town?
A.: I am scared to tell him this. This is how he frightens me. He says, "If you scold me, I will go away." He says that he can get food anywhere. I took his earrings away because I was afraid that he would run away and sell them." (This boy had frightened his mother badly at one time by running away to a neighboring town and staying there for two or three days. She had given him grain to sell, and instead of bringing the money back, he had spent it.)
Q.: Do you ever take God's name to frighten him?
A.: No one is frightened of God. He is not afraid of anyone. He will go anywhere at night. Reeshmī (her daughter) is afraid to go out at night, but not Sham. . . . Neither police nor ghosts can frighten him. If I lock him up, he tries to break a door. He is not afraid, so now I say that I will jump into

the well or go out of the village if he is not good. Then he is scared and sorry.

Q.: Do you do this most often? Or do you beat him most often?

A.: I have left off beating him because it hurts my hand. I beat him very hard and he just says, "Oh, that's nothing." So I say, "I will go away, and your brother and sister-in-law will be cruel to you."

Q.: Do you ever beat him with a stick?

A.: Yes, sometimes, but I cannot do that because I feel very bad.

Evidently this mother has reached the point where threats of suicide are her only effective means of controlling her unruly son. Luckily most boys have a father or uncle to take over discipline when the mother's control becomes inadequate.

Although this custom of differential caretaking is sanctioned by the belief that men are the best teachers for boys and women for girls, it sometimes leads to disagreement between parents who, in individual instances, do not approve of the action of their spouse. One man reported that if men do not think their wives are sufficiently strict with the girls, they will beat their wives, since retaliation against their daughters is denied them. Evidently such action can also be taken for the opposite reason because more than one woman could recall instances when husbands had scolded or beaten their wives for being too harsh with daughters. One informant, for instance, recalled the following incident from her own childhood.

Once when my mother was milking three cows, I untied the calves. She had told me not to do it. She was so angry that she threw a pot at me, and it cut my leg, which bled. She pushed me out of the house and I was crying there when my father found me. He went in, asked why she had done this, and beat my mother with a sugar cane. Then as soon as he left, mother started beating me again for having told him.

The mother is usually on the receiving end of such disagreements, since only a very bold woman would reprimand her husband for his treatment of their sons.

Although the men may reprimand their wives for severe treatment of the children, particularly the girls, they are usually more severe with boys than are the women. Probably the men do not utilize physical punishment more frequently than their wives, but when they do, it is likely to hurt more, not only because of the greater strength of the men but also because they are more apt to beat older boys with a stick or shoe, whereas women must frequently use only their hand. This seemed to be particularly true of the younger men. We noted that several 8- to 10-year-old boys were most afraid of an older brother or cousin. On inquiring, we found that such 18- to 20-year-old men, themselves low men on the family pecking order, not only assumed the disciplinary role of the elders but also administered this role with particular severity.

Since some of the men are severe in their use of physical punishment, tender-hearted mothers may cover up for their sons to protect them from father's wrath. Once we entered a household just after a mother had discovered that her 11-year-old son had stolen some money from her. She was very upset and loudly bemoaning her son's bad character. When he returned, she hit him several times, demanding to know what he had done with the money and threatening that when she told his father, who was out of town for the day, "He will beat you until you are dead." Despite this violent scene, we discovered the next day that she had not reported the incident to her husband and had failed, herself, to make the boy tell her what he had done with the loot.

The move to the world of men means that the boys are exposed not only to stricter discipline but also to masculine values, which differ, at least in emphasis, from those of the women. The daughters will soon marry out of the village and play no active role in village life, but the sons must be taught the patterns of loyalty and hatred which define the social groupings with which they must live throughout their lifetime. Therefore, whereas the wives usually do not extend their quarrels to their children and may welcome in their courtyard the offspring of families with whom their husbands are feuding, the men pass on their animosities to the next generation. It is they who point out the men's platform of an enemy lineage and warn their boys not to sit there or play with the children from that family. It is they who define the trustworthy, the untrustworthy, the relatives, the enemies, the false friends, and the neutrals who make up the participants in the intricate web of village factionalism.

Since the men live in a world in which they are surrounded, in fact and fantasy, by potential enemies, they cannot, as do the women, adopt a categorically negative attitude toward aggression. Although it is deemed best to remain on seemingly cordial terms with one's enemies, and although disputes are usually fought out in the arena of the courtroom when they do break into the open, nevertheless one can never be sure when a hotheaded, drunk, or tradition-minded Rājpūt will decide to settle a grievance with a "conversation of sticks." A youth, therefore, must stand ready to defend himself and his family in physical combat.

This does not mean that the men encourage aggression indiscriminately. Like the women, they say that they stop the children when they see them fighting and scold them. When questioned by Gurdeep Jaspal and me, a few of the men reluctantly admitted that they sometimes told their sons that they should fight back if attacked. Others, however, insisted that they never told their sons to fight. In view of the military tradition of these men and the fact that the adult men must defend their crops from thieves, and sometimes themselves or their relatives from attack, their answers seemed understated. We felt sure that the sons must be receiving more aggression encouragement from their fathers than the fathers were reporting. Hoping that they might be more honest in their answers if interviewed by a man, we requested one of the Indian men in the project to repeat parts of the father interview. Mr. Narayan Singh was kind enough to do this, and our conjecture proved to be correct. He interviewed nine men, asking them, among other things, "Do the men say that a boy must defend himself if someone hits him?" and "Do they say that a boy must defend another child from the family if someone attacks him?" Eight of the nine men said that they told the boys they must fight under these circumstances, and the ninth said that the mothers taught them this. Two other men said that women as well as men told their sons to defend themselves.

Evidently the men stop fights if they see them occur, but they do train their sons to defend themselves and their relatives. One should be peaceful, but one must defend oneself if attacked. The men's reluctance to discuss the topic shows their own conflict in this area.

The men reported, both to us and to Mr. Singh, that they did not instruct their sons in the art of staff fighting. This, they insisted, "They learn themselves." Some men said that they told their sons to hit the cattle with the staff (in order to herd them), and in this way they learned to use it. The following is probably an accurate description of how the boys learn to manipulate the staff.

In this way they learn. That when they are in the fields grazing their cattle, they hit the cattle with the staff. Then the children start fighting themselves and they beat each other with small sticks. Then like this slowly, they learn how to fight. While playing also they learn. They beat the other one and the other one beats them. Nobody teaches them this thing. They learn by themselves.

In general, the fathers' attitude might be summed up in the maxim: "Do not start a fight, but if someone starts a fight with you, finish it." The children do in fact readily retaliate when attacked, and they soon learn to appeal to a relative or friend for aid in their defense. This aggression training is given traditional sanction through the occasional reading of the Rāmāyaṇa and the Mahābhārata and the relating of stories about the bravery of Rājpūt warriors. There are many such stories which may be read or told by men in the course of an evening's entertainment.

Although girls are probably punished more severely for aggression, and although the cultural ideal for women condemns aggressiveness, a girl growing up in a courtyard is apt to witness bickering and verbal fighting among the women, and her mother's techniques of scolding and punishing are often expressive of anger. When questioned on the interviews as to what they would do if another child teased or hit them, there was little difference in the responses of boys and girls. Twelve out of 18 children said they would not hit a child who teased them, but 14 out of 16 said they would hit a child who hit them. The children, then, did retaliate to direct aggression.

The following observations give some idea of the kind of quarreling which is likely to occur among the children.

Biirwattī (girl aged 14), Raaj (boy aged 5), and Preem (girl aged 6) were playing on the road. Angurī (girl aged 8) came along the road. Angurī was carrying a dish of mud on her head. Biirwattī was with Angurī. She said to Angurī, "You take this home." (The mud.) Angurī: "I'll take it after some time." Raaj was lying on the road. He threw sand on Biirwattī. Biirwattī said, "Do you want to get a beating from me?" Preem threw sand on Angurī. Angurī threw back. Preem said, "Now don't you go and tell your sister. You have also thrown."

Dhuum (boy aged 10) went into the kitchen where his older sister was cooking. He said, "Give me some hot water." Sister: "You take it yourself. I won't give it to you." She got up and shook her fist at him. Their mother shouted at her, "Don't be silly." The sister hit him several times with a stick from the fire. He hit back at her. She hit him harder than he hit her but neither hit very hard. The sister sat by the chūla and picked up the tongs and shook them at him. Dhuum picked up a wooden sandal and shook it at her. The mother shouted, "Are you not ashamed of yourselves?" To the daughter she said, "Go and sit down and do not fight." Dhuum put on the sandals and went out.

Mukmal (girl aged 6) and Preem (girl aged 6) had a tussle. Mukmal said to Preem, "I'm going to beat you, bad character's widow. I'll set you right. Leave me, leave me." Preem was holding her and hitting her. Preem was stronger than Mukmal and she could not hit back so she was shouting. A big boy who is a relation of Mukmal's came along the road and Mukmal said, "Tell Preem to let me go." He grabbed Preem, who kept tight hold of Mukmal. Then Preem let go of Mukmal and held on to one end of her headcloth while Mukmal had the other end. The boy swung the two of them around him in circles, like cracking the whip. He was holding Mukmal while doing this. He let go and Preem grabbed Mukmal again. They were still tussling at the end of five minutes.

Although several competitive games are popular at this age, particularly with the boys, no one seems to take winning too seriously. An informal version of field hockey is played almost daily by the herd boys in the morning when their cattle are gathered under a grove of trees just outside the village. The game is played with a ball and the staffs which the boys use to control the cattle. As there are no goal posts, no goals, and no referee, the game consists mainly of the two opposing teams chasing the ball back and forth. Also popular is a hockeylike game played with a wooden stick ¾ of an inch long and pointed at both ends, which substitutes as a puck or ball. The players hit this puck with sticks, spinning it in the air, and attempting to hit it again in midair. It may be played alone or as a group game. Both of these games afford practice at handling a staff.

Older boys play a team game similar to the American game of Red Rover, played on a field which is divided into four equal rectangles placed lengthwise like the markings on a football field. The field is usually about 30 feet long and 15 feet wide. Members of two opposing teams line up at each end of the field. One member of a team attempts to run across into the section held by the opposing team, touch a member of the other team, and get back across the center without being tagged. While running, he keeps repeating, "kabaḍḍī, kabaḍḍī, kabaḍḍī" without drawing a new breath. If the boy is tagged, the opposing team wins a point; if he gets back to the middle line, his side wins a point; if he goes over and comes back without touching any boy, or is not touched, there is no score. The other team can only tag the boy when he is in the end section. A variation on the rules of this game is that if the boy is tagged, he is out. This game is potentially an aggressive game, but boys usually content themselves with tagging each other, although occasionally they will bring a boy down by tackling him.

Boys occasionally play a tree tag. The boy who is "it" attempts to tag the boys who have climbed a tree with a stick.

As popular as the first three games is a less strenuous one played by both boys and girls, which involves skill in pitching shells or small stones. The object is to toss the shell into the hole or to hit one of the opponent's shells. If a boy succeeds in doing this, his opponent forfeits his shell.

A variety of jacks is also played by boys and girls with seven or eight shells or pebbles. There are several variations of this game, involving manual dexterity; sometimes the children start by tossing the shells into the air one at a time, catching them, and increasing the number after each successful try; sometimes they try to catch the shells on the back of their hands; sometimes they throw one stone on two fingers and try to catch it again.

A third game of skill (tangī-tangī) is popular with both sexes and is similar to American hopscotch. Five squares are drawn in a row. The player throws the stone into each square consecutively and, hopping on one foot, tries to kick it out.

Little girls play a game similar to tag—frequently on the men's sleeping platform. All the girls stand in a group while one stands at a distance. She sings the following lines:

> Hul-hul a fly comes.
> The rest of the girls shout:
> If it comes, let it come
> The lone girl says:
> It will eat, it will drink.
> The girls say:
> Let it come.

All the girls then run round and round, and the lone girl tries to catch them.

When the play groups are mixed, the older children direct the play of the younger ones. They keep the small observers out of mischief. When girls and boys play together, the boys usually dominate the girls, although personality differences may upset the pattern. In short, the dominance pattern of the children follows the adult lines of authority, but, even as with adults, the tacit approval given to the dominant person may allow children with forceful personalities to assume ascendency over others who are structurally classed as their superiors. This does not mean that the older, stronger, or more dominant children bully or coerce the others. The mothers generally agreed that they would scold or beat children who persistently demand their own way with the other children. Individual dominance must not be allowed to upset group solidarity. If the child can successfully dominate his peers, well and good, but if his demands provoke a quarrel, he is punished. Again, this implicit "rule" is derived from adult standards.

Although the recreational activity becomes more organized and varied as the children grow older, they have less time to devote to play, since a portion of their day is allotted to school and work. Most children now perform at least a few chores fairly regularly. The girls may wash dishes, sweep, tend a baby, serve food to the men on the men's platform or bring food to them in the fields, pick water chestnuts, leafy vegetables, and sometimes cotton in season, bring extra water from the well, and wash clothes. The boys run errands, particularly for the men, water and pasture the cattle, bring fodder from the fields, and help the men with field work.

The extent to which the children must work depends largely (for girls) on the size of the family and (for boys) on the size and wealth of the family, since the custom of not requiring work of children if an adult can perform the task holds for older as well as for younger children. A family with few women, even if wealthy, requires the services of its girls, but a wealthy family can hire field hands, and even if short on manpower, may dispense with the services of the sons. Many families consider that school is a sufficient chore for a boy. Although some schoolboys may be expected to help with the farm only on weekends or during the harvest, others must skip more frequently or give it up altogether. Since school is not considered important for girls, they are more frequently withdrawn from classes during harvest seasons.

Children who are not in school usually have more work than those who attend classes. This is particularly true for boys, for a girl may be withheld from school because of the conservatism of her family, whereas a boy is not withheld unless the family needs his full-time services.

There are two boys in our sample, Shēr and Narayan, who did not attend school and who worked regularly. Shēr is 10 years old and Narayan is 7. Shēr's work is to pasture the family cattle. Every morning he drives the cattle across the bridge to the grove of trees standing just across the pond. Here he and the other herd boys play hockey while their cattle mill around under the trees. At noon Shēr returns for lunch, leaving his animals in the care of some other boys. In the afternoon he and his friends drive the herd to pasture on cut down fields. Small groups of boys and cattle leave the procession as they reach their families' fields. Shēr's fields are several miles from the village, and when he reaches them, only three or four friends of the group that started from the village remain to spend the afternoon with him. When he and his friends have herded their cattle safely into the center of a field, they sit down to rest, talk, or perhaps wrestle to pass the time. The afternoon is pleasant and leisurely, but the boys must always keep one eye on the cattle lest they stray into a neighboring field and invoke the ire of the property owner. Such an event will bring at least a flood of abuse for their carelessness, and in a community where so many grudges lie barely dormant, the results may be far more serious. It is dangerous to let cattle stray even into the fields of a relative if the family members are not on good terms with one another. One of Shēr's friends, Rājsingh, let his cattle stray into the field of an unfriendly uncle. The uncle and his wife were so enraged they invaded Rājsingh's home and beat his mother so severely that they knocked out one of her eyes. Shēr, whose uncle is also unfriendly, is careful to keep his cattle in bounds.

Narayan's family needs his services as fodder carrier as well as cattle tender. Narayan and his older brother leave their house between 7 and 8 A.M. and drive their few head of cattle to their fields, which are situated about 3 miles from the village. At noontime Narayan turns back to the village, often bringing a heavy load of fodder on his small head. After eating his own lunch, he returns to the fields, carrying food for his brother and father. At twilight he returns again with his father and brother, carrying another load of fodder or vegetables.

Of the girls—Dēvī, 10 years old, Rēshmī, aged 7, and Ohmwattī, aged 8—only Dēvī, the oldest, had extensive duties. Ohmwattī sometimes cleans dishes and sweeps for her mother. Although she has a 1-year-old sister, she does not carry her, perhaps because the baby is quite sickly. Rēshmī is a rather rebellious child who evidently does not care for her female status; she always uses masculine verb endings as though she were a boy. Her mother has trouble persuading her to be helpful, although, as we shall see, she is credited with less work than she actually performs.

Dēvī belongs to a family burdened both by poverty and lack of manpower. Her father is dead, and Dēvī and her mother live with her uncle Shanner and his wife, Dēvī's grandmother, her brother Rīrkā, and her male cousins Mugala and Baby Natū. Rīrkā and Mugala help Shanner in the fields after school and on weekends. Almost daily they may be seen trotting along the road with bundles of fodder so long that one must bend down to recognize them. When work is heavy, they must leave school. Dēvī's grandmother, old enough to ignore purdah restrictions, also goes to the fields to pick fodder and vegetables and carries large bundles of them home on her aged head. Dēvī is the steady baby carrier for her infant cousin, and when she goes on visits in the village, he is almost always on her hip. She also takes food to her hard-working uncle in the fields. She sometimes sweeps the floor, cleans the hearth, and, if the family exhausts their daily supply of water, delivered by their water-carrying girls, she brings an extra pot or two from the nearby well.

Adult recognition for this increase in the childrens' responsibilities is meager. Although one of the most frequent forms of praise reported by the mothers, when interviewed was, "You have done good work," we seldom heard a mother actually say this. Rather, there seemed to be a general tendency to belittle the tasks of children. Granting that the chores required of most children are neither long nor arduous, even those children who did work regularly were not accorded recognition. For instance, Narayan's mother, when asked about her son's chores, reported that he did not do very much work. It would seem that walking an average of 12 miles a day, and carrying a load for 6 to 9 of those miles might be considered a rather arduous undertaking for a slightly built 7-year-old boy, but his mother was not impressed.

Rēshmī's mother provided us with our most amusing example of this tendency to underrate the amount of work done by children. We interviewed her on this topic, and she responded as follows:

Q.: Can you tell us which work Rēshmī has recently learned?
A.: She has not learned anything special, but she can clean one or two utensils. . . .
Q.: What is Rēshmī's regular work?
A.: Besides the utensils, what does she do? What she will do, the immoral widow?
Q.: How often does she wash the utensils?
A.: (Sarcastically) Oh, she does them daily. No. Only sometimes.
Q.: How often? Every eight or nine days?
A.: She usually never washes them, but sometimes one or two she takes and washes.
Q.: How do you get her to do it?
A.: She does not do any work. Now I am telling her to take the baby girl and she won't do it.
Q.: Do you often ask her to take the baby?
A.: Every day she takes the baby, but I have to scold her and then she takes her.
Q.: What do you want of Rēshmī? That work which you tell her to do, should she do it at once, or do you give her a little time?
A.: What work? She does not do any work. Supposing you ask her. Sometimes she will bring one or two buckets of water from the well. That is all.

In one breath the mother denies that Rēshmī does any work, and in the next she mentions another task which the child performs fairly regularly.

Schoolwork is similarly ignored by most parents. Although education, as has been said, is by no means universal, even among the high-caste groups, at present most boys and a number of girls attend school. Since the school system is segregated by sex, those who do attend are effectively isolated from opposite-sexed children and adults, six to eight hours a day for five days a week, barring special holidays.

Although the Rājpūts send more of their children to school than do any other caste in the village, devoted scholarship is a rarity. The headmistress of the girls' school manages to keep her little band of students quiet and in their places, and the fourth and fifth grade boys spend most of their school time at least looking at their books or reciting, but the younger boys spend most of their time in minor horseplay. Their work is continually interrupted by frequent borrowing of books, pens, ink pots, and so on, usually accompanied by a good deal of bickering about who owns what.

Jagdish (boy aged 10) was in school, writing with some chalk on the floor. He turned to a boy and picked up a pen. He asked, "Whose is this?" The boy said, "It is mine." Jagdish picked up another pen and asked again. This time the boy did not reply. Jagdish took the pen and gave it to a boy in the corner. Then he sat down and wrote on his slate. A boy started using Jagdish's ink pot and Jagdish objected, saying, "Use your ink pot, not mine." He threw the boy's ink pot away from them. The boy said angrily, "I bought it for two pice."

The older boys sometimes take it upon themselves to stop the horse-play of their younger schoolmates. Indeed, some of the older boys act as official monitors and, like the older brothers and cousins, sometimes discharge their duties with a sharp blow. The following is a fairly typical example of the "study habits" of the beginning students and the attempts of a self-styled monitor to control them. All of the boys are Rājpūts.

Pralard, Puran, Jaipāl, and Bharat (all 6 or 7 years old) are sitting side by side; opposite them is Rūp, an older and stronger boy. They all have their slates and bags in front of them. The boy next to Bharat is attempting to write on his slate but is prevented by Bharat, who is twisting his hand. The boy keeps calling for the master (teacher) in a plaintive voice.
Jaipāl gets up, moves to the opposite row and then moves back. Puran follows him on both moves. Pralard is singing to himself.
Bharat twists the boy's hand again. He calls for the master.
Jaipāl again gets up. He pushes a boy sitting opposite him. He then backs away, returns to his seat and makes faces at him.
Rūp looks up at Jaipāl severely and says, "Why aren't you writing?"
Meanwhile Puran and Bharat are having a tussle. Seeing them, Rūp comes over and shakes his fist at Pralard.
Finally the master comes over and Rūp, seeing him, returns to his seat.

Although Rūp holds no official sanction with regard to the four boys, he does exercise a certain amount of control over them by virtue of possession of two of the three major sources of power of Rājpūt men, age and strength. The third source of power, wealth, does not enter into leadership patterns of the children. This informal control among the children is exercised among members of the same caste. Indeed, the Rājpūt children are in contact with only a few children of other castes in school, and they seldom associate with them. Their interactions while in school are primarily with their friends, relatives, and neighbors, all of whom are also Rājpūts.

Most parents do not press a child to attend school against his wishes. The teachers report that the school usually has about 80% attendance in the morning and about 60% in the afternoon. None of the younger boys attend school in the afternoon. Evidently their mothers feel the all-day session is too much for them. Any minor illness is sufficient excuse for remaining home. Furthermore, since the mothers are confined to quarters and the fathers are busy in the fields, there is no one to check on whether or not the children, after leaving the house, actually arrive at school. Since many parents are themselves illiterate, they cannot help the children with their homework, but older brothers and cousins, who have been to school, are seldom enlisted to supervise the work of the younger children. In fact, the children do very little homework in the afternoon. The possibility that they worked in the evening seems very remote in view of the poor lighting available to the villagers. In general, the parents show little concern for scholarship, and children do not expect them to. Out of 400 behavior observations, there was only one instance of a child seeking approval for good scholarship.

M. read his schoolbook to his brother. Every so often he would say, "Is it all right?" to the brother. He looked at us and smiled.

One can discern a number of reasons why children are not rewarded for working. We have already said that the attitude that a daughter is a guest in her own home leads mothers to be reluctant in demanding that their daughters work. The men, who consider farming a degrading occupation for Rājpūts and who hire, if possible, low-caste field hands, are unlikely to communicate to their sons any enthusiasm for work. Furthermore, the adults are impatient with the inept performance of children who are just learning a task and are more likely to scold the child for his awkwardness than praise him for his enterprise. A girl, just learning to spin, is ordered away from the wheel because she breaks the thread; a boy trying to feed grass into the fodder cutter is pushed aside by the man at the wheel; a boy who has brought a bread container from the bedroom in an attempt to feed himself is scolded and beaten by his mother when he drops it; a girl is making a fair attempt at embroidering on the petticoat that her friend has started but is told by her aunt to stop because she is ruining the work. In this way children are often discouraged from learning new tasks or undertaking work that is not well within their ability. The work they do is judged, not in terms of a reasonable expectation for children of a given age but in comparison with adult performance. Narayan works considerably harder than other neighborhood boys of his age. When his mother reports that he works very little, she can only mean that his contribution to the family manpower pool is meager in comparison with the amount of work done by his father and older brother, a comparison that naturally puts Narayan at a disadvantage.

In this atmosphere it is not surprising that the children are not notably self-reliant or conscientious. At school the boys seem unable to keep track of their own pencils and ink pots, and their books are often torn and dirty. When the work is difficult, they consult another student. Outside of school the children seldom undertake a task beyond their ability, nor do they persist in the face of difficulty. As reported earlier, when asked what they would do when having difficulty in some task, only one child in the sample said that he would attempt to solve the problem alone; all others reported that they would abandon the effort or seek help.

According to their reports, however, the children enjoy working. When asked to choose their favorite activity, 3 boys and 2 girls chose schoolwork, and 2 boys and 4 girls chose some household or farming task. The remaining 3 boys and 2 girls whom we interviewed chose some sort of recreational activity: playing a game, attending the mēlā, eating sugar cane, and so on, as their preferred pastime. Observed popularity of adult-role play confirms these reports. It may be that the children were giving socially acceptable answers. It seems probable, however, that, like most children, these children envy adult status, are anxious to grow up, and would be willing, if not eager, to shoulder increased responsibility if their parents were not so sparing of encouragement and impatient with their mistakes.

BIBLIOGRAPHY

Boquet, A. C. Hinduism. London: Hutchinson's University Library.
Blunt, Sir Edward (Ed.) Social Service in India. London: His Majesty's Stationery Office, 1939.
Carstairs, G. Morris. The Twice-Born. London: Hogarth Press, 1957.
Crooke, B. A. The Popular Religion and Folklore of Northern India. Westminster: Archibald Constable and Co., 1896, Vol. 1, 2.
Dube, Leela. Diet, health and disease in a North Indian village. Department of Anthropology, Cornell University, 1956 (Manuscript).
Dube, S. C. Indian Village. Ithaca: Cornell University Press, 1955.
———. India's Changing Villages: Human Factors in Community Development. Ithaca: Cornell University Press, 1958.
———. Some problems of communication in rural community development. Cambridge, Massachusetts: Massachusetts Institute of Technology, 1956.
Hawkridge, Emma. Indian Gods and Kings: A Story of a Living Past. Boston: Houghton-Mifflin, 1935.
Hitchcock, John T. A dilemma of dominant caste politics in a North Indian village. (Manuscript.)
———. Leadership in a North Indian village: two case studies. In R. L. Park and I. Tinker (Eds.), Leadership and Political Institutions in India. Princeton: Princeton University Press, 1959.
———. Surat Singh, head judge. In J. B. Casagrande (Ed.), In the Company of Man. New York: Harper, 1960.

Hitchcock, Patricia and Hitchcock, John, *North Indian Village.* A 16mm. 30-minute documentary film with sound and color. Distributed by International Film Bureau, 322 South Michigan Avenue, Chicago 4, Illinois, on either a rental or a purchase basis.

————. The Idea of the Martial Rājpūt. *American Journal of Folklore.* 1958, **71**, 216–223.

Lewis, Oscar. *Village Life in Northern India.* Urbana: University of Illinois Press, 1958.

Macdonell, A. A. *India's Past: A Survey of Her Literature, Religions, Languages, and Antiquities.* Oxford: Clarendon Press, 1927.

Planalp, Jack. Religious life and values in a contemporary North Indian village. Unpublished Ph.D. thesis, Cornell University, 1956.

Subcontractor's Monograph, Cornell-9 HRAF-56, *Uttar Pradesh,* Human Relations Area Files, Inc. New Haven, Conn.

Subcontractor's Monograph, Cornell-8, HRAF-44, *India: A Sociological Background.* Vol. 1, 2, Human Relations Area Files, Inc. New Haven, Conn.

Subcontractor's Monograph, California-3, HRAF-33, *India: Government and Politics,* Human Relations Area Files, New Haven, Conn.

Subcontractor's Monograph, California-1, HRAF-32, *The Economy of India,* Vol. 1, 2, Human Relations Area Files, Inc. New Haven, Conn.

Steed, Gitel P. Notes on an approach to a study of personality formation in a Hindu village in Gujarat, *American Anthropologist,* **57**, No. 3, Part 2, Memoir #83, June 1955.

Woodruff, Gertrude Marvin, An Adidravida settlement in Bangalore, India: a case study in urbanization. Unpublished Ph.D. thesis, Harvard University, 1959.

Index